STATES

OF

MIND

JONATHAN

MILLER

STATES

OF

MIND

Pantheon Books, New York

Library of Congress Cataloging in Publication Data

Miller, Jonathan, 1934–
States of mind.

Bibliography: p.
Includes index.
1. Psychology—Popular works. 2. Neuropsychology—
Popular works. 3. Scientists—Interviews. I. Title.
BF145.M476   1983   150   82-48953
ISBN 0-394-53014-4
0-394-72714-2 (pbk.)

Manufactured in the United States of America
First Pantheon Paperback Edition

Contents

Jonathan Miller

PREFACE

In 1854 the Scottish scientist David Brewster complained about the defective state of mental philosophy.

There is no department of knowledge in which so little progress has been made as in that of Mental Philosophy. The human mind has been studied as if it were independent of the body, and, generally speaking, by philosophers who possessed a comparatively small share of physical knowledge. No attempt, indeed, has been made to examine its phenomena by the light of experiment and observation, or to analyse them in their abnormal phases, when modified by external influences, or by the various conditions of that complex and mysterious organisation on which life and its functions depend. The science of mind, therefore, if it can be called a science, cannot boast of many indisputable truths, or many admitted laws. Without data, without axioms, without definitions, it proposes problems which it cannot solve; it draws corollaries from assertions which are not proved; and however ingenious have been its cultivators, their ingenuity has been more displayed in overturning the speculations of their predecessors than in establishing their own. Nor is this a result which ought to surprise us. Viewed as material by one inquirer, as spiritual by another, and by others as mysteriously compounded of both, the human mind escapes from the cognisance of sense and reason, and lies, a waste field with a northern exposure, upon which every passing speculator casts his mental tares, choking any of the good seed that may have sprung up towards maturity.[1]

Brewster's complaint, which typifies the frustration felt by many of his scientific contemporaries, was published at a moment when the study of the human mind was about to take a significant turn for the better. In fact, with the benefit of hindsight it's possible to recognise that the subject had already undergone considerable improvement.

Until the end of the eighteenth century psychology didn't really exist as an independent subject. It was as yet indistinguishable from philosophy, and its scientific accomplishments were negligible by comparison to what had been achieved in other areas of natural knowledge. Physics had already liberated itself from fruitless scholasticism, and although it still called itself natural philosophy it was 'philosophical' in name alone. Optics, mechanics and pneumatics had all profited from the experimental approach developed in the late seventeenth century under the influence of Isaac Newton. With the help of Benjamin Franklin and others, electricity had become intelligible, and after the publication of James Hutton's *Theory of the Earth* geology was well on the way to becoming a science. And when Lavoisier established the role of oxygen in combustion, chemistry also became the province of experimentally soluble problems.

[1] D. Brewster, *North British Review* 22 November 1854.

Having completed the first stage of what has been described as the mechanisation of the world picture, scientists were understandably eager to see the human mind yield to the same sort of analysis. But the progress was slow and uncertain, and it's easy to forgive Brewster for failing to recognise these early initiatives.

The process by which psychology began to turn itself into a science was made easier by the way in which philosophy had already shown a tendency to become psychological. With their belief that human knowledge was based on information provided by physical sensation British empiricists such as Berkeley, Locke and Hume encouraged a profitable interest in the function of the sense organs, and although this did not yield an immediate harvest of scientific results it certainly prepared the ground for it.

By visualising the sense organs as an interface between the physical world of matter and the mental world of ideas and feelings the empiricists sponsored the birth of psychophysics, enabling scientists to study the correlation between variable events in the material world and subjective experiences in the mental one. By 1830 there had been substantial advances in the psychology of vision. By exploiting the highly developed technology of optics Thomas Young was able to make valuable suggestions about the visual experience of colour. The sensations of touch and hearing also became subjects of experimental investigation, and by the middle of the nineteenth century sensory discrimination was undergoing sophisticated analysis. This work was further enhanced by discoveries about the structure and function of the nervous system. By 1822 physiologists had demonstrated the separate existence of motor and sensory nerves, and were able to prove experimentally that the route by which sensations entered the nervous system was anatomically separate from the pathway along which messages travelled to the muscles. This discovery sharpened the distinction between perception and action, and when the concept of the reflex was formulated as a result, it led to an inevitable interest in the quantitative analysis of reaction. By 1860 the collaboration between physiologists, physicists and introspective psychologists had borne fruit in a well-established laboratory science, although it was many years before British Universities followed the German example and established academic departments of psychology.

Although a lot of this research was productive as far as it went, there were two serious drawbacks. The empiricists tended to equate mind and consciousness, and since introspection depended on the reports of subjects who were aware of the experiments that were being performed upon their sense organs, psychologists neglected the importance of unconscious mental processes. The existence of such processes had been intuitively recognised since antiquity, and with the growth of Romanticism poets and writers paid tribute to the existence of this so-called 'stranger within'. Coleridge was one of the first thinkers to emphasise the dynamic function of the unconscious in his well-known reference to the 'esemplastic' power of the imagination, but such insights were unsystematic, and they did not represent a coherent body of psychological theory until Freud undertook his first clinical experiments with patients under hypnosis. Historians have successfully identified the extent to which Freud was inspired by literary romanticism. But it would be wrong to overlook the contribution that was made by the supposedly quackish work of Franz Anton Mesmer, a German who lived during the eighteenth century. For although animal magnetism had its roots in the European tradition of Rosicrucian mysticism, it led directly to the clinical discovery of medical hypnotism, and thereby provided a vantage point from which it was possible to catch a glimpse of mental activity which had previously been overlooked.

In such a short introduction it is impossible to do justice to the importance of Freud's contribution to psychology, and although the three interviews in this book may strike some readers as a disproportionate emphasis, it would take many more discussions to demonstrate the implications of Freudian theory. In popular mythology Freud is often represented as a mischief maker, who uncovered the roots of unacknowledged sexual desire. But as far as modern psychology is concerned it is the abstract dynamics of his theory which will probably be his most lasting achievement. His concept of active repression for example. Not to mention his startlingly original insights into the way in which prohibited thoughts undergo elaborate condensation and displacement.

But the concept of unconscious mental processes has also been reinstated in the work of psychologists who have little or no interest in Freud's exotic scenarios of infantile sexuality. With the birth of cognitive psychology not to mention the scientific study of linguistics, some of the other inadequacies of the empirical tradition have become clearly apparent. It is widely recognised that perception can no longer be explained in terms of passive reception, and that the mind is furnished with active powers of creative conjecture without which the information provided by the senses would remain disorganised and chaotic. And the same principle holds for the acquisition and use of language.

In the hundred-and-thirty years that have passed since Brewster first published his complaint, these and other developments have led to a remarkable explosion of psychological knowledge, and although it's difficult to know whether he would have been satisfied by all the investigations which are now conducted in the name of psychology, he could not fail to be impressed by the volume and variety. As George Miller points out in his introductory interview, departments of psychology include people who seem at first sight to have very little in common – engineers, logicians and mathematicians. Ethologists, educationalists, clinicians and social workers. Mental testers, pollsters, economists and psychiatrists. There are computer programmers and group therapists. Experts in children's play and in family relationships. There are anthropologists and physiologists, students of learning, memory, skill and perception. The only thing which gives this bewildering confederacy any sense of identity or coherence is the fact that they all represent contributions to mental life. This is a concept for which it would be difficult to give an explicit definition, but when William James first offered it as a way of identifying the domain of psychology it provided a loose framework within which investigators could confidently feel that they were pursuing a common aim.

In a series of fifteen interviews it is impossible to give a representative sample of what is now going on in psychology. With each interview I became aware that the topic in question deserved fifteen more, and that there were some important areas which were neglected altogether. Experts in the subject may be frustrated by the omission of some of the most interesting modern salients. And readers who look to psychology for some sort of wisdom about the conduct of ordinary life may think that too much space has been devoted to the technical aspects of cognition. As Professor Flügel[1] pointed out in his historical survey of the last hundred years in psychology, books of this sort make one aware of everything that has been left out. I therefore hope that these interviews will be read in the spirit that they were compiled. That is to say as a series of convivial conversations with people who have devoted their lives to the task of making the human mind intelligible.

[1] *100 Years of Psychology* 1933.

1

dialogue with
George Miller

THE
BACKGROUND
TO MODERN
PSYCHOLOGY

INTRODUCTION

In contrast to its derelict condition at the beginning of the nineteenth century, modern psychology has become so productive and so specialised that it would be unrealistic to expect any one authority to summarise its many aims and varied achievements. So when I invited Professor George Miller from Princeton University to undertake the task of introducing this series of interviews he agreed to do so on the understanding that there was no question of his providing a comprehensive survey. Recognising that the emphasis of his account would almost inevitably raise objections from those who prefer some of the ampler and more colourful issues of human psychology – anxiety, stress, love, hatred and aggression, not to mention human 'relationships' – Professor Miller discusses the great change which has overtaken the scientific study of perception and behaviour, and in doing so he develops a theme which recurs in many of the other interviews included in this volume. I am referring to the concept of mental 'representation', by which is meant some internal state through which the living organism displays to itself a conjectural model of the world in which it lives. As Professor Miller points out, this was an idea which early twentieth-century psychologists tried to eliminate in the effort to give their discipline the appearance of an objective science. In the doctrine which came to be known as Behaviourism, any reference to consciousness was carefully excluded for fear that it would introduce the scientifically unmanageable idea of a causal principle which was not immediately accessible to public observation. The Behaviourists developed a programme of research based on the assumption that conduct could be explained in terms of the measurable stimuli impinging on the sense organs and the nervous pathways which conveyed this traffic to the skeletal muscles. But as Professor Miller points out, this ambitious scheme came to grief as it failed to take account of the richly productive character of behaviour. It soon became apparent that the concept of stimulus and response was a misleading simplification, and that behavioural competence could not be explained as a straightforward reaction to the sensory input. In the effort to explain the way in which behaviour could transcend the information provided by the senses, psychologists began to suspect the existence of an internal representation of reality against the background of which the organism could (a) compute the probability of success or failure in its forthcoming plans; and (b) recognise the discrepancy between aim and achievement. But how could such a concept be introduced without resurrecting the discredited notion of the mind as some sort of ghost in the machine? Professor Miller argues that the problem was gradually solved by recognising the suggestiveness of certain mechanical metaphors created as a by-product of military technology during and after the Second World War. In the field of aerial combat for example, tasks such as radar tracking and gun aiming demanded an efficient co-operation between man and machine, and it soon became apparent that the vigilance and strength of the human operator often fell short of what was required. In the effort to create mechanical counterparts of otherwise dangerously fallible human skill, engineers recognised that any machine which was expected to reproduce or simulate the competence of a human operator would have to include some device capable of making mathematical generalisations about the behaviour of moving targets – some sort of conjectural model which could (a) predict the behaviour of the target; (b) formulate appropriate actions; and (c) make corrections in the light of what had happened. In order to satisfy these demands it was necessary to establish a physical medium in which all the relevant information could be represented and computed. The theory which resulted from such research brought about a revolution in cognitive psychology, for it reconciled the need for some sort of internal representation of reality with psychologists' understandable suspicion of a metaphysical agency which hovered over the nervous system like a spiritual superintendent. In summarising this theme, Professor Miller suggestively anticipates many of the arguments which appear later in this volume.

DISCUSSION

J. MILLER   As this is the first interview in the series, it seems appropriate, though I'm sure you'll say unfair, to ask you what psychology is. I expect an evasive but hopefully informative answer.

G. MILLER   It's difficult to give an answer that's both simple and intelligible, on the one hand, and honest and truthful, on the other. Modern psychology is an enormously complicated, multifaceted area, both as a science and as a profession.

I think we have to break your question into two. One is: what is psychology *about*? I believe that psychology is about precisely what William James[1] said it was about when he wrote his great textbook in 1890. James said that psychology is the science of mental life. I think he was right. Some people have disagreed, and we can pick up their disagreements later if you wish.

Then there'a a second question: what do psychologists *do*? That is the complicated question, because different psychologists approach the study of mental life in so many different ways.

Most people encounter psychology in one or another of its particular manifestations and, like the blind men examining the elephant, think the whole creature must resemble whatever part they happen to have their hands on. I see it sometimes when I meet strangers. I flinch a bit before I say that I'm a psychologist. Not because I'm ashamed of being a psychologist, but because I know I'm probably in for a lot of misunderstanding.

Some people say: 'So you're a psychologist. I think my wife's calling',

[1]William James (1842–1910). American philosopher and psychologist who wrote *Principles of Psychology*.

and off they go. Then there's the opposite reaction 'So you're a psychologist. Well, I'm something of a psychologist myself', and they describe how they trained their dog to bring in the newspaper. Other people ask about their children's test scores, and still others want me to interpret their dreams. All I can say is: 'I'm not that kind of psychologist!' If they ask what kinds of psychologists there are, I find myself right in the middle of this discussion of what psychologists do.

When the field was first defined, in nineteenth-century Germany by Wilhelm Wundt[1], it was defined as the science of immediate experience. Wundt meant much the same thing that William James meant when he defined it as the science of mental life. Immediate experience was the conscious, inner experience of normal, adult, educated, Western European human beings – usually male. But all of those adjectives have since been discarded – gradually as the original science began to expand.

In order to study human consciousness, you must put it into a context, you must look at it from some sort of perspective. The original perspective was given in terms of the mind versus the world: how does the mind get information about the world, how does the world influence the mind? That was the perspective formulated first by René Descartes and refined by John Locke, David Hume, Immanuel Kant, and the other philosophical forefathers of the new scientific psychology.

Scientific psychology was launched at a time when Darwinism was pre-eminently important, so it was natural to look at the mind from the perspective of evolution, to contrast man and animal. You can introspect on your own conscious states and processes, but when you study animals, no introspective reports are possible. You must look at animals rather differently. It isn't even clear that they have anything comparable to consciousness in the sense in which we know it.

Still another group of people sought their perspective by contrasting man and machine. Hermann von Helmholtz[2] and other nineteenth-century physiologists saw the body as a complex, biochemical machine that necessarily obeys all the laws of physics and chemistry. So we could take that perspective on mental life: the brain is a machine that 'secretes' conscious experience. In the twentieth century this perspective has been enriched by the development of intelligent computers: the brain is now seen as a machine that processes information.

Another line of psychological research contrasts man and child. Whatever adult consciousness is, it develops, it grows. Some aspects are determined at birth, of course; then the experience of the individual shapes how it learns to be the way it is. That is the developmental approach to understanding mental life.

[1] Wilhelm Max Wundt (1832–1920). A distinguished experimental psychologist, he wrote on the nerves and the senses, the relations of physiology and psychology, and logic.
[2] See footnote on page 47.

Still other psychologists have contrasted individual consciousness with social consciousness, studying the conduct that a social group imposes on an individual and the commitment that the individual feeds back into the social group.

Each of these approaches offers a different perspective on mental life. Not every psychologist looks at the mind from every perspective, of course. But even though people who take these different perspectives do very different things – often using methods and technologies so different that they can hardly talk to each other about their work – they are still held together by their shared interest in understanding the nature of mental life.

A modern psychology department is practically a college unto itself. There are people who know physics, who know biology and various branches of medicine, who know mathematics, statistics, logic, linguistics, computer science, anthropology, economics, philosophy; each of these is needed from one or more of the various perspectives.

What psychologists *do* about mental life involves an enormous variety of skills and activities. When the intelligent man-in-the-street meets one of these people, it is easy to think, incorrectly, that all psychologists do whatever that particular chap happens to do.

The layman generally encounters psychology in one of two guises: either as it is applied to education, learning and development, or as it is applied to mental health, or health generally. Thus he runs into psychologists who give mental tests, or who analyse dreams, or the like. But much that goes on in psychology is superficially unrelated to these familiar services. What really holds it all together is that even now, more than a hundred years after the founding of psychology as a science, we still feel that the constitutive problem of psychology is the nature of mental life. Anybody who contributes to our understanding of that is, to that extent, contributing to psychology, whether he calls himself a psychologist or not.

J. MILLER   If we can set aside for a moment a definition of what mental life might be – and it's very hard to really specify what we mean by it – can we say that it's one of three categories or areas within which people recognise knowledge to be divided? The material world, the living world, and the mental world?

G. MILLER   Before we set it aside, let's say one thing about this business of starting off with definitions. You should recognise that there are two kinds of sciences – we might call them deductive sciences and inductive sciences. In deductive sciences, you start with definitions and axioms, and you deduce all that follows as consequences of those. In such sciences, your definitions must be very clear.

In inductive sciences, on the other hand, you start with a rather vague notion: we're going to mess around a bit over here, and we're going to discover the definition of our science as we go along. Psychology is still learning what the definition of psychology should be. And it's changed. Definitions have changed from those made by William James to those derived from the behavioural period, and the current emphasis is now on cognitive phenomena.

But to return to your comment: yes, I think that the old-fashioned ontology, which the materialism of the nineteenth century almost destroyed, held that science can study only three things: one is matter and energy, which physics and chemistry study; another is life, the subject matter of the biological-biomedical sciences; the third is the mind. We know a great deal about physics. The twentieth century has been the century of biology – there's been enormous progress in understanding the nature of life, understanding it in terms of what we know about matter and energy. The project for the twenty-first century should be to continue this way, to understand the mind in terms of what we know about living systems.

J. MILLER But would it be fair to say that there was a time when mental life and mind or consciousness, with all that that implies, of urges and strivings and feelings and so forth, was felt in some way to be prior to the others? And far from trying to explain the mind as we now try to in terms of material processes, there was a time in primitive thought, when the physical world, the material world, and the living world in particular, was explained in terms of ideas borrowed from mental experience?

G. MILLER Yes. You can still see it in children. At first, when an object moves, the child thinks it's animate. Later the child thinks that things happen because people will them to happen; when they become aware of natural phenomena that no person caused, they assume a superior cause, a divine 'willer' who causes everything to happen.

The notion that the reasons for things derive from a human will, or from a supernatural analogue of human will, expires rather late in the life of each child. But even you and I will occasionally get angry and kick our automobiles or yell at them, as if we had regressed to the primitive way of thinking of objects as if they were alive.

But by the nineteenth century, our explanations reversed. Instead of the mind imposing its will on the world, the mind was reduced to a property of certain configurations of matter. For a materialist, all that really exists are concrete things that can be measured in centimetres, grams, and seconds. If you can put a metre stick on it, then there must be a physical process there. Those things *really* exist; we've got to build everything else from that, or reduce everything else to that.

Such was the spirit of Comte's[1] positivism early in the nineteenth century: the notion that you can explain how scientific laws govern everything that happens. Positivism was wedded to materialism, to the assumption that these explanations will involve nothing more than the scientific laws governing physical and chemical phenomena. Eventually

[1] Auguste Comte (1798–1857). Philosopher, founder of sociology and positivism – a system of thought and knowledge which limits knowledge to the facts of experience, and refuses to embark on speculation regarding the ultimate nature of things.

you should be able to reduce the mind to certain biological processes, which in turn will be reducible to chemical and physical processes.

J. MILLER　But this somewhat overambitious and perhaps misguided programme gradually became unstuck, presumably when people began to recognise that there was too much of a gap between what was known about the organisation of matter and what was recognised about the structure and organisation of thought or consciousness. And that introduced, did it not, the possibility of some mediating system of ideas, such as the reflex or the perceptual atom.

G. MILLER　Many of the founders of scientific psychology were rebelling against the positivistic, materialistic, elementalistic dogmas of the nineteenth century. They were saying: 'No, the mind is important; social processes are important; they have their own existence, independent of physical existence.' They said that positivism was not the right programme, that mental phenomena are not reducible to physical phenomena, and that they intended to study those irreducible mental phenomena.

J. MILLER　But even before the recognition of the indispensability of mental phenomena, there was a second stage, wasn't there, when psychologists began to recognise something which was crucially biological, rather than chemical and physical: the concept of the reflex. A *stimulus* that was put into the organism, followed by a response that was got out of it.

G. MILLER　Well, yes. A great deal of the history of neurophysiology could be told in terms of the history of the reflex, from its first clear description by Descartes down to the present day.

But I think what happened historically, was that the early psychologists were going to understand the mind by introspection, by looking inward on their own mental processes, under controlled and reproducible conditions. But as other psychologists tried to extend this programme to include organisms that can't introspect – the insane, children, animals – the initial programme became impossible to carry through.

Moreover, Sigmund Freud came along and said: 'Look how much of a person's behaviour is governed by motives of which he's not even aware. How can you say that psychology, the science of mind, is limited to being the science of the *conscious* mind?'

And I. P. Pavlov[1] came along with conditioned reflexes and said: 'We don't need introspections in order to study a dog that's trained to salivate or lift its paw. All we need is an objective description of the dog's behaviour.'

J. MILLER　And of the objective stimulus that was being inflicted upon it.

G. MILLER　Right. There were two great students of reflexes at the beginning of the twentieth century, two men who are interesting to contrast: Pavlov in Russia, and Sherrington[2] in England. Pavlov had won a Nobel Prize for

[1] Ivan Petrovich Pavlov (1849–1936). Russian psychologist.
[2] Sir Charles Scott Sherrington (1857–1952). A psychologist whose major work was *The Integrative Actions of the Nervous Systems*.

his explanation of the action of the digestive system; in the course of those studies he observed something psychological. Ordinarily you put food into an animal's mouth and it begins to salivate; that's the beginning of the digestive process. Pavlov noted there were times when the sight of food, or just the sight of the man who ordinarily fed the dog, started the dog salivating. He could make such observations because he had developed a way to record what is going on in a dog's digestive system, while the dog is still up and active like a normal dog.

Pavlov called these 'psychic secretions' at the time; he felt there was something peculiar because digestion began when there was not really any appropriate stimulus to the digestive tract. After he'd finished his work on the digestive system, Pavlov decided to investigate the source of these psychic secretions. He devoted the rest of his life to investigating the organisation of the higher centres in the brain by using these psychic secretions, or salivary reflexes, as his tool.

Now, think about the salivary reflex for a moment. It's not under conscious control. You can't say: 'I will now secrete saliva, and thereby cause my mouth to start watering.' Of course, you could think about a good steak dinner, and that might make you salivate, but that's a conditioned response.

You have a stimulus on the tongue, a message goes to some centre in the brain, and immediately the salivary glands begin to secrete. It's a simple little arc, from stimulus to response, and this very simple element was the analytical unit that Pavlov used. That was the building block from which he constructed his whole intellectual cathedral.

Sir Charles Sherrington, on the other hand, took a different reflex. Sherrington studied postural reflexes. You can condition a dog. Let's say that the dog is standing in a harness; you sound a bell and then apply a shock to its paw, and the dog raises its foot. After several repetitions, when you sound the bell the dog raises the foot in order to avoid the shock – the dog responds in anticipation. You can do that, but notice that it's a much more complicated response, a postural reflex. A dog cannot lift one limb without reorienting its weight and the whole of its body. . . .

J. MILLER So that it remains stable.

G. MILLER Yes, so that when it lifts its paw, it doesn't fall over. So it isn't that the message goes in and comes right back out over a simple reflex arc. Instead, the whole nervous system has to adjust. The postural reflexes that Sherrington studied are much more systematic and many things must work together or in opposition in order to maintain a stable base from which any kind of adaptive movement can be made. So Pavlov and Sherrington arrived at different conceptions of the reflex. Sherrington's work had much influence in physiology. Pavlov's had much influence in psychology.

Psychology has always had to wrestle with the problem of association. Once you have analysed the mind into elements, you need some principle that puts it back together. In the philosophical tradition of psychology, that principle had been called 'association'. Pavlov seemed to offer an absolutely objective way to explain how ideas become associated – the way Pavlov's dogs associated food with the sight of the caretaker. Pavlov showed that any stimulus a dog can perceive can come to evoke salivation after it has been paired with food often enough. That seemed to be an objective, scientific explanation of association – something that psychologists wanted very much. So psychologists picked up Pavlov and, along with him, a rather simplistic notion of a reflex arc, very different from the hierarchical system of interacting and counterbalancing reflexes that Sherrington had described.

J. MILLER   Sherrington, of course, was very well aware of the fact that the notion of the reflex, the simple stimulus going in and the response coming out, was essentially an abstraction, something that you could stencil into existence by creating artificial, experimental conditions.

G. MILLER   From scientists like Sherrington and Jacques Loeb[1] the belief grew that you could describe much of the behaviour of a simple organism as the result of integrated patterns and hierarchies of reflexes. This idea was taken over in a curious combination with the simple Pavlovian notion of a reflex arc, so that psychologists came to believe that they could build any arbitrary system or hierarchy by simply conditioning people.

Most psychological work on conditioning has been done, not with an involuntary reflex like salivation, but with voluntary movements. That was something Pavlov's rival, Bechterev, did first. The dog which raised its paw at the sound of a bell was the result of Bechterev's experiment.

So it was Pavlov's ideas and Bechterev's methodology that was picked up eventually by John B. Watson and the early behaviourists. They said in effect: 'Look, introspections are unreliable, different people introspect differently, there's no way I can verify that you really had the experience you told me you had. Let's throw the mind out of psychology – that's all religious superstition. We'll be hard-headed, hard-nosed scientists, we will do nothing other than what a physiologist would do.'

So the behaviourists redefined psychology in the 1920s. They redefined psychology, not as the science of mental life, but as the science of behaviour.

J. MILLER   The reflex being, as it were, the fundamental substructure.

G. MILLER   That was the building block. And it was thought that any complex pattern of behaviour – like the behaviour we're indulging in now, human speech – could with sufficient analysis be reduced to reflexes, to chains of reflexes. When a stimulus elicits a response and that response in turn becomes the stimulus to elicit the next response, and so on, it results in a reflex chain. It

---

[1]Jacques Loeb (1859–1924). A German-American biologist. He did pioneer work on artificial pathenogenesis and also carried out research in comparative physiology and psychology. His writings include *Dynamics of Living Matter* and *Artificial Parthenogenesis and Fertilisation*.

was thought, for example, that a grammatical sentence was merely a chain of vocal reflexes.

Scientifically, behaviourism was an enormously optimistic theory. How simple all this was going to be! People are not complicated after all! Psychologists had discovered the unit of analysis and the programme ahead was clear. That kind of thinking dominated both American and Russian psychology – it had less impact on British psychology – up until the Second World War.

J. MILLER   Presumably the reason it was so important in Russian psychology was that it offered some sort of route into the nervous system, through which the leaders of society could actually condition responses and render society uniform for the purposes of political conformity.

G. MILLER   Dialectical materialism needs some notion like that. I think there was a brief period when the Russian Communists thought of people as nothing more than complex machines, but then they found that that theory wasn't going to work. If people really ran like machines, when they did something that was not in the best interests of the commune or the State, you couldn't punish them; they were just doing what a machine had to do. But if people are responsible for their own actions, then they are subject to other kinds of control.

J. MILLER   Are you saying that the model of the reflex, with the system that was built upon it – an elaborate and organised system of stimuli and responses, either conditioned or unconditioned – was seen as the fundamental structure of behaviour, and there was no room in this structure for anything like the mind?

And are you saying that it eventually became apparent, some time before the fifties, that it was necessary to reintroduce something mental in order to account for a wide range of observable phenomena?

G. MILLER   No. It is not fair to say that behaviourists didn't believe in the existence of mind – to say that they didn't know whether they were conscious or not, and to make other bad jokes about them. In private life they were as intelligent as you and I; they knew they were conscious. They just believed that you can't study conscious experience *scientifically*. Whatever it is, consciousness is beyond the pale, and everything that a psychologist needs to know can be stated in terms of the correlation between certain stimuli and the responses that are conditioned to follow them. Given the response, you should be able to figure out what the stimulus was that led to it.

But you are right that it became more and more difficult for psychologists to live with that particular hair shirt, to confine their interests to nonmental events like stimuli, responses, and reflex chains.

One thing that the hard-headed psychologists used to beat their soft-hearted colleagues with was the materialistic claim that mental states and processes do not really exist. They would say: 'You talk about memory; you talk about anticipation; you talk about your feelings; you talk about all these mentalistic things. That's moonshine. Show me one, point to one.'

And psychologists interested in mental events were put off by this argument. Until, unexpectedly, during the Second World War, technological advances occurred that made it possible to talk materialistically about much more complicated kinds of physical things. Suddenly, engineers were using the mentalistic terms that soft-hearted psychologists had wanted to use but had been told were unscientific. It wasn't that the engineers were trying to reduce people to materialistic objects. What happened was that the concept of what a machine could be was greatly enlarged. And that change introduced a higher level of materialism. Whereas before we had been thinking of reflex arcs and rather simple processes of filling up and emptying containers at the energetic level, now we were given a much more complex set of theoretical ideas, ideas that can be instantiated in machines. 'It can't be moonshine if I can build one.'

The engineers showed us how to build a machine that has memory, a machine that has purpose, a machine that plays chess, a machine that can detect signals in the presence of noise, and so on. If they can do that, then the kind of things they say about the machines, a psychologist should be permitted to say about a human being.

J. MILLER   So that, in other words, the change was partly due to the fact that we had a greatly enriched series of metaphorical resources for thinking about the mind, because our machines themselves had become much more sophisticated and therefore provided useful metaphors.

G. MILLER   I know you've been interested in how science progresses by suddenly exploiting a new metaphor, a new analogy; we begin to understand the heart once we've understood pumps, for example. That's exactly what happened. World War Two involuntarily impressed psychologists into the laboratories of men who were developing complex machines. Many of those machines were hard for people to operate, so psychologists joined in with their knowledge of what the human ear can hear, the human eye can see, how far the human hand can reach; they tried to design the machines so that people could operate them effectively. In the course of this collaboration, psychologists picked up ideas from the engineers and the servo-mechanism was one of the first. This is strange, because the general notion of the servo-mechanism has a long history in physiology.

J. MILLER   I wonder if you could describe what a servo-mechanism is and then describe its historical discovery.

G. MILLER   Well, the usual tired but intelligible example is the home thermostat. Suppose you have a furnace in the cellar of your house and the furnace puts out heat. When the temperature of the house gets up to a certain level, a thermally sensitive element in the thermostat opens and turns the furnace off. The system takes a little bit of the output of the furnace and sends that back to control the input to the furnace, to turn it off. Then when the temperature falls, the sensitive element closes and the furnace comes back on. The furnace puts out an enormous amount of energy by burning coal or gas or oil or whatever, but just a tiny bit of electrical energy is turning that powerful furnace on and off, and the electrical energy is controlled by the output of the furnace. You take some of the output of the machine and feed it back to control the input. And you must feed it back out of phase. When the room is hot you turn the heater off; when the room is cold you turn the heater on. If you did it the other way, you would have positive feedback; the system would go into oscillation or explode.

This general servo principle was used in the military to develop systems to point a big gun at a target. For instance, if you want to shoot at something over there, some sort of mechanism must wheel the heavy weight of the gun around and point it at the target. You want a mechanism that's going to be sensitive to any deviation between the actual position of the barrel of the gun and its intended position, the direction you want it to point. The machine must be able to estimate that difference; as long as there's a difference, the system will feed that information back to keep the gun moving in such a way as to reduce the difference. As soon as the difference is reduced to zero, it stops.

J. MILLER   So that the behaviour of the gun is guided by the mismatch between the actual position and the desired one.

G. MILLER   Just as the behaviour of your furnace is guided by the mismatch of the actual room temperature and the room temperature that you desired when you set the thermostat.

With the servo principle it was possible to build machines that seemed to behave purposefully; the engineers talked about these machines as seeking goals. It's the purpose or goal of a machine to get a gun aimed at some particular point, for example. It has a goal in the old teleological sense that scientists had ruled out on the grounds that the future cannot control the present. But in the servo-system the *future position* of that gun controls the *present motion* of the gun in a very real, perfectly intelligible sense. So suddenly a mentalistic notion like purpose was given a physicalistic instantiation. A missile that seeks its target by sensing the target's position and reducing the difference between its direction and the direction it needs to go in order to intercept the target − that's a servo-system. And that missile looks just as purposive as a dog chasing a rabbit.

J. MILLER   So this allowed psychologists to reinstate the previously unrespectable notion of purpose, and this was due to the certain facts about machines, devices which were quite clearly material and could therefore be analysed in positivistic terms. But it wasn't simply in the area of servo-mechanisms that this relationship was discovered. Is it not true to say that advances also took place in the technology of signal detection?

G. MILLER   Oh yes. Radar. Early radar systems required a man to sit and look at a video screen, to try to pick up a radar echo, an electromagnetic echo that was displayed on the screen, an echo that indicated that there was an enemy aircraft at such and such a position. Now, men are very good at visual detection, but when you lash them down as part of an on-going surveillance system, they become unreliable. They make mistakes, their attention lapses, occasionally they have to leave their post, sometimes the signals are there and they just don't see them; they can become almost hypnotised by the display, or they look for the wrong thing or report something that wasn't an enemy plane.

So the engineers tried to invent a device that would replace the man in this job, that would detect the radar echo by itself and be more reliable. In the course of inventing this, the engineers and mathematicians who developed these electronic monitoring systems also developed a whole mathematical theory about them.

Psychologists who worked with these engineers learned the theory and applied it to how the ear hears faint sounds, how the eye detects dim lights, how the skin detects touches. They found that people detect signals in accordance with this theory, too.

One part of the theory says that you should be able to adjust your sensitivity in such a way as to reduce the cost of your mistakes. You're always going to make mistakes as long as there's some overlap of the signal and the background noise. You will sometimes say there is a target present when there wasn't one, and sometimes when there is a target you'll say that there wasn't one. You'll have both false reports and misses. Signal detection theory predicts the trade-off between the two kinds of errors. Sometimes it's very expensive to miss a signal, but it's not expensive to give a false report. In that case you want to make your detector very sensitive, so that you don't miss many signals. But in other cases the values can be the other way round: the costly thing is to make the response, that is to say, the cost of the response is high relative to the cost of what you're preventing. In that case, you make the detector less sensitive, so it doesn't respond unless you are extremely sure that there was a signal.

It turns out that people can adjust their sensitivity in this way. I can instruct you to listen for tones, for example. 'I will pay you ten dollars for every tone that you detect; if you should give me a false report (say there was a tone when there wasn't), I'll penalise you one cent.' Under that payoff condition, you would be reporting a great many tones. Or I can switch you around by making the payoff go the other way: 'I'll give you a penny for every tone you detect, but if you tell me about one that isn't really there, I'm going to fine you a thousand times that.' Then you'll switch, you'll be very conservative about reporting tones. Under these different instructions, people adjust their sensitivities exactly as if they were turning a knob on one of those machines that the engineers developed, and they adjust in such a way as to maximise the expected payoff to themselves.

So signal detection was a second line. But another idea grew out of the design of communications systems. In designing a communication channel you have to decide what band width and what signal-to-noise ratio you need in order to get your signals through. To get voice signals through, for example, you need something from about 500 to 3000 Hertz, and you would like a signal-to-noise ratio of, perhaps, at least twenty decibels.

J. MILLER   Could you explain what you mean by a signal-to-noise ratio?

G. MILLER   The intensity of the signal must be about a hundred times the intensity of any interfering noise or static in order to be easily intelligible. Forgive me for dropping into technical jargon. The signal must be clearly distinguishable from the background noise. Moreover, the channel must pass a range of frequencies, and that range determines its bandwidth. For speech, you don't need a high-fidelity system like the one you probably have in your living room. You can use something like that which the telephone company provides; this is really a narrow-band system with a not very good signal-to-noise ratio compared to a high-fidelity system.

But the general question is, what are the dimensions of the channel you need in order to transmit any signal at a given rate without exceeding some given probability of error? You can use a narrower channel and transmit information more slowly, or you can open up the bandwidth and transmit information more rapidly, but bandwidth is expensive.

What the engineers came up with was a scheme for measuring information, a way to say how much information has to pass through a channel per unit time. Once they knew that, they could design an inexpensive channel capable of transmitting the required amount of information per unit time. So the measure of information was very important.

J. MILLER   Perhaps I can summarise then, very briefly; out of those three broad areas of development – information, signal detection, and the recognition of the importance and relevance of the servo-mechanism – is it true to say that some sort of counterpart to the old notion of mind was reinstated, some idea of an internal state, the idea that there had to be something *represented*?

G. MILLER   Yes. For instance, in information theory, it turns out that the unit of information depends not on the characteristics of the signal as much as on the size of the set of alternative signals that might have been sent. The channel must be large enough to deal with that range of alternatives. What is important isn't so much the particular signal you're getting as the range of alternative signals that you expect. Now, *there* is a mentalistic word: 'expect.' As soon as psychologists heard that engineers had a way to talk about expectations, they realised that that was something the behaviourists hadn't allowed them to talk about before. Expectation was another of those forbidden mentalistic concepts.

J. MILLER   In exactly the same way that the servo-mechanism enables people to reinstate purpose.

G. MILLER   Yes, exactly the same way.

J. MILLER   So, in your own phrase, the mind came in on the back of the machine.

G. MILLER   It's ironic.

J. MILLER   So this allowed us, and indeed made it important in psychological explanation, to reintroduce consciousness, not merely by default, but as an almost indispensable concept for thinking about how we thought.

G. MILLER Consciousness? Now you've run a bit beyond what I've said so far. A great many mentalistic concepts came back into use. Whether we have to reintroduce the notion of immediate experience, immediate conscious experience, and whether this new conception of what machines can be and do is adequate to explain consciousness – those are still open and debatable questions. But certainly, vastly enriched possibilities for talking about mental phenomena resulted from engineering, technological developments in World War Two and shortly after. And we haven't even mentioned the most important development of all: the stored-programme, high-speed, digital computer, which can do all sorts of things that we had previously assumed only intelligent people can do. We call the machines intelligent because they can do things that, when people do them, we say are intelligent. It's anthropocentric to deny the word 'intelligent' to a machine if it's doing it, too, even though the machine may be doing it in a very different way.

J. MILLER So without necessarily using the ambiguous term consciousness, can one say as an alternative that the experiences with these machines at least made it respectable to reintroduce the idea that there were internal representations?

G. MILLER Right. Think about computers at the most general level. A computer has two main parts: there's the processor and there's the memory. You use the computer to perform transformations on information, but in order to do that you have to have something that holds the information while you're operating on it; you have to have a stored representation of the information, and you have to have an active element that works on the information. So you must have both a memory and a central processor.

J. MILLER And this representation exerts a very powerful influence upon what is going to be regarded as an acceptable, interesting or important stimulus.

G. MILLER Right. People seldom respond to stimuli. They respond to what they think the stimulus was. I remember doing some experiments once where people tried to predict messages; I'd give them a string of letters in a sensible message and ask them to guess the next letter. They might say, 'I think it's the letter "T",' for example; and I'd say, 'No, it's not "T".' Then they'd go on and guess something else, and later they'd come back and say again, 'I think it's the letter "T"'; 'I told you it wasn't "T"'; 'Oh, you told me it wasn't the "T" in *water*. Now I am thinking about the "T" in *Watneys*.' The same physical response – 'T', in this example – can result from very different psychological processes. And in other cases, different responses can result from similar psychological processes.

J. MILLER I get the impression that you are getting to the point where you regard the achievement of the nervous system in terms of the world it constructs.

G. MILLER Oh yes. I think the main intellectual accomplishment of the nervous system is the world itself. Physicists and chemists tell us that the surface I see there is not really a surface, but a bunch of little particles dashing around each other in some mad dance. But to me, it's a solid surface; I can reach out and touch it; it resists; it exists in space – all of which I have created by virtue of having a human nervous system that takes information in through receptors, puts it together as objects, locates the objects out there in space, gives them colours and three dimensions, sees purposes relating those objects, distinguishes people from other objects, and eventually begins to look at *me* as different from *I*, to look at myself as an object 'out there' as well as an agent 'in here'. That is the great accomplishment of the nervous system.

Human beings have laid on another level of representation beyond this one that we call the world. It is the level of symbols. Our capacity for symbolisation, most obviously expressed in our ability to speak, to use language, gives us a way to represent things at levels quite different from the concrete, perceptual level. And so we develop a world of culture and tradition. That symbolic level exists only in the most primitive way in other species. Man is an animal that represents the world symbolically; responses are important insofar as they control the information that shapes these representations of the world – and not as responses to penny-in-the-slot stimuli.

THE GROWTH OF COGNITIVE PSYCHOLOGY: DEVELOPMENTAL PSYCHOLOGY

INTRODUCTION

In a long and productive career Professor Bruner has witnessed and contributed to the revolution which has overtaken the study of mental life in the last twenty-five years.

In its understandable effort to be regarded as one of the natural sciences psychology paid the unnecessarily high price of setting aside any consideration of consciousness and purpose, in the belief that such concepts would plunge the subject back into a swamp of metaphysical idealism. Research was designed on 'positivistic' lines, so that the emphasis inevitably fell on measurable stimuli and observable behaviour. It soon became apparent that such a programme could not be sustained, and that psychology would begin to stagnate if research failed to take account of the inner state of the living organism.

Professor Bruner points out that 'the first sign that all was not well in this positivistic heaven' came with the discovery that the effect of a stimulus could not be predicted on the basis of its physical characteristics alone and that the outcome depended to a large extent on the range of alternative stimuli which might have occurred. By including the notion of probability amongst the factors which determine the effect of any particular stimulus, psychologists were forced to concede the existence of some sort of mental structure capable of sustaining states of differential expectation. Conversely it soon became apparent that behaviour was not simply a question of observable movements, and that what a creature did had to be considered as an act as opposed to a mere event; and that an act could only be intelligibly described in terms of some intention which it was designed to realise. Psychology as a result became recognisably mentalistic but without any of the unmanageable spiritualism which had embarrassed some of the early pioneers. The paradox is that by embracing the concept of mind, instead of exiling it as an unmanageable phantom, psychology has become more scientific rather than less.

Professor Bruner has developed these themes in many different areas of psychological research, but in the last fifteen years he has explicitly devoted himself to the study of cognitive processes – 'how we acquire, retain and transform knowledge of the world in which each of us lives'. Apart from his imaginative research in the laboratory he has acquired a world-wide reputation for the work which he has done on children with 'learning blocks', and more recently he has turned his attention to the nature of the teaching process, in the effort to formulate the outlines of a 'theory of instruction'.

DISCUSSION

MILLER In your Herbert Spencer lecture, which you delivered in Oxford in 1976, you expressed a feeling of crisis, implying that the subject of psychology had undergone a revolutionary change. You also expressed anxiety about the fact that as yet psychology as an expert discipline did not seem to have had an immediate impact upon the commonsense life of ordinary people, and conversely that the commonsense life of ordinary people seemed to have had no impact upon expert psychology.

Perhaps we could start by trying to describe what psychology was trying to do in those years before this revolution which you described in the lecture.

BRUNER Well, you can well imagine why one would be disturbed. Here is a field which presumably has expert cognisance concerning the nature of man. Yet somehow, its way of looking at man doesn't get discussed when it comes to matters of jurisprudence, of economics, of social policy. All those models for describing and regulating human affairs take virtually nothing that comes from 'expert' psychology into account. I brooded as to why this was so.

Let me go back and trace what psychologists had been up to before the change to which you referred. Psychology was born in a period that was essentially very positivistic in spirit. Objectivity was the motto. You must use no subjective data. Psychology must be objective science, the way in which physics was thought to be objective (though this turned out not to be quite the case). It very quickly became the rule that you do not look to the nature of ordinary experience, to the world of phenomenal experience – what Freud later called 'psychic reality' – as the basis for the new science. You looked instead to the relation between physical stimuli and observable, public and physical responses. In the interests of respecta-bility, it was agreed to stay away from private experience and subjectivity; from mind itself. It achieved the status of a four-letter word: m-i-n-d, Mind.

Let me quickly say that there was one thing that was good about this new intellectual puritanism. It kept people from doing 'armchair psychology' – from working on matters that seemed obvious though they were in fact untestable. Untestable means simply that there is no way of choosing among alternative assertions about the truth. The historical purpose of the objective approach was to save us from that.

The battle cry for objectivity, particularly in its exaggerated behaviour-istic version, soon began limiting psychology to issues that were no longer humanly interesting. What occurred then was a series of 'soft' explosions that created a revolution before anybody quite realised what was happening. How should I describe this? For one thing, there was a transformation in physics and in the 'philosophy of physics' concerning 'objectivity' and 'science'. This transformation probably starts with Ernst Mach, the great physicist-philosopher working at the turn of the century. He became interested in the *sources* of data on which science depends. All data, he argued, came out of experience, direct experience of the senses. The origins of knowledge, then, were subjective. From this subjective base we construct science.

One way of interpreting subjective experience is to project it *outside* and say: 'That is the physical world.' We then assign properties to these external constructed entities of the physical world and build upon them new experiences that are congruent with this constructed world. This is the way of physics.

The other way to proceed is to project experience *inside* and to say, in effect: 'This is the structure of our sensory, perceptual, ideational life.' We explore experience further and hope, as with physics, that we will find regularities that will allow us to elaborate this constructed world of psychology.

What Mach did to physics and the philosophy of science was to make theorists realise that the data of physics were related to the models in the physicist's head – the models that he had constructed in order to build his theory of the physical world. There was no way of getting direct access to an external world. Objectivity itself was a construct from experience, the product of subtle ways of making experience both reproducible and conceptually relevant.

It was, I think, a crucial breakaway from the programme of the British empiricists. The 'world' that impinged on mind, the 'world' that the mind somehow reflected, was *not* an image of the world that existed by virtue of Locke's primary sensations that gave direct access to external reality. The 'world' was the resultant of intellectual processes.

But there was also a second thing that entered: the change in technology. Nineteenth-century technology was overwhelmingly preoccupied with energy. The machine was envisaged as essentially an extension of the arm and the hands. It boosted energy, channelled it, and so on.

MILLER   Like steam engines, for example.

BRUNER   Yes, steam engines, mechanical shovels, gears, and governors. It was the age of mechanics and of energy transfer. Not surprisingly, the machine models of mechanics, the guiding metaphors of technology, were transferred to the human domain. In their tremendous pride, technology-dazzled philosophers sought to explain *man*; man, too, was really just another machine. '*L'Homme Machine*'.[1]

Then technology shifted. A tremendous amount of interest in the notion of control and the transmission of information developed. Information began to replace energy as the central concern of the emerging technology. The new emphasis grew steadily between the two great wars.

Kenneth Craik[2], who worked in Cambridge during the Second World War, was one of the first to see the implications of this shift for psychology.

---

[1] From the eighteenth-century French philosopher, La Mettrie.

[2] Kenneth Craik was a brilliant experimental psychologist who worked in the laboratory of Sir Frederick Bartlett at Cambridge. He wrote *The Nature of Explanation* in 1943 and published a collection of papers on experimental psychology. He was destined to become the most influential experimental psychologist in his field but he was killed in a road accident when in his thirties.

Interested in the man-machine relationship and the limits of human control of machines, and trying to assess how people managed machines, he took off on a new tack. He began to look into the nature of the human ability to know, into limitations on human information processing, how we deal with uncertainty, how we use the feedback of our own actions to regulate those actions. It was the dawn of cybernetics, and all this exerted a very powerful influence on psychology.

Gradually we began to realise, as the science of computing began to grow, that 'stimuli' were forms of input, and that their 'significance' depended upon how you coded the input, where you put it for storage, how you then put it back together again with other coded inputs. Now you could not only store inputs in memory, but instructions as well. The instructions were like thought processes: what to do 'if'.

The older psychologists could only talk about stimuli and responses and their 'linkages' as physical entities. The younger ones could and did talk about matters which were far more interesting than that. Before long, the post-war generation was deep into such mentalistic matters as the selective filtering of experience, the construction of selective representations of the world in memory, strategies for co-ordinating information. Its sum total amounted to 'the cognitive revolution'.

Some people say the cognitive revolution took place in 1956. Why then? Well, for example, in 1956 Herb Simon developed a programme called the General Problem Solver, a good enough computer programme to solve some theorems found in Whitehead and Russell's *Principia Mathematica*. It was not just a 'logic cruncher'. It embodied an effort to simulate thinking. Something called 'artificial intelligence' was in the process of being born.

In that same year, some colleagues and I published a book, *A Study of Thinking*. It was the first to take rational problem-solving as something to be explained psychologically rather than simply to be evaluated logically. Under Freud's tremendous impetus, it was *irrational* behaviour that was thought to need explication. In our book we showed, I think, that there were 'strategies' for achieving rational outcomes that were psychologically quite as interesting and subject to folly as those that produced 'the psychopathology of everyday life'. Logic is not a *process*. It is a characterisation of the results of *processes* at work.

The moment you assume that *everything* is essentially constructed, you are required to account for 'successful' and rational thinking as well as the unsuccessful and irrational. The year 1956 was also when Noam Chomsky began presenting some new ideas about language as a generative system, of which more later. And here in Britain, the work of Kenneth Craik was finding new expression through people like Donald Broadbent and Richard Gregory.

But if I had to choose a date, I think I would consider 1932 as the most significant in this area and for an odd reason. In 1932, there were two

Nobel Prize winners. One of them was E. D. Adrian, the neurophysiolo-
gist whose work had to do with how an 'outside' world of continuous
fluctuating energy could get into and be carried by a nervous system whose
individual elements, neurons, operated on an all-or-none principle.

MILLER   Could you explain that in more detail?

BRUNER   Each individual neuron has a threshold. That's to say, at a given level of
stimulating energy, it fires. Each individual fibre either goes off totally or
its doesn't go off at all, depending upon whether its threshold is reached.
Patterns of firing represent patterns of stimulation: those patterns are the
world in code. Understanding this was the beginning of the powerful
modern conception of the nervous system as a highly sophisticated
apparatus for coding and sorting input. To me, it is the antithesis of the
ancient Greek notion of the world entering the mind as an 'eidolon', the
idea that pictures introduce themselves directly into the mind. That idea
had to be abandoned. And Adrian's work provided a working alternative.

But Heisenberg won the prize for physics in the same year, 1932. His
work, to paraphrase Niels Bohr, was eventually to show that there are
certain kinds of knowledge that, canonically speaking, cannot be considered simultaneously, even in physics. There is no way of understanding
simultaneously the position of a particle and its velocity.

MILLER   So that if you determine the velocity of the particle, you are in no position
to know where it is, and if you know where it is, you can't tell how fast it's
going.

BRUNER   That's right. Bohr realised that this poses a deep problem for anybody
interested in how we cope with information and knowledge. I met him
quite by accident during the war, and later at the Institute for Advanced
Study. He told me during our first meeting that what had led him to accept
this notion were two things, both psychological. His son had committed a
certain misdemeanour, a petty bit of shoplifting. He then confessed it to
his father voluntarily.

'It was very difficult,' Bohr said, 'to know my son both at the same time
in the light of love and in the light of justice!' 'Could you,' he asked me,
'have both love and justice in the same psychological system?'

I've been brooding about that chat ever since!

MILLER   So the experience of moral complementarity led him to consider and
intensify his investigation of physical complementarity.

BRUNER   How far all of this was from the original positivistic notion of science!
Newton's notion was that science is a voyage of discovery on the sea of
ignorance to find the islands of truth. The islands were there for anybody
to discover, no matter what hypotheses they might hold.

MILLER   So we are working towards a psychology which visualises perception as a
series of constructions and hypotheses which we act upon until they prove
to be erroneous. Then we abandon them, or modify them, and reconstruct
them.

BRUNER   We place emphasis on one other thing as well. Rather than man being a recipient in the Lockeian sense, a *tabula rasa*, on which experience is written, we *selectively test* hypotheses. The most practical thing you can do is to have an hypothesis that you can reject on the basis of experience.

It is in that sense that Karl Popper[1] can talk about the proper business of science being the rejection of hypothesis. I think Professor Popper perhaps overlooks the processes needed to generate an hypothesis, but that is another question.

MILLER The Popper view of the scientific enterprise is (to summarise it briefly) that science proceeds not by accumulating facts and then building theories out of them, but starts out with some sort of conjectural hunch which often goes way beyond the information provided. It then checks the hypothesis against the world, and abandons it if and when it proves to be faulty or erroneous.

You're saying, then, that the mind is furnished with theories, or models, which determine to some extent *what* we perceive and even how much. You've got a nice experiment with the visual perception of letters which makes this point.

BRUNER Here's the experiment. (fig. 1) We begin by constructing different orders of approximation to English. We make up eight letter 'words' or rather eight letter sequences which can be gradually made to resemble spoken English.

0-Order	1-Order	2-Order	4-Order
YRULPZOC	STANUGOP	WALLYLOF	RICANING
OZHGPMTJ	VTYEHULO	THERARES	VERNALIT
DLEGQMNW	EINOAASE	CHEVADNE	MOSSIANT
GFUJXZAQ	IYDEWAKN	NERMBLIM	POKERSON
WXPAUJVB	RPITCQET	ONESTEVA	ONETICUL
VQWBVIFX	OMNTOHCH	ACOSUNST	ATEDITOL
CVGJCDHM	DNEHHSNO	SERRRTHE	APHYSTER
MFRSIWZE	RSEMPOIN	ROCEDERT	TERVALLE

FIG. 1 *Pseudo Words Constructed at Different Orders of Approximation to English*

To get sequences with what we call a zero order approximation to English you pick letters at random from the alphabet. This yields impossible, unpronounceable words like the ones in the first column.

OK. Now let's prepare a column of words with a first order approximation to English. To do this you pick letters at random, not from

[1]Sir Karl Raimund Popper (1902–). An Austrian philosopher who wrote *The Logic of Scientific Discovery* (1958), in which he refuted the long-established Baconian principles of scientific method and argued that testing hypotheses by selective experimentation rather than proof was the essence of scientific induction. For Popper, to be scientific, a theory must in principle be falsifiable, not verifiable in the logical positivist sense, and this criterion marks off a genuine science, such as physics, from what he calls the 'pseudo-sciences', such as Marxian economics and Freudian psychology which instead of challenging falsification impose a rigid finality from the outset.

the alphabet this time, but from any old page of English text. The letters will appear in the words with the same relative frequency that they occur in English. The more frequent a letter is in English the more likely it is to occur in one or other of your eight-letter crazy pseudo words. But the order of the letter is still at random. That's column two.

MILLER OK. How do we get the next order of approximation?

BRUNER To get words which have a second order approximation to English, you start by picking your first letter at random. You go to your English text and look for any word which happens to contain that particular letter. Take the letter that follows it in that word and write it down. You've now got a duet of letters one of which follows the first in the same way as it sometimes does in English. Now take the last letter in the duet and look for it in yet another word, and write down the letter that follows it and so on. Working like this you generate charming pseudo words like 'wallylof', 'therares', 'chevadne', and 'nermblim'.

MILLER Nothing like English, but words of a sort. How do we get to the next stage?

BRUNER Take any triplet of letters which have been arrived at by the method I have just described, and look for any occurrence of such a triplet in your page of English text. Pick the letter which follows it and write it down. And so on. You begin to get pronounceable nonsensical words like 'ricaning', 'vernalit', 'mossiant' and 'pokerson'. You can actually say words like this over the phone and people invariably say: 'What did you say?'.

MILLER And working like this you can get closer and closer approximation to real English.

BRUNER Right. You have now got four columns of pseudo words with column one containing unpronounceable sequences with no resemblance to words in any language, and column four containing words which are verging on recognisable English. You now present these words for recognition by flashing them onto a screen for a fraction of a second. And when you ask the subject to report the letters that he or she has seen, you get a very interesting result. With pseudo words taken from the first column the subjects correctly pick up two or three letters at the most, whereas they get all eight from the nonsensical words in the fourth order column.

MILLER It is as if the letters become more perceivable as the sequence in which they occur approximates more and more to the sequences which appear in actual words. Am I right in saying that the difficulty in recognising letters in the random sequences is due to the fact that the probability of any one letter is completely independent of the occurrence of all the other letters. Which means that each letter has to be perceptually processed as a separate alphabetical item.

BRUNER That's right. Whereas in 'words' which have a fourth order approximation to English you can use your internal model of the English language to fill in, predict and extrapolate. Now, one is tempted to ask whether this is perception or inference. But there is no way in which you can make this distinction. How can experience be independent of the perceptual hypothesis which is generated by the model of English which you have in your head?

MILLER   So you're saying then that perceiving is the result of our imposing hypotheses on the incoming information, and that the internal models which generate these hypotheses are labour-saving devices which exempt us from the otherwise overwhelming task of handling perceptual information item by item.

BRUNER   Yes. Man lives in a stunningly complex world. But he can only deal with a limited amount of information at a time. Modern psychologists refer to this as 'limited channel capacity'. But if I have an internal model of the world, I can 'chunk' the information into manageable packets, and I can also use this model to guide my search for, and processing of, present information.

This idea led to some radical changes in work on the nervous system and particularly led to new studies on attention and alerting. Arousal of the nervous system with active scanning was seen to occur when the model of the world stored in the brain was violated in some way, i.e., when it was inconsistent with the incoming information. You can see how different this is from the classical empiricist view of perception.

MILLER   You mentioned the word 'scanning' just now, which brings up yet another way in which modern neuropsychology differs from its predecessor. I'm referring, of course, to the role of motor activity in perception. This was largely overlooked during the nineteenth century, although the English neurologist Hughlings Jackson once said that no one ever says anything without moving his eyes, or felt anything without moving his hands. Now if this is so, if perception is a question of actively exploring the sensory world, there must be some mechanism inside the brain which enables us to tell the difference between sensations which result from our own movement, and sensations which result from the world's movement.

BRUNER   That's basic. The German physiologist Von Holst put the question beautifully. How does a monkey tell the difference between shaking a branch himself and having his arm shaken by the branch? Von Holst proposed a sort of 'intention process' – something signalled to the rest of the nervous system to say that an active movement is about to take place. A copy of the order for the act is shipped around the nervous system to all departments concerned.

Let's take an example. Voluntary eye movements. Whenever we move our eyes, or our head for that matter, the image of the outside world streams across the back of the retina. And yet we never get the impression that the world has moved. This can only mean that some neurological mechanism has signalled the forthcoming movement of the eyeball which allows us to compensate for the image shift which results from that movement. We don't know what neural language this signal is written in, but it's impossible to imagine a nervous system which could operate without it. Mechanisms like this, which anticipate the state of affairs which will result from a forthcoming action are called 'feed-forward' mechanisms to distinguish them from feed-back mechanisms which provide information about the actual result of such movements. In fact, the comparison between feed-forward and feed-back represents one of the most important processes in the nervous system. The difference between what was intended and what actually occurred is what we process to correct the movement.

So we now regard perception as a constructive process, in which we build a perceptual world from samplings of the sensory field.

MILLER   This notion has played a very important part in your study of the cognitive abilities of children, has it not?

BRUNER   Yes. Children faced with simple visual displays explore them just as much as adults do. But when they get into more complex displays they lack a perceptual model to guide their search, and therefore don't explore them.

MILLER   OK. Let's take an example of what an infant does when he is confronted by a relatively simple visual display. I'm referring to the experiments you did on the behaviour of young babies when confronted by a blurred picture.

BRUNER   Contrary to folklore, infants don't like blur. They don't like things out of focus. Buzzing, blooming confusion is not their scene at all.

MILLER   And you're saying that they take action to reduce this blur. But as babies have so little control over their muscles it's difficult to imagine what they can take action with.

BRUNER   Well the one thing babies can outdo us in is sucking. With those marvellous fatty pads in their cheeks plus the facial muscles they can produce thirty-pounds of pressure in long bursts of sucking without batting an eye. We used this capacity in our visual experiments. We took a rubber dummy and put some expensive electronic machinery into the teat and linked it up to the lens system of a magic lantern projecting a picture onto a screen above the baby's head. This meant that the infant could bring blurred pictures into focus by sucking on his dummy. Having established the basic rate of sucking – i.e. the rate at which the infant sucks in order to comfort himself – we found that the infant soon learned to step up this rate if he could bring the picture into focus by doing so. Presented with a blurred picture, he began to suck faster, and when the picture came into focus he would stop and look at it. That pause however, allowed the picture to drift out of focus again. And when that happened he would turn away, suck, and as the picture came back into focus he would start looking at it again. Quite an accomplishment for a little baby. He would then become so dazzled by this gorgeously clear picture of a womanly face – as powerful a stimulus as there is – that he would again stop sucking and so let the picture drift out of focus. We also found that he could master the opposite situation. We linked up the dummy with the projector in such a way that sucking drove the otherwise clear picture out of focus.

MILLER   I see. So that he was now confronted with a dilemma. The pleasures of sucking and the gradual realisation that this pleasure deprived him of the reward of seeing a clear picture. How did he reconcile this contradiction?

BRUNER   He would look at the clear picture without sucking for as long as possible, and then have an exuberant burst of sucking while looking away.

MILLER   That's very elegant. In a task which is as simple as this the infant can learn to control the visual world on its own. But earlier on you suggested that when the child is confronted by more complex visual situations he may be at a loss for want of good models to guide his motor behaviour. Am I right in saying that this may require the participation of an adult?

BRUNER   To some extent. There are some interesting experiments which show that although a child may try to explore his visual world by moving his head, he is often reluctant to shift his gaze beyond the point where the adult conducting the experiment can still be seen. It's as if the child is using you to register the most profitable direction.

MILLER   You mean that although the infant is actively exploring his visual world, he is taking cues from an adult in order to guide his gaze?

BRUNER   Yes. There's a certain element of appreciation of the adult's line of regard.

MILLER   So over and above the internal models which determine perception you're saying that perception is also directed by social factors, and that instruction plays an important part in exploration.

BRUNER   Yes. Learning is not simply the kid operating solo in a random environment. Learning is being part of a society, with that society trying somehow to keep the error rate down to a minimum by arranging manageable encounters. Which reminds me of the point which was stressed by the great Russian psychologist Vygotsky[1], who insisted that when talking about intelligence what matters is not so much intelligent action as it exists to be measured here and now, but the extent to which a person is *instructible* given optimum conditions.

MILLER   I hope this interview will have proved that point.

[1]Vygotsky, a Russian psychologist whose book, *Thought and Language*, was very influential in this field.

dialogue with
Richard Gregory

VISUAL
PERCEPTION
AND ILLUSIONS

INTRODUCTION

In his long and productive career as a laboratory scientist Richard Gregory, Professor of Neuropsychology at the Brain and Perception Laboratory at the University of Bristol, has repeatedly asked himself a question which he and many others regard as the central issue in experimental psychology. The question is this. To what extent is perception determined by current information provided by the senses, and how far is it shaped by what is already represented in the central nervous system? As a result of the research which he has done over the last thirty years Professor Gregory has become increasingly convinced that the emphasis must be in favour of the latter, and that it is impossible to explain perception in terms of the current sensory input. There is, for example, a puzzling discrepancy between the relative poverty of the image on the retina and the complex richness of what we seem to 'see'. When someone is driving along a wet road he 'sees' a three-dimensional vista of slippery tarmac, but since the retinal image has none of these properties – the visual image being neither slippery nor three-dimensional – it can only mean that the subjective appearance of the road is actively created by conjuring up a conjectural model of external reality and that the visual stimulus 'cues' one amongst a number of alternative perceptual fictions. This analysis represents a startling contrast to the traditional view according to which the subjective appearance of the world is a straightforward copy of its sensory image – as if the mind's eye were a phantom spectator looking at the coloured picture projected on to the ground-glass screen of the body's eye.

Gregory's cognitive approach to perception establishes a much more fruitful method for explaining the otherwise difficult problem of illusion. There are, as Professor Gregory points out, well-known situations in which the same sensory information can call up at least two mutually incompatible perceptions. One of the best examples is the spontaneously reversing Necker Cube, in which the same pattern of lines can be seen as the far corner of a room or the near corner of a solid block. According to Gregory's analysis such an alternation is due to the fact that the information on the retina 'is insufficient to decide between rival internal hypotheses, and each comes to the fore in turn'. In other words, perception can no longer be regarded as a straightforward matter of seeing what is there, but must be regarded instead as a process of guessing what might be there and then making the appropriate adjustments if further experience shows that the perceptual choice was incorrect.

Professor Gregory would be the first to acknowledge the debt which his ideas owe to the work of the almost legendary Cambridge psychologist Kenneth Craik, who was one of the first to introduce the idea of the brain as a conjectural model maker. 'If the organism carries a "small-scale model" of external reality and of its own possible actions within its head, it is able to carry out various alternatives, conclude which is the best of them, react to future situations before they arise, utilise the knowledge of past events in dealing with the present and the future, and in every way react in a fuller, safer, and more competent manner to the emergencies which face it'.[1]

DISCUSSION

MILLER   There was a time when vision was regarded as the experience of some privileged spectator seated behind a ground-glass screen, watching a perfectly formed image of the outside world. In recent years however vision has been studied as if it were a creative skill. I think it's true to say that the study of optical illusions has played a very large part in this change of attitude.

GREGORY   Well, first of all, I take the view that perceptions are representations of reality and not, so to speak, samples of reality which a passive theory of perception would maintain. They are, rather, brain descriptions in a sort of internal brain language. Brain states represent the world rather as letters on a page represent fiction or truth. Now once one says it's representation, then we can classify illusions rather as one classifies errors in language or in other forms of representation. One can have a distortion; for example, if I say that the moon is ten million miles away, that's a distortion of the truth. And similarly in perception you get visual distortions.

The second kind of illusion, I think, is ambiguity: where you've got the same input into the eye, or the ear or the other senses, but the awareness 'flips' from one perception – one seen object let's say – to another. Or it might change in space or orientation, with no change in the input. So it's like a sentence with two meanings, or more than one meaning with the same words on the page; it's ambiguous in that sense.

The third kind of illusion is paradox. For example one can say that one has a 'dark-haired blonde girl friend', which is paradoxical, in that it has an incompatibility built in; and one can also get visual perceptions which look impossible. They may be resolvable, or they may not; but they certainly appear impossible.

The final one I think you might call fiction – something like ghost stories. It's when you see something which is not there. It turns out that this is very important, the generation of fictions, for seeing the richness of reality from the very limited amount of data, or information, which the senses can handle or have available to them. So generation of fiction is intimately bound up with generation of fact.

MILLER   Your point being that the objective visual input is somewhat impoverished by comparison with the relatively rich experience which you have as a subject. This can only be accounted for by suggesting that some positive contribution is made by the viewer other than simply, as it were, sitting behind a ground-glass screen.

GREGORY   Yes, I think it's partly that the sense organs themselves are highly limited

[1]Kenneth Craik: *The Nature of Explanation* (1943) p. 61.

in what they can accept at any one moment, and secondly that objects are often partly hidden. For example, if I put this pen behind this spectacle case, you 'see' it, as a continuous thing, in spite of the fact that you don't actually see the stretch of pen behind. So either perceptually or conceptually one is maintaining an assumption of an object although the information is simply not available to the senses. This is an extremely important part of perception, and it can of course go wrong – it can generate bits of pen which are not really there.

MILLER   Perhaps we can go through each of those four examples in terms of visual illusion. Could you show examples of *distortion* in perception?

GREGORY   Yes. Well these are classical, rather well-known examples. They're good in that they're very simple. The Ponzo illusion (fig. 1) is essentially a pair of lines which are converging, and anything which is placed between them is distorted in such a way that a feature which is near the narrowing end of the lines gets expanded, and looks longer than it would below. But it's also true if I rotate the figure.

MILLER   So that it's nothing to do with position relative to up or down. It's to do with the position relative to its placing in the converging lines.

GREGORY   That's right.

MILLER   How would we explain that it terms of a contribution made by the spectator?

GREGORY   Well, the whole of perception is controversial. This is the way I look at it. If one looks at a picture like this one (fig. 2) it looks as if it's in depth. It's, in fact, a photograph of a railway track. And it's a very similar shape to this illusion (fig. 1) which is, as it were, a simplified line diagram of a very common type of scene. Now the narrow part (fig. 2) is obviously further away from you, so the issue is this: are you, by indicating that something is further away, getting the expansion? The information of the converging

FIG. 1   FIG. 2

lines, which are typically perspective convergence, would apply to the image in the eye looking at an actual railway track. This shrinking will occur in retinal images with true distance. But when that's on a flat picture, you're presenting the eye with a very silly situation, because you're indicating distance when in fact, in the case of the picture, the whole picture is at the same distance from you.

Now the argument is a little bit complicated. It goes like this. If you've got an object which is in fact going further away from you, the image in your eye shrinks as the object gets further away, by geometrical optics. But you don't see it *getting* that much smaller. In other words it's compensated by what we call Size Constancy Scaling. There's a scaling process in the brain which compensates for the shrinking of the image with increasing distance. So if, for example, your hands are at different distances from your eye, they look much the same size.

MILLER   In other words, although the actual image projection on the retina is shrinking quite dramatically, one does not infer that someone is really shrinking as they go away. You simply say that the same size person is moving away.

GREGORY   Exactly. And one actually *sees* them as much the same size. Now the argument is this. The mechanism works fine in normal space, three-dimensional space like this room. But if you've got a flat *picture* of normal space, you're asking the visual system to do something quite impossible – and you find that the features which normally activate the compensation to the shrinking of the image – which as you say occurs in real space with increasing distance – that compensation is now set up by the perspective in the picture. But since the picture's flat, it cannot be correct, because there's nothing to compensate. Any point on the picture is at the same distance as any other point. So you get an expansion. This is very much in line with the kind of thing Helmholtz[1] was saying, when he said that normal processes can become inappropriate to generate error, in certain atypical situations of which pictures are one.

MILLER   Of course this picture (fig. 2) is a comparatively rich portrayal of a concrete situation; but it still works when you have this relatively impoverished representation of perspective (fig. 1), merely with two converging lines – so that it's as if the perceptual system is capable of making these conjectures on the basis of very inadequate information, and then makes its other judgements on that basis.

GREGORY   Yes. It's as if there were a preliminary setting up from limited features which are first of all accepted. And it's also interesting, of course, that one doesn't have to see this in depth. It occurs at the early stages of perception, which is setting up the initial scale of things.

MILLER   Early psychologists failed to see that this was the explanation. They failed

[1]Hermann von Helmholtz, a nineteenth-century German physicist and psychologist. Author of *Handbuch der physiologischen Optik*, in which he developed the notion that perception involves 'unconscious inferences'.

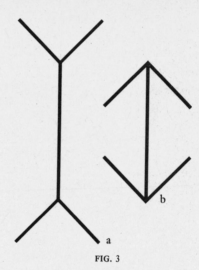

FIG. 3

to see that they themselves, as ordinary perceivers, were actually reading these converging lines as something *going away* in *three dimensions*, rather than something *converging* in *two dimensions*.

GREGORY   Absolutely. And indeed this is still to some degree controversial. I've actually been arguing for that theory for twenty years and there are probably a lot of psychologists who will still not agree with it. It is the way I look at these distortion illusions.

MILLER   You make the same argument, don't you, about the famous Muller-Lyer illusion? (fig. 3). I wonder if you could explain what's going on with those two lines.

GREGORY   Well it's exactly the same argument. These are the shapes that you get on the retina when you look at a corner. In this case (fig. 3a) an inside corner.

MILLER   In a room?

GREGORY   Yes. This is in fact a perspective drawing of a corner and the other way round (fig. 3b) you've got a corner at the outside of a building or something similar.

MILLER   So that the apparent lengthening of one of the vertical lines (fig. 3a), although those two vertical lines are identical in length, is due to the fact that one is reading *that* one (fig. 3a) as further away.

GREGORY   Yes. That's exactly right. Because this vertical line (fig. 3a) is taken to be further away than these end diagonals, by this mechanism we're talking about – Size Constancy Scaling – it gets expanded, which is appropriate for a room, or a model, but not for a picture, because a picture's flat.

MILLER   And again, although there's very very little spatial information there, it's got enough of a *clue* as to its spatiality to convey that sense.

a

b

FIG. 4

GREGORY   Yes. And again we can look, if you like, at a richer example. Here's a not
           very scintillating picture (fig. 4a) of a building, which I took myself.
           There's an inside corner with this typical shape of the Muller–Lyer
           illusion, and an (even worse) picture of an outside corner (fig. 4b).

MILLER   So that, then, is distortion. How about ambiguities?

GREGORY   Ambiguities. Well they're great fun. You really do see a sort of
           spontaneous activity of your perceptual system with ambiguities. This
           (fig. 5a) is the most famous example, and I think it's right to look at these
           simple, though perhaps well-known, examples. Let's try to explain them.

           Well, this obviously looks like a three-dimensional cube and that in
           itself, of course, is interesting, because it is just lines on a flat piece of
           paper. Sometimes you find that one face looks like the front and then
           suddenly it'll flip and become the back. Now there are a lot of lessons to be
           learned from this. First of all, you can make it happen when you blink, or
           when you move your eye about; but it will also flip entirely spontaneously.
           You can actually fix this image on the back of the eye, on the retina,

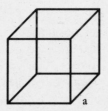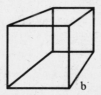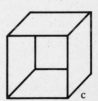

a   b   c

FIG. 5

optically, so that although the eye is moving about a bit, there's no movement of the image on the eye. In other words you stabilise it on the eye.

MILLER   How would you do that?

GREGORY   Well you can either do it by looking at this with a flash of light, and looking at the after-image, which is a very easy experiment. One can do it if one has a photographic flash. Or one can do it optically with a contact lens carrying a little mirror, which is put in the eye; then you reflect the image from the mirror with some rather cunning optics. As the eye moves the image remains stationary on the retina.

MILLER   So although exactly the same pattern of lines is retained on the retina – the subject supposedly looking at his retina – which of course is nonsense – is in fact seeing two mutually exclusive spatial pictures of a cube.

GREGORY   Yes, and this happens when you've got a retinal pattern, if you like, which can be, or is, with roughly equal probabilities, either of two or more objects. Not necessarily two, it could be three, four, five or more stable states, or, if you like, possible objects, but two is the most dramatic example.

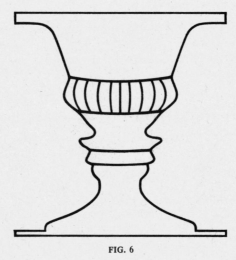

FIG. 6

MILLER   So that one's making two alternative hypotheses about what sort of object could be responsible for that sort of pattern of stimulation on your retina.

GREGORY   I think that's exactly the point.

MILLER   Just before we go to the *third* kind of illusion there is of course the famous Rubin vase (fig. 6) which is another of these equivocal figures.

GREGORY   This is a switch between two different kinds of objects, namely the vase or the two faces – which are really quite frightening. I always get quite frightened looking at this thing. The cube, of course, is a change in space, not a change from one object to another. These (fig. 6) are actually two different objects, and to get this to work, the objects – the vase as an object and the faces as objects – must have roughly equal probabilities. By biasing the probabilities, as I think we can probably see in a minute, you can prevent this being ambiguous and make it stable. So it's nothing really to do with the physiology – it's to do with the relative probabilities of these shapes as representing objects.

MILLER   You mean the relative probabilities of their occurrence in your world.

GREGORY   Yes. I don't know of any experiment using a subject who had been brought up with no vases – or, even more difficult, no faces – but that ought to upset this experiment: they ought to get a different result.

MILLER   So it might happen in a Martian world where in fact they'd never seen a species that had profiles of that sort, but where they were accomplished vase makers, that they wouldn't understand why we thought of this as an illusion at all. They would only see vases.

GREGORY   Yes. That ought to be the case.

MILLER   I see. So that takes us to the third category – to paradoxes. Have we got an example of a paradox?

GREGORY   Well again this is fairly well known (fig. 7a). It was designed about twenty years ago. It's a very nice example of a simple sort of figure which

FIG. 7a

shouldn't present any sort of physiological problems to the eye, and yet it's very difficult to see it, to interpret it as an object.

The question, of course, concerns where the different features lie in space. Well, one sees it in a way as a flat thing, but the perspective of these corners doesn't tie up. Now this is actually a model in three dimensions and yet it still looks impossible from a critical point of view. You may have seen that there is in fact a solution to this paradox. There are other visual paradoxical figures which have perhaps no actual solutions. So, there are contingent paradoxes and there are, if you like, logical paradoxes.

MILLER   So there are two equally possible interpretations which are actually locked here into a situation which is so mutually exclusive as to produce a ridiculous figure which is internally inconsistent with itself.

GREGORY   Yes. What's really happening is that the visual system is making the assumption that all the parts of the figure are at the same distance from the eye. Having made that assumption the figure is then very difficult to see. It's really impossible. But when (fig. 7b) you can make a solid model of this thing you simply make this part (a) lie behind that point (b). Then all these angles work out perfectly naturally. The paradox is based on an assumption which could be false and the false assumption then generates the paradox.

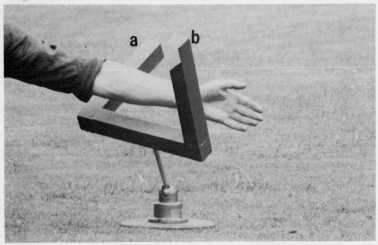

FIG. 7b

MILLER   Once again, it emphasises the importance of the contribution made by the perceiver as opposed to the information provided by the world.

GREGORY   Yes. And by the assumptions that he holds to interpret the evidence. Which again is true in science. After all you can't interpret an experiment unless you've got assumptions.

MILLER   And that's a point we're going to come to later on. Now we come to the fourth type, the illusion which is a fiction.

GREGORY   Yes. This figure (fig. 8) is due to an Italian psychologist, Gaetano Kanizsa.

FIG. 8

The central white triangle is in fact illusory, and the edges, although sharp clear edges, are not there. That is, there's no actual brightness difference across the edges, so that it must be constructed by the observer. Let's look at some more examples.

One can make the lines curve (fig. 9) by simply reducing the angles in those sectors and the visual system kind of joins up an imaginary curved triangle . . .

MILLER   And it's not just that one is *intellectually* making a hypothesis. One is actually *seeing* a white triangle, although all that there is, is an interruption in the black triangle and some little bites out of the black circles.

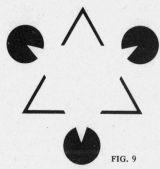

FIG. 9

GREGORY The key to it is having, so to speak, a gapped figure. If it's a figure that's got surprising gaps, which are unlikely to occur by chance, then it's more likely that there's something getting in the way, producing the gaps. And this reminds one of looking at the pen which is partly hidden.

But with the pen, we correctly either conceive, or perhaps even perceive, that the object is continuous although partly hidden. Here (figs. 8, 9) we've got actual gaps in this figure, and the same mechanism is creating lines or figures which are not really there – because normally it's very useful to go on seeing parts of objects, or at least to believe that they're there, when they're hidden by something nearer.

MILLER   It's again a question of making guesses on the basis of the probabilities in the world one knows. One knows about triangular objects, and something as interrupted as *that*, would only be explained in terms of an overlapping white triangle, which was actually cutting off the edges.

GREGORY But regarding that curved one (fig. 9). Some people have argued that these are a sort of Gestalt 'closure' effect, or something of that kind.

MILLER   Now what does that mean exactly? 'Gestalt' is a famous term from the twenties but what did the Gestalt psychologist really mean by a 'Gestalt'?

GREGORY Well I think at least two things. These psychologists said that there were 'preferred forms' which in a way is right, because objects generally are rather closed. Their parts move together if the objects are in movement. There are certain characteristics of objects, as opposed to different objects, lying separately in space, or just at random. There are certain characteristics of objects and they were very good in pointing that out. But they also said that the form-making processes by which the brain perceives objects were due to the physiology of the brain, in a way which they described as isomorphism. This idea is that you've got little models of the object world in the brain.

And it's as if the brain, as it were, preferred certain stable geometrical shapes – like soap bubbles forming spheres. This is wrong; that is, the theory behind what they were saying is, I think, physiologically quite wrong.

Now it's interesting that if you take this figure (fig. 9) you find that it is a very bad Gestalt. In other words, you've got concave edges here which is *not* what the Gestalt psychologists would predict.

MILLER Because they would have predicted that a straight sided triangle would be a much more regular figure, which the brain would prefer.

GREGORY Yes, or preferably a convex one.

MILLER And yet because of those smaller angles, combined with the place at which the black triangle is interrupted, one cannot avoid inferring a curved object lying between you and the black triangle and black discs beyond.

GREGORY Yes I think this is right. I think it's an *inference*. It's a postulate, if you like, and is not due to the physiology of the brain, in the sense of it having preferred forms in the Gestalt sense.

MILLER Well I'm sure we'll come to that point about the difference between brain processes and mind processes, a little later. I can see from all that you've said so far that you're suggesting that perception is really a hypothesis-making process: that we're making conjectures or guesses about what's out there, and the intellectual guess that you're making – if it is intellectual – is actually framing the experience you're having.

GREGORY Yes. I think the experience that one has in perception *is* a hypothesis. I wouldn't separate the hypothesis from the perception. The way I see it, perceptions are predictive hypotheses. They're suggested by available data; but interestingly the data can be the surprising *absence* of signals. In those Kanizsa figures it's the gaps – which are really the absence of stimulation – which are the data for the overlying object. It can be surprising absence of signals, just as much as signals, which are the data.

MILLER Which, of course, by the classical view of perception would have made no sense at all, because that view would have insisted that only the presence of a stimulus would allow you to see, whereas some sort of inference is the only thing that accounts for these actual experiences.

GREGORY Yes. I think actually this presents some difficulties to physiology. I'm sticking my neck out a bit here; but I don't think one can equate activity in the nervous system with the resulting perception – at least peripheral activity in the nervous system – because, again, it's a surprising absence of activity which can actually produce contours, and can produce brightness changes, and can produce the triangle in those figures, and many other things.

One has to be able, I think, to read the physical signals in the nervous system as information representing presence or absence of features according to a sort of internal code; until we've learnt that code we can't really relate the physiology to the perception.

MILLER   In other words, as far as the nervous system is concerned, the *absence* of an otherwise expected positive signal can be just as informative as the presence of something which might have occurred in a gap.

GREGORY   That's right.

MILLER   So that the information is to do with the probability or improbability of an event occurring.

GREGORY   Yes. It's only when it's improbable that it's conveying information, and it can be, as you say, the improbability of its presence or its absence; and the physiologist needs to know that in order to interpret his results.

MILLER   It's like that wonderful example from Sherlock Holmes when he said, 'Did you notice anything about the dog barking in the night?' and Watson said 'I didn't hear the dog bark.' 'Precisely,' said Holmes. It was the fact that the dog did *not* bark that was significant.

GREGORY   Yes.

MILLER   So that, in all of this, the notion of conjecture and hypothesis is the important part. And we've got another example of that here with this dotted picture (fig. 10). If you inspect it closely you can see that it is a dog. Now presumably what one is doing is making some sort of hypothesis about the probabilities of what's out there. Among the likely probabilities, in a dotted world, is a Dalmatian dog.

GREGORY   I think in a situation like this, it's very difficult to see (or unlikely that one

FIG. 10

would see) a highly unlikely object. One is picking up typical features, which in this case is the ear of a Dalmatian dog, which then suggests the hypothesis 'Dalmatian dog'. I think this is a matter of selecting the most probable object given this rather poor signal-to-noise ratio. In my laboratory we have a system by which we can produce what we call dot sampled pictures, which you might like to look at.

MILLER   Now what is this (fig. 11) exactly? What have you done here?

FIG. 11

GREGORY   Well each dot is selected electronically from an object, and I won't say what the object is. It's a sort of really crummy picture – and we can quantify the crumminess.

     We will now make it a bit less crummy.

MILLER   Okay, so crumminess mark two.

GREGORY   Crumminess mark two (fig. 12). You can possibly see what that is.

FIG. 12

MILLER   Let's de-crummify it a bit more.

GREGORY   Which is simply having more dots.

These are electronically generated with a video system, and we count the dots electronically, so we can quantify the information. Here (fig. 13) it's fairly obvious what it is, surely. You begin to see the shapes much more accurately. You can see the shape of that telephone (fig. 14), which you couldn't in the earlier pictures, as you get more and more information.

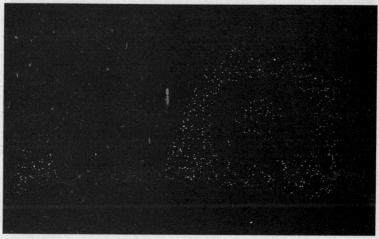

FIG. 13

Once you know what that object is, we could go back to the first one (fig. 11) now and it's rather difficult to see it as anything but a telephone once you know the answer.

MILLER   So, in other words, once your ranking of probabilities has been biased by the experience, then it reintroduces itself into the perception that you make of that relatively impoverished information.

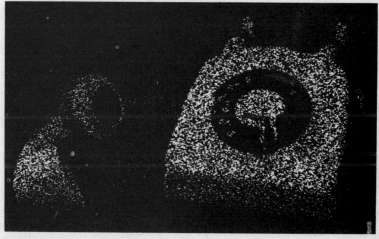

FIG. 14

GREGORY   Yes.

MILLER   So you're looking up a stock of images of objects with which to interpret what you see.

GREGORY   It's rather interesting that this guessing from inadequate data can go overboard. It's a part of all perception but it can generate fiction, which indeed we saw with those Kanizsa pictures. I'd like to go back to that and look at a rather more elaborate form of Kanizsa picture. In fact there is going to be a series of pictures. I think that this one (fig. 15) just looks a bit of a muddle. As a whole it doesn't make much sense. Now suppose we join

FIG. 15

up some of the lines in this figure and then have a look at it (fig. 16). Bingo ... you see a cube lying behind those bars.

MILLER   And all that you've done, all that you've added, is the black lines down those white rivers.

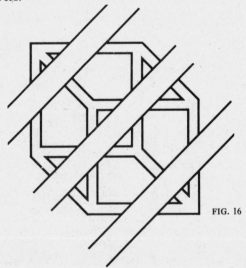

FIG. 16

GREGORY   Right. Now what happens if we remove the end lines (of fig. 15). You surely see illusory bars (fig. 17) which you've postulated or created, which allow you to see that cube as an object. So there's a sort of two-stage

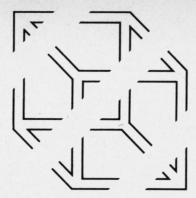

FIG. 17

process of creation here in that when they were blocked off in the first place (fig. 15), you can't do anything much about it; when you put in the explicit bar lines (fig. 16) you then perceive it as one object lying partly hidden. If we remove the blocking ends of the figure (fig. 17), then you can postulate the bars which also allow you to see it.

MILLER   And as in the earlier Kanizsa figures, you can actually see the white strips although they have no contours themselves, or at least no outside hard lines.

GREGORY   That's right, and they're kind of serving a purpose. They actually allow you to see a cube figure. The postulate of the strips seems to be necessary.

MILLER   The funny thing is that once you've seen it and you've gone through the tuition of the intervening process, if we go back to the first of the three figures (fig. 15) you can now, by an effort, actually see that cube. It's quite hard to do though, isn't it?

GREGORY   I find it still quite difficult to do. There's a very big difference between that (fig. 15) and the end one (fig. 17), although I know the answer. It's still jolly difficult to apply one's knowledge to modify the perception. And this is, I think, a very important point – that what we *perceive* and what we *conceive* can be different. In other words we can know that we're wrong perceptually and yet we can't really correct the perception in many cases. At the same time, knowledge is important for perceiving objects, that is for handling the information from the eye, but the knowledge is kind of built in – stored – and most of it is not available to consciousness. We can't juggle with it with our intellect very much to affect perception. They're almost separate processes.

MILLER   And yet we do use the phrase 'trying to make it look like a cube' and I find it quite hard to know exactly what force one ought to give to that phrase. What would one want to say about *trying* to make the Necker cube reverse, what does one *try* with, how does one *do* the trying?

GREGORY   I feel that's extremely difficult. It has been suggested by William James, and it's also been suggested by Popper and Eccles more recently, that when you look at a Necker cube you can *will* it to switch, to flip, and that this is an example of mind imposing itself on brain. It's been used as an argument that mind is causative – not part of the brain, but able to affect the brain. Now I don't like this argument, frankly, and I'd like to fight it by suggesting that *one* brain mechanism, associated here with *will*, can affect *another* part of the brain mechanism. Here (fig. 5) in the analysis of the lines which form the cube perception, we've got one bit of brain affecting another bit of brain, rather than the mind – as something separate from brain – affecting brain. I don't think these phenomena are evidence of a causal link between mind and brain. I think that both the will *and* the processes of perception, are physical processes going on in the brain. It's *not* a case of mind hovering above one's head, affecting one's brain like a sort of ghost.

MILLER   As Gilbert Ryle[1] once pointed out in *The Concept of Mind*, the idea that the mind might be a ghostly exertion behind the hardware leads to an infinite regress, because one would have to postulate some sort of mechanism which was responsible for mind, which enabled it to exert its effect on the hardware.

And that in itself would then set up another mind behind the machine; that mind would itself have to have machines to operate it, and so there would be presumably an infinite regress of these agencies. Nevertheless there is a problem, because one wonders what it is one does the willing *with*.

GREGORY   Yes. One does it with one's brain I suspect. And then you get a sensation which you call the sensation of will when there are certain channelled operations going on. I don't think that is a complete explanation either. I agree, this is frightfully difficult.

MILLER   But it's strange that one does feel much more puzzled by the problem of willing a perceptual figure to change its shape than one does with the more commonplace experience of willing one's hand to go up. And yet presumably the same problem is involved.

GREGORY   I think, going back to Ryle, one might say it's wrong to say there's a sort of ghost in the machine, but at the same time when you look at complicated machines such as computers they *are* a little bit ghostly, because they are carrying out procedures which you don't describe in terms of mechanics.

If a computer is carrying out mathematics, you need mathematical concepts to describe what is going on; electronics is not adequate, mechanics is not adequate. So there's a dualism in a machine, but not a metaphysical dualism in the sense of a hovering mind affecting a machine. But rather that the procedures carried out by the machine are richer than, and different from, the mechanical and electronic processes described by the engineer, and I think this is also true of the brain.

MILLER   You're not suggesting then, or perhaps you are, that there comes a certain

[1]Gilbert Ryle (1900–1976). An English philosopher. In 1931 he became a convert to the view that 'philosophy is the detection of the sources of linguistic idioms of recurrent misconstructions and absurd theories'. His *The Concept of Mind* (1949) displays brilliant linguistic detective work in exorcising 'the ghost in the machine' or the philosophical remains of Cartesian dualism.

point at which the machine actually begins to create something transcendent to the specifications introduced by the engineer and that at a certain point in the complexity of the design, the machine, by virtue of its complexity, mysteriously secretes a ghost of its own?

GREGORY   Not quite that, but in a funny sort of way, not miles away from that. First of all, the machine can do things that the engineer, the designer, never thought it could do, which is even true of a simple computer. It can solve problems that nobody imagined it would be set to solve, and, secondly, it is carrying out procedures with its programmes, which are not really described by the physics or by the engineering of the machine, but by the logic or the mathematics of the program itself, which you can think of as very separate from the machine, although it's carried out by the machine.

In other words you've got two languages. You've got the physics or the electronics of the device, let's call it a computer, but you've also got the procedures carried out by it, which needs a different language. The concept of logarithms, even of multiplying, is not really in the description of the machine itself. It's in the description of what it does. This is even true of a sewing machine – it's carrying out processes, and you've got to know about sewing and what's required in order to make stitches in cloth, in order to understand the function of the sewing machine, although of course it's just a mechanical system. So it *is* a sort of ghost, but not quite Ryle's ghost, both in machines and also in the brain and mind situation. The distinction here between brain and mind would be that you've got the physical structure – which you can put electrodes in, which you can record from, and which you can study anatomically – and then you've got the processes which this is carrying out. These are dynamic processes which are, essentially, following rules, which might be rules of mathematics or might be rules of logic. They're probably rules that we can put into a computer, to make a computer itself perceive, though possibly not become conscious. We can begin to make computers that will recognise objects, and curiously and interestingly, they suffer from many of the same illusions when the processes that are carried out by the very different physical structure of the computer (or if you like the robot) are inapproripate to the situation. So again, the illusions are due not to inadequacies of the *physics* of the system, but rather to the inappropriateness of the strategies or procedures that are carried out by the physical structures. When it's working appropriately, with the correct assumptions, you can say it generates truth or that we perceive reality without error or distortion. But inappropriate assumptions can generate mistakes and perceptual distortions.

MILLER   But we haven't yet produced a computer which is capable of detecting the fact that it's in the presence of an illusion – or capable of undergoing some sort of exploratory process which would enable it to tell that something is illusory.

GREGORY   Well, there are strategies called 'hill climbing' strategies which are of such a kind that when the computer cannot get a better and better solution and gets stuck, it can be programmed to be dissatisfied with the progress it's made, and to take a step back – and even accept worse solutions in order to get to a vantage point from which it can make progress towards a new line of development. This is a rather recent kind of computer program in Artificial Intelligence.

MILLER   But the notion of satisfaction is in fact borrowed, slightly dishonestly, from our own sense of conscious *dis*satisfaction. What would it be for the computer to experience restlessness or dissatisfaction? We're inferring what *might* be dissatisfaction, from the fact that it behaves in what, in a human being, would be a dissatisfied way.

GREGORY   Yes I agree, but I think as soon as a computer is put into a robot which can explore, which can touch and handle objects, the computer situation is more like the situation for humans and exploratory animals. I don't think a baby would ever come to see things unless it could touch them as well – in other words carry out experiments, validate the hypothesis, much as a scientist does. I think once a computer can actively interact with the world, then it can discover dissatisfactions or inadequacies, though they are not represented in consciousness.

MILLER   So you're saying that the way in which we *perceive* the world is analogous to the processes by which scientists undertake to *explain* the world.

GREGORY   I would think they are extremely similar. If you take, say, a radio telescope, you've got a sensing system; you've got signals coming up the cable, some of which is rubbish; the interpretation always depends on knowledge of where the aerial's pointing and so on. From how the calibration of the instruments is set up, and by following assumptions with various rules, you extract what we may call 'data' from those signals, and those data are used to suggest and ultimately test hypotheses of the nature of the object – which might be a quasar, or it might be anything you like.

MILLER   So science would never have got anywhere, or wouldn't have got beyond the starting line, if it had simply been the passive accumulation of data from which it then built theories. It has to leap beyond the information provided.

GREGORY   It has to leap ahead in stages, then test by whether it's going to work or not in practice. I think it uses a series of check procedures – a series of leaps ahead in a very dynamic way – and it develops its own rules for its progress as it goes along, so the rules are based on successes and failures and generalisations from the past. They ought to go on applying into the future, but the actual objects discovered might be unique and still be discoverable, still perceivable.

MILLER   But in making these leaps, in the process of perception, to some extent we're guided by previous experience. We're looking up records of things that we've seen or experienced before. Would it be true to say also that some of the guesses or conjectures and leaps are determined by innate propensities? Although again it goes against the seventeenth- and eighteenth-century idea of 'no innate ideas in the mind', we are gradually beginning to favour the notion that there are built-in rule-observing capacities in the brain.

GREGORY   Yes, well I think there isn't really a philosophical problem here, so long as one says that the rules, or even indeed knowledge of objects, is innate in the individual as a result of the experience of past generations. There's no reason why this should not be so. Why shouldn't the structure of the brain be modified, just as noses have been modified by rain having fallen downwards for millions of years? If one's nostrils were the other way up one would have drowned. As a result, the nose is shaped like a roof.

In other words it's the experience of past generations, by natural selection – the fact that organisms that can see a bit better or organisms which have better shaped noses, survive – which ends up as innate knowledge. You have an innately appropriate shape to your nose, and you have appropriate rules, built into your brain structures, that must be followed in order to see the world.

MILLER   But we have to emphasise that this is not because of the immediate experience of one's parents. It is not the fact that one's parents have learnt that the world is furnished with this or that object, and that that is handed on by some Lamarckian[1] process to the offspring, but rather that natural selection has gradually weeded out those creatures which have not been endowed through mutations with some sort of rule-observing idea about the universe.

GREGORY   Yes; so that what gets inherited are structural changes, but these are carrying out appropriate procedural operations. So in that sense, you can say natural selection develops the processes of perception just as reflexes get developed by natural selection. After all the knee jerk, or the fact that the pupils of your eye contract in a bright light, are innate responses: they don't have to be learned.

MILLER   So would it be true to say that as the process of natural selection refines and improves the brain, what we're getting in some strange and paradoxical way is a brain which incorporates inside itself, through natural selection, a more and more accurate model of the universe in which it lives?

GREGORY   Yes, and rules for being able to accept limited data: or should I perhaps say inadequate signals interpreted as data, according to rules which you've discovered to hold in the world, even in rather unfamiliar situations.

MILLER   So if what you're saying is true, then the brain is progressively incorporating rule-observing processes in its circuits which are more and more accurate pictures of the world. One ought to be able, if one could read the 'brain writing' on these circuits, by looking inside the brain of a creature which had experienced some other world, get a pretty good model of the world it lived in, or am I going too far?

GREGORY   No, I think it's a nice idea. This is really it – how can we read the brain language? Why don't we look at how information is encoded in structures

[1]See footnote on page 102.

of the brain? I suppose the only answer is that we don't yet know how to do it. It's been done for the gene code in molecular biology to a great extent; but we don't yet know the corresponding features to look at in the brain structure.

MILLER But are you saying that if we actually knew the language – if we knew the alphabet and knew the grammar of the brain script – that we could look at this sort of Lascaux painting of neurological activity inside the brain; and that even if one had never seen the world in which the creature lived, if that brain is an accurate representation of the world, it should be a way of actually getting information about that creature's world?

GREGORY Yes in principle, provided of course the 'language' hadn't changed for that creature, which it might. In other words, a given bit of brain structure might represent one thing at one stage of evolution and a different thing in another stage of evolution; parts of the brain get used for different things, like the parts of the brain used for smell in dogs becoming associated with emotional activity. You sometimes get a takeover of function. So I think the argument would perhaps never be very secure because that 'language' – brain language – might evolve just as human languages evolve and change.

ARTIFICIAL INTELLIGENCE AND THE STRATEGIES OF PSYCHOLOGICAL INVESTIGATION

INTRODUCTION

There was a time, not so long ago, when psychologists shunned questions about the philosophy of mind in the belief that they were tedious and unanswerable compared to the problems which could be settled by experiments carried out in the laboratory. To some extent their attitude was justified by the fact that until recently philosophical speculation seemed vague and unhelpful, added to which discussion was often conducted without paying any attention to the discoveries of experimental psychology.

But as Professor Dennett points out, both philosophy and psychology have taken a turn for the better, and there are already signs of a fruitful *rapprochement*. 'Psychology has become "cognitive" or "mentalistic" and fascinating discoveries have been made about such familiar philosophical concerns as mental imagery, remembering and language comprehension'.[1] Conversely, philosophy has become noticeably less metaphysical, and by asking questions about the language which we use to describe mental processes it is at least in a position to provide helpful methods for thinking about the design and significance of psychological experiments.

Professor Dennett's career epitomises this change in the history of ideas. Trained as a philosopher both in England and the United States, his interest in logic and language has played an important part in the contribution he has made to the conversations which are now going on about the meaning and methodology of the cognitive sciences. The problem to which Professor Dennett has directed much of his attention is the traditional puzzle of the relationship between brains and minds, between a universe of discourse which includes words such as 'neurons', 'circuits', 'synapses' and 'neuro-transmitters'; and one which uses so-called intentional concepts such as belief and meaning. There are those who insist that the gap between these two domains is logically unbridgeable and that some of the traditional efforts to mediate between them have resulted in conceptually absurd proposals such as the well-known theory of an immaterial substance halfway between mind and matter. An alternative theory is the so-called reductionist one, which argues that with improvements in neurophysiological knowledge the language of mental states will eventually be replaced by an accurate account of so-called brain states. Philosophers who support this theory look forward to the time when it will be possible to characterise someone's beliefs by reading the nervous inscriptions written within the substance of the brain. What makes Professor Dennett's analysis so interesting is the way in which he breaks down the logical implications of such proposals, and instead of supplying yet another theory about the relationship between brains and minds, he provides a versatile and productive method for weighing the value of any theory which might be offered. In the interview that follows, Professor Dennett has restored philosophy to its proper place as the handmaiden of the exact sciences.

[1] Daniel C. Dennett, *Brainstorms*, Harvester, 1978.

DISCUSSION

MILLER   Nowadays there seems to be a division between those who believe that the most profitable way of understanding how the mind works and how the brain works is to go at it from the top down, by analysing and examining and experimenting with the whole person. And there are those, on the other hand, who say that it's much more profitable to try and analyse the whole process from the ingredient elements upwards. Where would your money be? Do you think that it's going to be more profitable to go from above-down, or from below-up? Or is this in fact even a reasonable or understandable distinction?

DENNETT   The top-down, bottom-up division is perfectly real and the subject of debate among people in this field. The neuroscientists, generally, are in favour of an abstemious bottom-up approach, in which one says: 'We're all agreed that the brain is an information processing organ of some sort, and we can tell that the *atomic* information processors, the basic building blocks, are the neurons. So now if we can just understand how each neuron processes information, we can then build molecules, larger structures of neurons. In effect: combining the effects of the individual neurons, we will determine what these large structures process in the way of information and gradually we'll work our way up – not really analysing but synthesising: building larger and larger structures of brain tissue which can be seen to process information.' This, they say, is the only proper way of doing the science involved.

Whereas the other group, the so-called top-down cognitive scientists, say that this is grasping the wrong end of the stick. You'll never make much progress that way. Rather you should start with the whole person, and say:'here's a whole person, and these are his cognitive talents. This is what he knows, this is what he believes, this is what he can see and these are the problems he can solve. Now let's try to decompose this whole person into assemblies or sub-systems, which in complex interaction can explain the talents of the whole person. Then we can decompose each sub-system in turn into its component sub-systems, and so on, until we have finally reached components that can be securely identified by the neuroanatomists.' That is the top-down strategy.

Now, both strategies ought to work in principle, because both ought to end up having completed exactly the same task. In the end both sides want to understand the relationship between the brain and the mind. And you can either start with the mind and work down, or you can start with the bits of brain and work up. So if you compare this with the analogy of building a trans-continental railroad, you *do* start at both ends, and plan to meet somewhere in the middle. I would bet, however, that most of the track is going to be laid by the people who are working from the top down, rather than from the bottom up. For a very simple reason: top-down is much easier, as it turns out.

MILLER   Now exactly why is it easier? One would have thought that there is certainly something easy about sticking a needle into the brain, finding a neuron, and then actually recording the action potentials and then doing it again to another neuron. There's something easy about the hardware of such a situation. It's ticklish, but it's easy.

DENNETT Yes, each little bit of data-gathering is easy enough, but the trouble is there's so much of it, and you don't know what further questions to ask. Those who think that the bottom-up strategy is the best way to proceed should be reminded of a system which is, in fact, much more simple than a human brain; a commercial chess-playing computer of the sort you can buy in the stores for Christmas. There it is, a little box, with a chessboard on the top, and it plays chess. It plays pretty good chess. How does it do it?

Well exponents of the bottom-up approach would say: 'Let's get our microscope and start taking the thing apart and looking at the individual tiny microchips and the relays on them and see if we can understand how each little part works, and then build up from there.' The trouble is if you start at that level of detail, you don't know what questions to ask. It's virtually inconceivable that somebody who didn't already know how a chess-playing computer was organised, and how computers in general were organised at a much higher level, could ever work his way up from a physical analysis of those little tiny parts.

For one thing, when would one ever get to the level at which one would be describing chess-playing, which after all is what the thing does? The top-down theorist on the other hand says: 'Let's think about it in a more or less *a priori* fashion first. The thing plays chess – what do you *have to know* to play chess? Well you have to know the rules, for one thing, so we'll bet that somewhere in this there's a representation of the rules – at least implicitly. That information is somehow in the system. You also have to know the principles of chess play. So somewhere we're going to find explicitly or implicitly represented, in something or other in there, the rules and principles of chess. Moreover, to play chess one has to know the position of the pieces on the board, so the system has to know what its move has been, and has to know where all the pieces are.'

MILLER And all of these questions can be asked of the machine, without ever asking oneself questions about the sort of material out of which these representations are going to be made.

DENNETT Not only can you be ignorant of the *sort* of material, you can even be ignorant of the *structure* of the material. That is, you can treat the question first purely at the level of the information – the beliefs and desires if you will – of any agent that can play chess. What information and what goals does such an agent require, whether it's an electronic agent, a sort of pseudo-agent, or a full-blooded human agent? What is the *content* of the strategic information, the tactical information, and the information about the rules that would enable *anything* to play chess, except by sheer magic?

So the top-down advocates ask those questions first. They then postulate interacting sub-assemblies of information processors that might do the job. Then one can test these postulates by designing and actually building models, and gradually working down to the level where one can finally tell somebody doing the bottom-up approach: 'Look for something in the brain that does the following rather fancy jobs; it should have the following sorts of features.' At some point (they hope) they are going to be able to say: 'now we've described some sub-assemblies that have certain talents; we bet you bottom-up people can find those – maybe you already have. If you haven't we can at least give you hints about what to look for.'

MILLER   So you're saying that unless one has some sort of idea about what that machine is out to do, or what it's set up to do, one wouldn't actually know what to start looking for at the bottom level.

DENNETT   Well, of course, the people who do bottom-up research can engage in informed speculation; they frame hypotheses about what the functions are going to be that they should look for. But that's not really their line of country, and they haven't developed a perspicuous vocabulary for describing such functions; they haven't trained themselves to think in terms of information processing models. Everybody says the brain's job is information processing, but that's a very tricky notion.

MILLER   But presumably even the fact that they approach it with that sort of theoretical preconception means that they have imported, perhaps without knowing it, ideas from the top-down approach, in that they're already looking at the elements with a view to there being an information processing device, which itself is a top-down idea, isn't it?

DENNETT   Yes. We shouldn't over-dramatise the division here. And after all there are people doing brilliant work who are trying very hard to pay attention to both ends of the track. And each strategy – and that's what they are; they aren't really competing methodologies, they're just competing strategies – each has its own foibles. The weakness of the bottom-up strategists is, as I've already said, that they don't know the right questions to ask; they don't know what hypotheses to test. The complementary weakness of the top-down people is that very often, they don't know enough about what the constraints on the hardware finally are going to be. They don't know enough about what nerve tissue can and can't do, so they are apt to design a model which might work in some other world, but couldn't really be done by the brain, given the way the brain is actually composed.

So one should, of course, try to keep alert to both of these. But people *do* specialise, and as I say, I'm putting my bet on the top-down approach to be much more dramatically fruitful in the foreseeable future, simply because it generates more fruitful hypotheses to test.

MILLER   Why does that approach generate so many serviceable hypotheses about the brain?

DENNETT   Well, it's because the idea of information (which is still not very well formulated) is nevertheless a very powerful generator of experiments. It's powerful because it allows you to abstract from messy details, in a certain way. When you're ignorant of a lot of messy details, if you can find a way of abstracting from them so that the account you give is neutral with regard to them, then sometimes you can make great leaps.

MILLER   Perhaps we should first of all clear up the concept of information, because it's one of those things which has obviously got a popular connotation and several technical ones.

DENNETT   In fact the concept of information that is in the forefront in the top-down approach is closer to the popular idea than it is to the technical one. Now, many people have heard that there's something called information theory, which was devised by Claude Shannon and Warren Weaver[1] and several other people, back at the close of the war, and in the 50s, and they know that this is very mathematical and very precise, and that it's at the foundation of computer science, and, for that matter, television transmission.

Let's call that the Shannon–Weaver sense of information. That's *not* the sense we're really talking about. We're talking about what is often called *semantic information*, which is information about meaning and about the 'aboutness' of what's being carried in some informational channel. We can bring out the distinction very clearly in terms of an analogy. The Shannon–Weaver sense of information is to the semantic senses as spelling and handwriting are to journalism and playwriting. Now here's some good advice for playwrights: write legibly. That's a principle from the domain of the Shannon–Weaver theory of information. It says: 'We want to maintain high fidelity transmission so that messages don't get garbled along the way; we want to have a lot of redundancy and clarity; we don't want noise interfering in the transmission. (Redundancy may sound like a bad thing, but in the domain of Shannon–Weaver theory, it's not. Everybody can fill in the missing lett r in this sentence, because the surrounding context so strongly demands it that its presence is scarcely required. It's redundant. Coding systems that exploit this redundancy feature are relatively impervious to noise.) This sense of information says nothing at all about what you might write *about*, what you might portray, what themes or ideas were going to be presented. It simply prescribes that whatever you present should be presented clearly and efficiently. Use a system which is proof against noisy interference and garbling.

MILLER   And for this there is a mathematical theory about what will count as clarity and about what will count as muddiness and confusion.

DENNETT   That's right, and it's a very powerful theory with many beautiful technical applications. For instance, it's thanks to that information theory that a television signal can be designed that will convey a high fidelity image over a long distance. It doesn't say whether the images will be of a football game or whether it's going to be news from China or a discussion. It's completely topic-neutral as to what information *in the semantic sense* is going to be carried over the channels.

[1]Claude L. Shannon and Warren Weaver, *The Mathematical Theory of Communication*, University of Illinois Press, 1949.

Now when we turn to the semantic information sense, we can see that illustrated in the products of the journalist or the playwright. It's a very abstract but also very familiar sense of information. Suppose we want to compare two different works of art, even in different media. We have, say, *Romeo and Juliet*, Shakespeare's play, and then we have *West Side Story* – let's talk about the film, not the original Broadway musical. Now these have something in common, as we all know. There's thematic structure, there are characters that can be paired off, and so forth. We can say that Juliet and Maria are really very similar; they have a lot in common, and we can spell out the various features they have in common. That's a perfectly possible objective analysis, but notice it has nothing to do, directly, with the actual physical details of the medium. It doesn't tell you how the portrayal is done; it doesn't tell you even what words are used, or what frames are in the film: it just tells you what both works of art are *about*. Now that sense of information is, as it were, *syntactically* neutral – there's nothing about the shapes and structures of the signs – it is all about what the signs portray. It's that sense of information which is also really a very common and popular sense of information. It gets slightly clarified in the theories of the cognitive scientist.

MILLER   What you're saying has something in common with that fashionable term structuralism, doesn't it? For example there are surface differences between different myths; nevertheless if you pierce below the actual narrative surface, they have something in common which people will recognise. Certain elements are to one another as the elements in myths are to one another, and it's *that* which one is recognising as being the 'aboutness'.

DENNETT   That's right, and that sort of investigation is conducted at a notoriously high level of abstraction. It is none the worse for that. If you want to make such points, you have to leave the messy details behind, and then you can make very powerful, very compelling points.

Of course the main difference in an application of this idea to structuralist literary criticism is that there we are dealing with static objects for the most part. That is, there's a text and there it sits. It doesn't process information itself. It may convey a certain amount of information, it may embody a certain amount of information, but it doesn't *do things* with the information; the information doesn't get moved from here to there, and it doesn't leak and it doesn't get transformed in the object itself.

But if we think of an application in the theory of the mind, where we do want to talk about information moving about and being processed, we can see the strategy of the top-down semantic information method much more clearly. A nice analogy occurred to me recently. Think of intelligence and counter-intelligence – spies and counter-spies. Suppose you've been given the task of catching spies. You've been told: 'We've discovered that information is getting out to our enemies about various matters, and we want you to plug those leaks; we want you to catch the spies.' Well now how do you proceed?

The first thing you want to do is to find out what sorts of information on what topics are leaking out. And if you find out that it's information about submarines then you will say we should look at the navy first rather than at the postal service, if we want to find the likely source of this information leak. Suppose you then get some pretty good idea of what the information is that's going out; that is, you know what topics, what things in the world, are referred to in the information that's getting out.

At this point you haven't the faintest idea of the physical embodiment of the actual channel of communication. Maybe the spies are using carrier pigeons, maybe they're using teletype, maybe they're using English messages printed in newspapers. Who knows what they're using.

MILLER   But at that level of information, it's got to satisfy some minimal requirement of information in the Shannon–Weaver sense in order to count as information at all.

DENNETT   That's right. That's the foundation on which this all has to be built.

Somehow they have a channel which is good by Shannon–Weaver criteria for getting information on any topic from A to B.

MILLER   In other words, there's a certain recognisability of signals, in that the noise is not so great that you can't make sense of it.

DENNETT   The channel, whatever it is, is insulated against noise but that leaves open a thousand possibilities. Once you've got some sense, though, of the semantic information that you're losing to the enemy, then you can begin to run experiments.

You can say: 'Let's see if we can just cordon off some particular part of this institution – the Government or whatever – and block any information on any topic from getting out, and see if we plug the leak.' You can sometimes get results that way. A more telling strategy, which is also nicely analogous to many experiments in cognitive psychology, is to plant a little *mis*information at a particular place – deliberately put a little falsehood into the system.

MILLER   And once again, this is misinformation at a level above the purely Shannon–Weaver one.

DENNETT   Oh yes, it's not just garbling. You don't just put a little typographical error in somewhere.

MILLER   Nor is it scrambling the telephones.

DENNETT   You put in a bogus 'fact' of some sort, some utter falsehood. You casually drop it into the system where you think there might be a leak, and then you see if, in a little while, the enemy shows signs of relying on that proposition, that bit of information, in its counter-thrust. And if you find that, then of course you know that there's an informational link between the spot where you dropped it in and the enemy. You're on the way to catching your spy. You still don't know what the medium is, but you know that there's a channel that's open and you know moreover what sort of information is going across the channel.

MILLER   And this information is at fairly high level of conceptual abstraction.

DENNETT   Absolutely. We can illustrate that. Suppose that you leave a phony blueprint of a bomb lying around somewhere in the War Office, and sure enough a little later information about that bogus bomb appears, say, in the international espionage markets: you know that the bait has been taken.

MILLER   Or if the Russians release a bomb which goes off with a resounding silence.

DENNETT   Yes, that might be another good clue that they picked up the bait. At that point, you know that the information has got out, but you don't know how. It may have got out in pictorial form; maybe somebody made a Xerox copy of the blueprint and carried that bodily out of the country. Maybe somebody looked at it, then wrote down a description in English, and mailed it out of the country. Or the description might be in German or in French, or in some code. Maybe the information wasn't sent that way at all; maybe a courier simply studied the diagram, then walked across the border and redrew it. Those are all different channels, and at this point you're completely in the dark about what channel was used. But that doesn't prevent you from proceeding with your experiments. You might even catch the whole ring of spies, and only after you'd caught them would you be able to tell how they'd done it. Only then would you be able to see what the mechanisms were that they'd actually used.

   To compare the top-down with the bottom-up strategy with this analogy is perhaps unfair because the bottom-up people look particularly forlorn if you think of their strategy applied to a case like this. What would they do? Suppose they are asked to catch the spies: they might say, 'Well, we're going to intercept every letter mailed out of the country, and we're going to monitor every radio signal and waylay every carrier pigeon, and we'll see what we find.' But now, how are they going to tell what to look for? We imagine all these people opening letters, but how are they going to tell the innocent love letter from the coded message? It's hopeless unless they've narrowed down their task by top-down sleuthing. They need some hypothesis to the effect that certain semantic information must be moving through a certain channel. 'It's got to be in that letter somewhere.' Then one can turn the letter over to the cryptographers and hope they can find that information there. It can work only if they already have a hypothesis about what the letter is about; it's about bombs, not about meeting in Paris for a drink. Only then can they solve the problem. Otherwise it's worse than looking for a needle in a haystack.

MILLER   But even if they are examining every single one of the transmissions, they cannot avoid examining the transmissions at the level of their semantic content, because they are themselves, human beings, and will therefore be scrutinising them for their 'aboutness', for their topics. The very word 'topic' is built into the top-down approach to meaning, is it not? It's very hard to think what the word 'topic' would mean if one was going from the bottom upwards, if one was dealing entirely in nerve impulses or in pulses in a cable. Because these things don't *have* topics.

DENNETT   Yes. They are just matter and motion. But as you said at the outset, virtually everybody in the neurosciences is prepared to make that leap and to talk about information. It's just that they want to do it in their abstemious bottom-up way, rather than in this more risky but also potentially more powerful top-down way.

MILLER   But as you say, there are obvious advantages in there being people working at the lower level, if only because it provides us with the physical constraints which would have to be observed in any system which we happen to have identified by the top-down approach. If we start to put forward hypotheses about how this semantic information is transferred, and we have empty fantasies without some sort of reference to what nerves can do, then we're going to come unstuck fairly soon.

DENNETT   Right. And that of course is the recognised danger in that brand of cognitive science, of the top-down approach, known as Artificial Intelligence. The rationale of Artificial Intelligence research runs this way: we want to do top-down psychology, and eventually even physiological psychology, but we've found a way of simplifying the task. In order to ask the question, 'how does *Nature* solve this design problem?' we ask the related question, 'how could *we* solve the problem if we were to design, as engineers, a system that had a certain informational capacity?' That's a much more indirect way of trying to get at the truth, and notice, for instance, that while chess-playing computers do play chess (they are *a* solution to that top-down problem) very few people would claim that they are *our* solution. That is, chess-playing computers do not play chess in the way we do; they're really quite different even at the most abstract level of organisation. You can compare different programmes to see which are more psychologically realistic as models of human chess-playing competence. The bold claim of Artificial Intelligence is that even when you design a system that is both physiologically and psychologically unrealistic, you may still be able to extract, from the highest levels of analysis of the problem, some principles that will transfer. You may be able to get some concepts out of this engineering exercise that can be fruitfully applied to the empirical investigation of how we play chess.

MILLER   Are there limits to what we can learn in this way?

DENNETT   If you look at the actual products of Artificial Intelligence you find they're a relatively unimpressive lot; they're typically a bag of tricks and even when they do mimic the human being, it's usually for spurious reasons. But one shouldn't judge the field by those gimmicks and illustrations, which is really all they are.

The real products of the field are conceptual. In fact, that's why I am interested in it; it seems very much like philosophy. When you look at the theoretical discussions by the people in AI you see that they are dealing with issues that have been around since Descartes, since Hume, since Kant, and they're dealing with them with new conceptual resources, new ideas, new methods, and with a greater sensitivity to the ultimate problem of taking these 'semantic engines', these hypothesised systems of information processing, and actually making something physical that can do all the wonderful things that a semantic engine clearly can do.

I think perhaps the best example of this, and it's a very abstract point, is something that I call Hume's problem, not because Hume solved it, but because he laboured mightily with it. Hume wanted to have a theory of the mind, and like others before him – Locke and Descartes – he had his basic building blocks: he had impressions and ideas. They were like little pictures, little mental pictures. They represented in virtue of resembling; the idea of *cow* was cow-shaped presumably. I mean, that's roughly the way it seemed to work. He was conveniently vague about that.

Now he thought that a mind could not work unless it were filled with lots of little representations which he called ideas. But he also recognised that a representation, something like a picture, isn't really a representation at all unless there's a sort of observer, a sort of agent that's looking at it, and understanding it. If you put a road map under the bonnet of a car this is utterly futile unless you've also got some wonderful gadget under the bonnet that's going to look at that road map in some way and interpret it – perhaps in order to keep the car on the road. Otherwise you've got an entirely gratuitous attempt at representation.

So Hume saw that representations without representation *users* were futile. But he also saw that if he put a smart observer in the mind to look at the ideas, then we have the problem simply postponed. What was in the smart observer's head – more ideas and another tiny observer watching them? We generate an infinite regress of representations and watchers, and the representations in *their* heads, and so forth *ad infinitum*. Now the fear of that regress has loomed large ever since Hume. For instance, it was a major impetus to behaviourism, and B. F. Skinner[1] often talked about this infinite regress and how preposterous it was.

MILLER   And Ryle as well.

DENNETT   And Gilbert Ryle[2] as well. Virtually every theorist has had at least a tacit appreciation of the danger of this idea. As soon as you introduce mental representations you seem to be off on an infinite regress. And there the situation would sit, were it not for the advent of Artificial Intelligence, which showed us a way out. It hasn't necessarily shown us the way *we* do it, but it's shown an abstract way out of this problem. People working in AI saw a way of doing with representations something that at first looks miraculous. As a student of mine once said: 'Hume's problem was to get the ideas to think for themselves.' And that really was his problem. He couldn't solve it. He couldn't see how to get the ideas to do the work for themselves. But models of this is just what AI has given us. The basic idea is that you start at the top with your whole intelligent being, with all its

[1] B. F. Skinner, *Beyond Freedom and Dignity*, NY, 1971; London, 1972.
[2] Gilbert Ryle, *The Concept of Mind*, Hutchinson, London, 1949.

beliefs and desires and expectations and fears – all its information. Then you say: 'How is all that going to be represented in there?' You break the whole system down into sub-systems, little homunculi – little men in the brain. Each one is a specialist, each does a little bit of the work. These sub-systems are organised into a sort of society of interacting parts that can co-operate. Out of their co-operative endeavours emerge the whole activities of the whole system.

MILLER But when one introduces the notion of homunculi, isn't one sneaking in through the back door, in place of an infinite regress of spectators and representations, a crowd of spectators who are each of them observing their own little tiny province? That's another way of being mentalistic in the way that so alarmed Hume, is it not?

DENNETT Yes, you do replace the little man in the brain with a committee, but the saving grace is that the members of the committee are stupider than the whole; they are less intelligent and they 'know' less. The subsystems don't individually reproduce all of the talents of the whole. That would lead you to an infinite regress. Instead you have each sub-system doing a part, so that each homuncular sub-system is less intelligent, knows less, believes less. The representations are themselves, as it were, less representational, so you don't need an inner *eye* to observe them; you can get away with some sort of an inner process which 'accesses' them in some attenuated sense.

Take our chess-playing computer. We first break that down into a number of experts. We have a move generator, a bright-idea person; and then we have a move critic who will criticise the moves generated by the move generator; and then we have a referee who makes sure the rules are being obeyed; and then we have a time-keeper who makes sure that nobody spends too much time on any one job. Then if you focus on the move critic, who has just some of the information, and look at him more closely, you see that he's broken down into a team of smaller, stupider sub-critics, petty clerks each doing a little job. You get specialists, and as we all know, specialists know more and more about less and less, and these in fact know not very much about very little. But put together into large armies, mustered like Chinese boxes, a whole system of these stupid elements can exhibit behaviour which looks distinctly intelligent, distinctly human.

MILLER Now although one uses the vocabulary of knowing or believing for each of these congeries and little assemblies, that is not to say that they are, as it were, in 'states of mind' about whatever it is they know.

DENNETT That's right. They're not supposed to be full-blooded conscious mind-havers, or minds, at all. They are diminished minds; they are only quasi-minds; they are only pseudo-minds. There's a debate one can enter here which is finally just lexicographic. One can say: 'Well, in that case, they really don't represent at all; they don't have mental representations that they manipulate at all.' If that's the way one side goes then the other can respond: 'If that is how you understand the terms, it turns out that we don't really need mental representation to explain the mind. Pseudo-representation will do just as well.' Or on the other hand one can say: 'Well I guess representation is not quite such a marvellous and mysterious thing as we thought. If there can be representations in a computer, then maybe we can harmonise the idea that the mind is a system of representations with the idea that the mind is just the brain, just ultimately a physical organ.'

MILLER One can imagine, then, some sort of hyper-elaborate machine which is capable of accomplishing most of the human repertoire, without having to attribute to that machine some sort of self-conscious state of mind or a screen on which its overall operations were represented to itself.

DENNETT Yes, there's a strong inclination, when one starts developing models of this sort always to exempt the *self* and say: 'Maybe I do have all of these little sub-systems in me, but then there's the king sub-system, the boss; there's the one at the centre who knows it all and who controls all the others and that's the really wonderful and mysterious one. That's the seat of the soul.' But I think that's a bad mistake. It's an immensely compelling idea, but I for one have been trying to talk people out of the conviction that it's compelling and get them to see that there isn't any king homunculus, there isn't any all-knowing central boss 'I' at all.

To revert to the spy analogy again, what we want here is a principle like the CIA's principle of 'need to know'. Your agents in the field only need to know a little bit so you don't let them know any more than what they need to know to do their jobs. The rationale in the CIA, of course, is that if an agent gets caught, you don't want him unravelling the whole system. The rationale in the case of the mind is rather different. It's that only by building up a whole system out of proper parts which are genuinely proper parts – that only do part of the work – can you avoid the infinite regress which is threatened by Hume's problem. Now if we take that idea to its conclusion it would seem that there shouldn't be any homunculus, any sub-system, that is itself *in charge*. Such a sub-system would be too powerful, and would threaten an infinite regress. And in fact I think there's lots of evidence, now, and somewhat disturbing evidence, which shows that if there were any homunculus in our cognitive committee with which we would be inclined to identify the self intuitively, it wouldn't be the boss; it would be the director of public relations, the agent in the press office who has only a very limited and often even fallacious idea about what's really going on in the system. He's the one whose job it is to present a good face to the world, to issue press releases and generally try to tell everybody on the outside what's going on. He can be wrong, he can be massively misinformed, he can be massively ignorant of what is really going on in the system. And many results of experiments in cognitive and social psychology now strongly suggest that our own access to what's going on in our minds is very impoverished. We often confabulate, we tell unwitting lies and we are often simply in the dark; we have no idea at all.

And so the notion, which was overpoweringly obvious to somebody like John Locke or Descartes, that the mind is transparent to itself, that each one of us is the ultimate authority on everything that's going on in our minds, that we are incorrigible, infallible observers of our own mental life, has been completely overthrown.

It begins to appear that we have, in Keith Gunderson's[1] phrase, 'underprivileged access' to the goings-on in our own minds. We make mistakes even about what we're thinking.

MILLER And this underprivileged access that we have to our own minds is not because of what Freud said – that we are actively prevented from gaining access to our own minds – but more because it is a constitutive character of having a mind at all. Nine-tenths of it is subterranean machinery which it would be impossible to know.

DENNETT Yes, this was the point that was hidden from the classical representation theorists like Descartes and Hume. They conducted the entire enterprise at the purely semantic level, where they could think of thoughts and ideas which were just *pure meaning*, in effect pure reference, pure 'intentionality' to use a jargon term. They never really addressed themselves – they didn't know how – to the question: 'How could anything actually perform these functions; how could anything as marvellous as a mental representation actually work?' It was convenient for *them* to say that it's all done in the non-physical mind which is beyond the ken of science. But now that we are embarked, for better or for worse, on the research project of trying to understand the brain as the mind, we have to raise these questions. And the beauty of it is that once we raise them, particularly in the top-down approach, we uncover new problems. We uncover new issues, and some of the old home truths of the introspective psychologies of everybody since Descartes no longer seem true. In particular the idea that each of us is some sort of infallible explorer of his own mind and can just read off what his ideas are, is no longer compelling once these new results begin to come in.

MILLER So the mere fact that one is able to introspect *at all* should not lead one to be over-confident about being able to introspect everything.

DENNETT Yes. This is an old idea. Karl Lashley[2], many years ago, delighted in shocking his psychologist colleagues by saying that no activity of mind is ever conscious. It seemed a flat contradiction of what everybody knew. What he meant was that we're not conscious of the *processes* at all, but only of their products. He gave an example: suppose I ask you to think a thought in dactylic hexameter. Well, try it and you can come up with one, if you know what dactylic hexameter is, but how do you come up with it –

[1]Keith Gunderson, 'Asymmetries and Mind-Body Perplexities,' in D. N. Rosenthal, ed., *Materialism and the Mind-Body Problem*, Prentice Hall, Englewood Cliffs, N. J., 1971.
[2]Karl S. Lashley, (1890–1958) 'Cerebral Organization and Behavior,' in *The Brain and Human Behavior*, (Proc. of the Assoc. for Research in Nervous and Mental Disease) Vol. 36, ed. H. C. Solomon, S. Cobb, and W. Penfield, Baltimore, Md., 1958.

what do you do, what do you consult in your mind? Clearly there's a very complicated process going on in there, one that has to compose a sentence which has a certain metric analysis and has to be grammatical; and one that has many other constraints which have to be met. We haven't the faintest direct evidence, and only the slightest clues, about what we do in order to achieve this. It's all that backstage machinery about which the top-down approach in cognitive psychology is beginning to frame enticing hypotheses. This is a newly opened domain which was not even imagined by earlier introspectionists.

dialogue with
Jerome Fodor

IMAGERY AND THE LANGUAGE OF THOUGHT

INTRODUCTION

As a result of the colourful publicity which has often been associated with psychoanalysis it is almost impossible to visualise the unconscious mind in anything but Freudian terms. In other words the concept has become synonymous with one of repressed sexuality, and this region of the mind is widely regarded as the province of instincts whose free expression would contradict the demands of co-operative social reality. But the development of cognitive research has introduced yet another picture of unconscious mental processes, one which has nothing to do with conflict, guilt or repression, but without which it has become increasingly difficult to account for some of our more distinctive capabilities.

In the field of linguistics for example, the rapid acquisition of language can only be explained on the assumption that the infant mind is endowed with some sort of unconscious competence which enables it to make productive generalisations about the meaning of what it hears. Inspired by the original work of Noam Chomsky at MIT (Massachusetts Institute of Technology), modern linguists have come to the conclusion that the ability to learn and use a natural language presupposes the existence of some mental structure which is itself not unlike language. And that although this structure is not directly represented in consciousness, one can infer its existence from the efficiency with which we recognise the meaning of sentences which we have never heard before.

The same principle probably applies to the psychology of perception. As Professor Gregory has already shown, perceptual skills cannot be explained in terms of sensory input alone, and since there is often a considerable discrepancy between the image on the retina and the picture in the mind, one can only assume that the deficit is made up by some kind of hypothesis supplied from an unconscious store of previous experience.

From these and other considerations, cognitive psychologists such as Professor Jerome Fodor, Professor of Psycholinguistics and Philosophy at MIT, have been led to stipulate the existence of some sort of represent- ational system which enables the human organism to perform comput- ational processes on the often inadequate information provided by the physical senses. And as Professor Fodor points out in his important book on the language of thought, *The Language of Thought*, it is the task of psychology to identify a formal system rich enough to give our conscious experience of the world its characteristic meaning and coherence.

DISCUSSION

MILLER   It has become apparent to me that the concept of mind has been reinstated as a respectable idea. Now I suppose that the popular and long-held view of the mind is that it is a sort of inner chamber in which there are pictures of the outside world and conversations conducted in English. I suppose that it's impossible to hold that view any longer, as a result of what's happening in the cognitive sciences, so I wonder if we can start by discussing the language of thought, which is quite obviously different from the language in which thought is expressed.

FODOR Well I think there's something to be said for the popular notion. It captures a fact the philosophers in particular, and psychologists recently, have been seriously interested in. If one thinks about how the mind might work, one of the things one is struck with very early on is this: there is a parallelism between the properties of certain kinds of mental states, the kinds that Bertrand Russell called 'propositional attitudes' (beliefs and desires are the ones that turn up most in cognitive psychology), and certain properties of symbols. In particular I suppose that mental states and symbols are the only things in the universe – at least the only things we know of – which have semantic properties. Beliefs for example are about things, just as pictures and sentences and words are. And beliefs can be true and false, just as linguistic objects like sentences and statements can. If you're trying to construct a theory of the mind, you don't want to treat that parallelism as simply an accident.

So about 300 years ago, certainly as early as Descartes, and coming to full flower in the writings of people like Hume and Kant, somebody developed what's been called the 'Idea' idea. That is, the idea that there are somehow mental symbols (ideas spelled with a capital 'I'), and that thought and cognitive processing in general is a matter of deploying these symbols in some disciplined way. The picture of the mind is thus essentially as a symbol processing device. (Indeed, that same picture underlines the contemporary psychologist's analogies to computers and other fancy technology of that kind.) So the philosophical programme was to account for the parallelism between psychological and symbolic objects by assuming that the mind is actually stocked with symbols, and that mental processes are somehow causal processes in which these symbols are implicated. That is: what gives thinking what philosophers call its 'intentional' properties, its properties of being *about* things, and of being true and false, is the semantic properties of these symbols, and the way these symbols are deployed. That kind of picture has haunted the philosophical (and recently the psychological) imagination, as I say, for some 300 years, and it's not all that different from the popular idea that thinking is a matter of having images or somehow talking to yourself. In fact the early versions of this model, the kind that you get, say, in David Hume, *did* take the mind to be a repository of images; images enter into causal relations with one another via presumed principles of association; that's what is supposed to make chains of thought. And they enter into semantic relations with the world in virtue of resembling the things that they're images of. That's what is supposed to explain the 'aboutness' of thought.

So that this picture of the mind as a repository of images is a sort of early version of the current computational model of the mind. However, what's happened in modern resuscitations of this view, in the contemporary so-called 'cognitive science' movement, is, among other things, that the presumed mental processes have gone underground. Unlike Hume or Descartes, cognitive scientists now assume that the most interesting thought processes are unconscious. So if thought is talking to yourself, then most of the time you're not, maybe, listening. At least not with the conscious inner ear.

And there is some doubt about how close to imagery the presumed mental symbolism might be. There is some very pretty recent experimentation which does suggest the involvement of some kind of mental imagery in a lot of thought processes, and those experiments are fairly convincing. But what I think nobody believes now is what Hume believed: that these images are *about* the world because they resemble the things that they're images of. So those aspects of the classical story which were primarily concerned with consciousness, and with resemblance as the key to how thought is about the world, those have been largely abandoned. But the picture of the mind as somehow conversant with symbols – that it's essentially a symbol-processing system of some kind – is very much with us again, and the major research goal is now to say, in as much detail as we can, and with as much evidence as we can marshal, what this symbolic system might be like, and what the mechanisms that deploy it might be like; what the mental processes are in which these symbols are involved.

MILLER I'd like to talk about mental imagery and about why you believe that a thought process which was based on a succession of images simply won't count as a satisfactory explanation of thinking.

FODOR Well look, whatever mental representations are like – whatever these mental symbols are like – they've at least got to be the right kinds of symbols to express the kinds of things you can believe, because the underlying picture is that believing is in some way entertaining these mental representations. Now, it's certainly possible to *believe* that something is *not* the case. But try to imagine drawing a picture of something not being the case. It's easy enough to draw a picture of a man scratching his nose, but it's very hard to draw a picture of a man *not* scratching his nose. And yet a man not scratching his nose is a perfectly reasonable object of thought.

Well this is a way in which one can go about asking what mental representations might be like. They've at least got to be the right kind of vehicles for expressing the kinds of things you can believe or think about. One problem about imagery is that its, as it were, 'expressive capacity' is extremely limited in comparison with, say, discursive symbols. There is, for example, no difficulty in *saying* of a man that he is not scratching his nose, however difficult it may be to have an *image* of his not doing so. In short, we can use facts about what kinds of things we can think about to set a sort of lower bound on how rich the expressive power of systems of mental representation must be. In this respect, imagery looks like a bad candidate.

MILLER So there is something about internal visual images which disqualifies them as being the currency in which thought is transacted: that is, in thought, one is able to make claims about what is the case, or what is not the case – but you can't do that with pictures.

FODOR Right. Or at least not with sufficient richness and subtlety to capture the richness and subtlety of objects of thought.

MILLER Although one can imagine a mental world in which you put up a picture of a man scratching his nose, and then, as you sometimes have with no smoking signs, had a diagonal line passing through it.

FODOR But one has to be very careful, because one doesn't want that symbol to represent a man scratching his nose with a diagonal line through him. Somehow one needs interpretive text – or at least conventions of interpretation, and these annotations can't themselves be a piece of imagery. That again suggests that images are inadequately rich symbolic vehicles for the kinds of semantic content that thought seems to be involved with.

MILLER But nevertheless there is, on commonsense grounds, a basis for thinking that mental images play a large part in our conscious thoughts.

FODOR Indeed they do. In fact I suspect that the representational system in which we think, if that's the right way to describe it, is so rich that if you think up any form of symbolism at all, it probably plays some role in thinking. There's a lot of anecdotal evidence and some recent experimental evidence of a rather charming and striking kind, which suggests that there must be some deployment of image-like intellectual apparatus, along with whatever else is going on in thought.

MILLER I wonder if I can coax you into describing some of these experiments.

FODOR I guess it started with some work done at Stanford by a psychologist called Roger Shepard. He had subjects do the following thing. He would present nonsense figures of one kind of another, or it might be letters of the alphabet. These would be presented in different orientations, so one of them might be sticking straight up and the other one might be sticking up at an angle. The subject is instructed in the following way. He's told that he is to decide whether the two figures are congruent. The interesting cases are the ones where the right answer is 'yes'. There are also 'catch trials' where the right answer is 'no' but for present purposes, we needn't worry about those.

MILLER By congruent you mean that if overlapped, the figures would match.

FODOR Yes. So the subject has to make this determination and he's told to do it as rapidly and efficiently as he can. What Shepard did was to measure the so-called 'reaction time', the time it takes the subject to reply correctly, as a function of the angular distance between the two figures. By the angular distance, we mean the amount of rotation you would need to perform on one figure to make it overlap with the other.

MILLER So you mean he would have a letter 'E', say, lying with the prongs downward, and a letter 'E' standing up.

FODOR   Right. And perhaps one facing 45° to either side. So one has various amounts of rotation separating the two figures. Then Shepard plotted these data as a graph, so that the amount of time that it took the subject to give the answer is on one axis and the angular disparity between the figures is on the other. What you find is that the reaction time is directly proportional to the angular disparity. That is, the more the figures have been rotated relative to one another, the longer the reaction time. It's very much as though what the subject was doing is exactly what he *says* he's doing, if you ask for his introspections about how he performs the task. Namely, constructing an image of one of the figures and rotating it through 'internal space', until he can see whether it matches the other. That's very much what the subject's intuition is, and the reaction times, the data, come out just as though that's what he's doing. There's a plethora of other experiments that have been done since Shepard's, all with very much the same motivation. What they suggest is the following: take the crudest kind of picture you can imagine of how mental imagery might work. Imagine that the subject has a snapshot in his head and can turn it upside down, look at the colours, lay a ruler across it – that sort of thing. Take this crude picture of mental imagery which any philosopher will tell you can't be right, and the data come out exactly as though that picture *were* true.

Now how exactly one is to interpret these experiments is a bit of a puzzle, because, of course, the philosophers are right; people *don't* have snapshots in their heads. That's one thing we're very sure of – brains don't work that way.

MILLER   But in what sense do people *not* have snapshots in their brain?

FODOR   Well there can't be a real image – a literal spatial display – that is being somehow turned around in the brain. One thing that is very clear about brains is that visual signals get turned into discrete digital code very early on. The brain doesn't preserve the optic properties of the visual array.

MILLER   Exactly as television cameras don't. Once the image has entered the lens, it's transformed into a stream of signals.

FODOR   Right, it's electronic code; it's not at all like a snapshot. So it can't be that you literally have pictures in your head and are turning them around. Not at least if any mind-brain identity theory is going to turn out to be true.

MILLER   And yet that's what the subject consciously reports as going on.

FODOR   That's what he reports and the data certainly look that way. So whatever this suggests – to come back to the earlier part of the discussion – it gives some degree of scientific respectability to the introspective reports that it *feels* an awful lot as though there were images in there, and as though they were being deployed in some kinds of thought processes.

What nobody now believes is that the mechanism of reference for these mental images – the properties in virtue of which they get to be *about* things, to be true and false and stuff of that kind – is resemblance to the world. That's a line of enquiry which took a terrible drubbing from a succession of philosophers from Wittgenstein through Nelson Goodman.

MILLER I wonder if you could outline some of the basic objections to the idea that a mental image could resemble something in the outside world.

FODOR If you really assume that people think in something like a language – that there is something like a system of mental representations and that the brain is a mechanism for manipulating them – then you have to face the question of how these representations ever get attached to the world. And a very natural kind of view is that it's just like a photograph being attached to the world. That is, that in both cases there's a sort of resemblance relationship which ties a picture, be it mental or photographic, to what it's a picture of. That may not even be right about photographs, but still it's the kind of view which, barring the anachronisms, Hume probably had in mind. But if one tries to take that view literally – that is, if one tries to base a theory of the way thought might be related to the world, on some relation of resemblance – it breaks down very rapidly. Wittgenstein has these thought experiments: you're to form an image – a stick figure, it might be – of a man climbing a hill with a cane. And Wittgenstein says: 'Right, how do you know what that's a picture of?' Answer, 'Well it looks like a man climbing a hill with a cane.' Wittgenstein replies: 'Yes, but it looks equally like a man sliding back down the hill, dragging his cane after him.'

In fact the mappings that resemblance produces between symbols in the world are just too undifferentiated, too ambiguous for a well-behaved symbol system. A lot of philosophers have had fun at the expense of classical mental representation theory, by taking the idea of resemblance as the central thesis in this theory. Whereas, in fact, it's not. The *central* thesis is the existence of mental symbols, images or otherwise. In fact very early on, Descartes had worries about the plausibility of the theory that Ideas could resemble what they are ideas *of*. Descartes said: 'Look, I have an idea of a thousand-sided figure. But it can't possibly be that having that idea consists of having an image, because I couldn't tell the difference between an image of a thousand-sided figure and, say, a thousand-and-two-sided figure.' Yet the two concepts are perfectly distinct. The point is that the notion of mental symbolism – languages of thought and stuff of that kind – might be dissociable from resemblance stories about how thoughts refer to the world. That point enters the literature very early and it's very much part of the current revival of the mental representation approach to cognition. The current candidates for languages of thought are built on formal logics and on computer languages, and on a whole lot of mathematics. In effect, on notions of symbolism which simply weren't available to the classic progenitors of this kind of theorising.

MILLER Although, of course, what *was* available to them was natural language itself, which was the medium through which people declared beliefs, asserted things to be true or false, and made statements about what was the case in the world. Why didn't people use natural language as a model for what might be going on inside the head?

FODOR   I think it's because they had the intuition which, unlike many philosophers, I'm inclined to think is correct, that the order of explanation must be the other way around; that you have to explain the semantic properties of natural language – explain the meaningfulness of natural language symbols – in terms of people's thoughts. You explain the symbolic properties of language in terms of the intentionality, semanticity, however you like to talk about this, of people's thoughts rather than the other way around. So the answer to a question like: 'Why is the sentence, "John went to the store" about John?' is something like: 'Because that sentence is a vehicle for expressing thoughts about John.' The internal language is, in short, assumed to be prior to the external one.

That's why, I think, it was taken absolutely for granted that the language of thought couldn't be English or German or Urdu or something of that kind. Even so, I don't know why people didn't take more seriously the possibility that mental symbolism might be syntactically, that is, in its grammar, and even semantically, rather similar to natural languages. The image theory had an enormous grip on people's imagination. It kept getting refuted, it kept getting knocked down, but it kept being resuscitated time after time.

MILLER   It may well be that visual imagery is so powerful that it was rather hard to consider thought in terms of some sort of symbolic manipulation.

FODOR   Well, part of it may have been this. One gets a lot of talk in the classic texts about natural versus conventional symbolic relations, and the picture goes something like this: what connects the English word 'magazine' to magazines is a convention. I mean, we just learn at our mother's knee that the way you talk about magazines in English (as opposed to French, German or Urdu) is by using the noise 'magazine'. So natural language meanings are based on convention, and we can build further conventions on top of them; for example we could agree that for the next twenty-four hours when I say 'up', I really mean 'down', and *vice versa*. But the question then arises, if it's *convention* that associates the word 'magazine' with magazines, what could it be that associates thoughts about magazines with the very objects themselves? Well, the meaning relations on which these conventions depend cannot themselves be conventional, because that would lead to an infinite regress of conventional associations. So between thoughts and the objects to which they refer, there must be a non-conventional, natural relation which acts, if you like, as the foundation for the conventional associations of natural language. And what could this natural relation be? Well how about resemblance? So it was like the fly and the fly-paper. Philosophers and psychologists buzzed and buzzed but it was very hard to get free of that notion of resemblance.

And indeed, I don't know anybody who's very happy about how the question of the relation between thoughts and the world is to be solved. What's happened is that people are indulging in what I think of as the Scarlett O'Hara manoeuvre – namely, that's too hard a problem, we'll worry about that tomorrow, and get on with setting out whatever we can of the format of these mental representations, leaving the question of how they get connected with the world – how they get their semantic properties – as a hard problem with which we will eventually have to struggle.

MILLER   Meanwhile, even if natural language – the language in which we actually express our thoughts – is not a suitable candidate for being the language in which thought occurs, progress has been made in rethinking natural languages themselves, and presumably one would have to say that this was mainly under the influence of Noam Chomsky.[1] Could you give some sort of account of what's happened as a result of looking at natural languages from this new viewpoint?

FODOR   Well there are two kinds of issue that have been thought about seriously. One is the question of the character of the mental representation that a hearer must compute if he is to understand a sentence uttered in his language; (the same representation, presumably, that the speaker has in mind when he utters that sentence). One can treat the noise that someone makes when he talks as a perceptual object, something that needs to be analysed and understood by the hearer, just in the same way as tables and chairs, cows and television screens are perceptual objects to be recognised and understood. And one can ask: 'What's the nature of the representational capacity that has to be brought to bear in order to get the right perceptual analysis of this object; a perceptual analysis rich enough to specify which object the thing is; in the case of language, which sentence one is hearing?' An enormous amount of work has been done on that problem, and a lot is known about it. Language is of interest, from the point of view of the whole cognitive science project, because sentences are probably the first class of perceptual objects, the first class of things that people can cope with in terms of perceptual processing, where the representational capacities involved are well enough understood so that one can actually develop something like an axiomatic theory of them.

That's one direction in which the work on natural language has gone. The other direction is this. Given an understanding of the cognitive capacities you deploy when you use a language, the question then arises: where do those capacities come from? The direction that much of the theorising in this area has taken is to suggest that basically they're unlearned; that they're part of the innate endowment of human beings as human beings.

MILLER   In other words, that newborn babies must already know something in order to learn a language like English.

[1] Avram Noam Chomsky (1928–). Professor of Modern Languages and Linguistics at the Massachusetts Institute of Technology. His book *Syntactic Structures* was the first to outline and justify a generative conception of language, currently the most widely held view. Apart from his technical contributions within linguistics, he has written at length on the philosophical and psychological implications of a generative theory of language, in particular developing a view of the integral relationship between language and the human mind, and it is this which has made such an impact on disciplines outside linguistics.

FODOR Yes.

MILLER I see. So this deals with the apparent paradox that the hardest task of which human beings are capable is the one thing which they learn at eighteen months.

FODOR Yes, and as linguistics has developed and we've been given a clearer picture of how hard sentence comprehension is – how much information and how much computational machinery must mediate the ability to speak and understand a language – the capacity of a child to assimilate these skills becomes more and more bewildering. I think there's a very widespread feeling that unless there is a good deal of preprogrammed material available to the child, unless he or she knew a great deal about how the language learning task was to be coped with, as it were, at birth, it's hard to imagine any learning procedure that could work. All the more so since what evidence is available suggests that the operation of these mechanisms will tolerate wide variation in the child's verbal environment; that it doesn't, for example, much depend on explicit teaching being provided for the child.

MILLER As opposed to the traditional view of the learning of language, which I think was first expressed by St Augustine, that one learns by hearing people speak and seeing them point things out. According to Chomsky there wouldn't be time to learn the language if one had to be exposed to all the samples of it.

FODOR There wouldn't be time, and also, although the environment presumably provides you with a lot of examples where people utter words in the vicinity of things that the words refer to, it doesn't provide you with any very explicit information about the syntactic regularities of a language, the mechanisms that allow you to put words and sentences together and make up new sentences. All that apparatus turns out to be extremely complicated and very delicate, and apparently, to some considerable extent, universal across natural languages. Striking similarities emerge between English and languages to which it's historically unrelated as far as anyone knows. All that apparatus, which is what we best understand about how languages work, is certainly never taught to the child in any very explicit kind of way. Although in some sense the child must be imitating what he or she hears, what the child hears is so abstractly structured that the idea of imitation is itself equivocal in this context. It's difficult to see how imitation could account for the development from hearing Mother say: 'Daddy will be home soon', to a capacity to produce sentences with relative clauses, and questions, and all the whole complex apparatus of adult language.

MILLER And even asking questions like: 'Is Daddy going to come home soon?'

FODOR Indeed, yes.

MILLER And also it's very hard to see how one would point to examples of 'if' or 'but'.

FODOR Yes, this very primitive model, according to which what is learned in learning a language is some sort of naming relation that holds between individual words and objects in the world, is hard to take seriously, if one ever listens to a three-year-old. They prattle along in ways that have very little to do with naming what's going on in their immediate environment; they have a linguistic sophistication which is very hard to differentiate from that of the adult. By the time they're three or so, most of the syntactic apparatus is likely to be under control. All the interesting stuff in the language, all the stuff that allows you to build long sentences out of short ones, is likely to be pretty much under control by that age.

MILLER   And in view of that speed of acquisition, one would have to assume that the child enters the world with some sort of linguistic competence built into its brain which allows it to survey the samples of its native language that it hears.

FODOR   What is wanted is an exact and exhaustive characterisation of what this pre-structuring is like. It's a very difficult problem because the solution has to satisfy a lot of conditions that are hard to meet simultaneously. For example, it's very unlikely, if children are innately biased to learn their natural language, that they're innately biased in favour of one language rather than another. I mean, pop a child down in a Chinese-speaking environment and it learns Chinese; pop it down in an English-speaking environment, and it learns English. There seems to be no bias in the language learning mechanism. It seems to be completely neutral. So you want a theory which on the one hand is sufficiently complicated and rich to explain how, given this innate endowment, the child could learn a natural language very rapidly, and on the other hand sufficiently abstract so that it's not biased toward learning one language rather than another. That's a trick that the theoreticians have not yet been able to pull off. It's the question that everybody in linguistics would like to be able to solve, and which is still very much 'pending business'.

MILLER   Nevertheless there must be some mental structure which, although not cast in the form of the language you eventually learn, is nevertheless linguistic in its essential character. Do you want to say that this pre-linguistic language is a good candidate for the language of thought, which we use for thinking even if we're not thinking in language?

FODOR   Well that would be the most gratifying suggestion. There are really two ways that one can look at this. One is to suppose that what you know innately about the language you're going to learn is highly specialised; and highly specific to language though, of course, neutral as between one language and another. With that picture, the apparatus that mediates language learning is specific to that one purpose; it exploits, as it were, a fragment of the language of thought, which is pre-moulded to describe natural languages. The alternative view is that learning a language is a special case of a very general cognitive capacity: language learning is thus the application of general learning procedures to the special case of learning to talk. It's a matter of considerable controversy in cognitive science as to just how specialised the various psychological mechanisms actually are.

MILLER So it may be that only part of the language which is being employed for thinking in general is used for acquiring the language which we actually express our thoughts in; the rest of it is being used for other aspects of thinking, which don't necessarily enter consciousness.

FODOR That's a plausible picture.

MILLER Perhaps we ought to add that when we talk about the unconscious aspects of this language, we're not talking about unconscious in the sense that Freud referred to it. It isn't a repressed and censored system. It's simply inaccessible to direct consciousness.

FODOR Right. It's not unconscious for any reasons of motivational dynamics. In fact one of the ways in which Freud had an advantage over contemporary theorising is that he had an explanation of why all this stuff *had* to be unconscious; namely that repression would serve no purpose unless the things that get repressed ended up being unconscious. From the point of view of a cognitive psychologist, I suppose the total inscrutability of almost all the processes that one has to postulate in order to explain how behaviour and thought are organised is a bit of an embarrassment. No one is quite clear why one should have as little access to one's mental processes as it turns out one has. People go around saying in a slightly downcast tone of voice that maybe one ought to put the question the other way round, and treat consciousness as a sort of pathological mental condition, the exceptional case.

MILLER As a sort of oil slick on the surface of the mind?

FODOR Yes. There just happen to be things about one's thoughts that one can report with more or less accuracy. But most of the real stuff, most of the interesting stuff is simply inaccessible. And of course thought isn't primarily intended, I suppose, for introspection. What it's for is the organisation of behaviour and getting around in the world. Fundamentally that's the biological basis of the thing. So it's not so clear what massive introspectability would buy one. It would just make psychology a lot easier.

MILLER In terms of natural selection what do you think would be the advantage in having one part of this thinking process available to inspection, when the other nine tenths of it are sunk into some sort of subterranean machinery?

FODOR I think that's very hard to say. I think the question of selectional advantage is extremely obscure. It may be that what you get out of introspectability is the possibility of conscious correction. Insofar as one can look at one's thought processes, they're sensitive to instruction and re-examination and self-criticism.

MILLER But could you not conceive of a system which was capable of exercising the same sort of self-scrutiny without it having to enter consciousness? There are all sorts of automatically self-correcting devices which can monitor their own behaviour, detect that an error has occurred, and put the thing back on line again. Why could thinking not have this character right the way through?

FODOR   I really don't know, and as I say, unlike Freud's situation, ours in respect to this problem is a bit embarrassed. We don't have a clean aetiological explanation in terms of say selectional advantage or something of that kind, of why those things that are conscious are conscious and why the rest of them aren't. It is also possible that there isn't going to be such a story.

MILLER   Do you think we'll ever succeed in identifying the mechanisms involved in the languages of thought?

FODOR   The answer you get to that question depends very much on who you ask. There is a whole spectrum of optimism and pessimism in this field, and I find myself on the pessimistic end. I think that you can divide the kinds of processes that people have been studying into roughly two kinds. On the one hand there are topics like natural language, topics like the perception of visual form, topics like face recognition – a scattering of research areas – in which there's been a fair amount of success. Not that we're able to actually make machines that can simulate these capacities. But a great deal more is known about them than was known say ten or twenty years ago. On the other hand, there are processes that people speak of loosely in such terms as 'general problem-solving', and 'thought' as opposed to 'perception'. The kinds of 'central processes', in short, that one takes to be paradigms of the higher cognitive activities. It seems to me that we know very little about them indeed. It's a little hard to say just what the things we have made some progress with, have in common. But they all seem to be systems where the class of phenomena that the mechanisms operate on is highly limited. People talk a lot, these days, about *modularised* psychological systems; as it were, little bundles of special purpose computational mechanisms.

What seems to be characteristic of such modular systems is that they are concerned with highly specific problem structures. For example, there seems to be one such system involved in speech perception, in translating the utterances one hears into internal representations of sentences. There seems to be another one that's involved in rather low level analyses of visual forms – mapping from the retinal array that one gets when one looks at a visual scene, onto some sort of analysis in terms of three-dimensional objects in space. There may be another one involved in face recognition; there may be one involved in voice recognition. What's characteristic of all these mechanisms is that they do very highly specialised jobs (in a way that thought at large does not). When we encounter a cognitive system that specialises in this kind of way, we can ask quite detailed questions about what kind of cognitive domain it operates in, what's the structure of that domain, what kinds of transformations or operations have to be performed on objects in that domain, what kind of output does the system produce; and that kind of research strategy has been reasonably successful.

By contrast, when we try to understand less specialised intellectual processes: solving problems, writing plays, experimenting in science, and so forth, it seems to me that the dark ages are still upon us. There's really very little about such processes, it seems to me, that's understood.

MILLER When you describe these modular units it sounds as if you're reviving nineteenth-century phrenology.

FODOR There's a certain recurrence of popularity of phrenology, but without the bumps – I mean nobody's going round feeling heads. But it seems that there may be something to be said for the picture of mental organisation that was proposed by people like Francis Gall, the founding father of the phrenological tradition. According to that picture, neural organisation involves highly specific mechanisms which do restricted jobs, and which as computer theorists would say, don't 'talk to one another'; they're relatively independent in the performance of their computations, and they don't share capacities like memory and attention and so on with one another. They're isolated specialised computational systems, according to this picture.

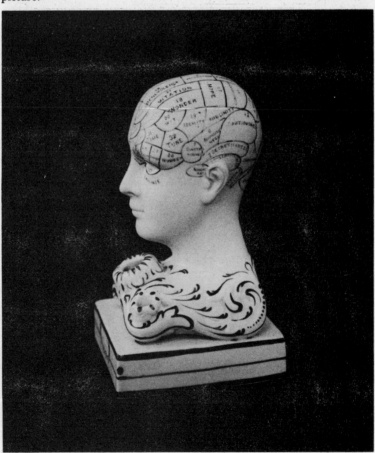

PLATE 1

That treatment seems to capture more of the story about mental organisation than was supposed, even quite recently. Just which such systems there are is unclear. The language mechanism is certainly a paradigm candidate.

MILLER That was shown, I suppose, fairly early on in the 1860s when people like Broca[1] first showed that disruption of language abilities could be caused by very localised damage to certain parts of the cerebral cortex.

FODOR Right. In fact, a characteristic feature of these modularised systems, is that they're associated with specific neural architecture. In fact if you think about a sort of rough first approximation of how the brain is organised, it seems to suggest just the kind of picture that I was talking about before. That is, you have some areas of the brain which seem to be task specific; visual areas and tactile areas, and language areas and so on. And then there's a lot of what people used to call 'association cortex', where roughly speaking everything seems to be connected with everything else. The suspicion has always been that that's where the real thinking goes on. In any event, there's a lot of the brain that doesn't *appear* to exhibit highly specialised neural organisation. So perhaps we can postulate a dichotomisation of the brain into parts that the phrenologists would have recognised, namely modularised special purpose computational units; and a part they wouldn't have liked at all: something structurally diffuse and functionally 'equipotential'.

MILLER A sort of generally smart area of the brain as opposed to the specific talents.

FODOR Right. The hope is, too, that wherever you find neural specialisation and modularity you will find independent evidence for genetic specificity – that is, for innate structures of the kind that one apparently has for language.

MILLER Nevertheless, even if we accept the idea that the brain might be divided into two separate types of function – as you say, a very general capacity which is to do with problem solving of a very general sort, and then these highly modular units which deal with very specific tasks – might it not be the case that even within these small modular units, the language of thought which was employed by them to process the task that they had to do was analogous, if on a smaller scale, to the type of language of thought which was used by these more diffuse areas?

FODOR Well I think that's certainly a possibility; no one yet knows what the answer is, but I think that to be optimistic in this area is to hope that that's not true. That is, that the representational capacities of these systems are quite specialised and quite finely tuned to the jobs which they have to do. The reason it would be nice if that were the case is that the smaller the system is, the more likely we are to be able to understand it in some finite amount of time, and in relative isolation from other problems in the field.

[1] Paul Broca (1824–1880). A French surgeon and anthropologist, first located the motor speech centre in the brain and did research on prehistoric surgical operations.

Success in science very often depends upon being able to find a way of dividing research problems into manageable bits.

If you look at the case of language (and again, I think that's the most elaborately and successfully studied of these modularised systems), it looks like the kind of representational capacity you need, the kind of information you have to represent, the kind of structures that you have to be able to display and the operations you have to be able to perform upon them, are really very highly specific to language. The analogies between, say, language and visual perception seem to be really pretty weak and unimpressive. So it might be that, not only are there these specialised computational systems, but that they, as it were, talk individual private languages; that the representational systems you use for doing visual form perception are really quite different from the ones that you use for doing, say, the syntactical analysis of utterances.

MILLER   Now if there is this loose confederation of specific capabilities on the one hand – the modular functions you speak of – plus the more generalised ones on the other hand, would one have to postulate some higher function which was capable of bringing them all together, so that there was a sort of federal government which said: 'Well now, come on fellas, come together and actually agree to make this thing into a person?'

FODOR   Right, that's where the soul lives these days. The kind of line that I've been considering and that I think is now becoming fairly widely held, is that you have this loose federation of special purpose processors which are interested in giving you news about what's going on in the world, and also integrating behaviour. That is, the modular systems seem to be largely involved in perception and in the integration of physical acts and responses. But these mechanisms have to communicate with some more central system which puts all the news together. I suppose that that's the kind of system that mediates problem solving and higher cognitive processing at large. I have no idea how that works, nor am I convinced that the currently available theoretical and experimental techniques are very likely to throw much light on that question.

6

dialogue with
Stuart Hampshire

Notions Of The Unconscious Mind

INTRODUCTION

When man began to take an intelligent interest in his own mental processes, he became increasingly aware of psychological facts which could only be explained by postulating a region of the mind into which thoughts and ideas could vanish without ceasing to exist. The unexpected return of forgotten experiences and the apparently effortless solution of problems which had been previously given up as too difficult, suggested that consciousness existed against a background of unconscious mental activity. Sigmund Freud, who is often credited with the discovery of this domain, insisted that it had already been identified by poets and philosophers and that what he discovered was a scientific method by which this otherwise inaccessible region of the mind could be studied. Such a claim gives a somewhat misleading impression of Freud's contribution to modern psychology, and although the interpretation of dreams and the analysis of 'free associations' make up a distinctive part of the psychoanalytic enterprise, it is the theoretical picture which Freud developed on the basis of such evidence which represents his most controversial achievement.

By the middle of the nineteenth century artists and philosophers had developed a concept of the unconscious mind which played an important part in shaping Freud's ideas on the subject, and historians of psychology have recognised the debt which psychoanalysis owes to European Romanticism. But Freud's ambitions were scientific rather than literary, and although he was peculiarly susceptible to themes expressed in art, his concept of mind was also influenced by a deep commitment to scientific materialism. As far as he was concerned, mental events were dictated by physical processes, and he was convinced that psychological function was rigidly determined by natural laws. If thoughts, dreams and fantasies often seemed unintelligible, it could only mean that they had their source in a region of the mind whose processes were not accessible to conscious introspection, and that special methods were needed to elucidate their hidden grammar.

The framework within which Freud began to elaborate these investigations was provided by biology as much as physics, and it is almost impossible to visualise the outcome without the presuppositions of evolution. Admittedly Freud was never a committed Darwinian, and throughout his working life he continued to sponsor Lamarckian[1] notions about the inheritance of acquired characteristics. But as far as psychological theory was concerned such a distinction is not altogether relevant.

[1] Jean Baptiste Pierre Antoine de Monet, Chevalier de Lamarck (1744–1829), was a highly distinguished French naturalist, and a pre-Darwinian evolutionist. He published his famous *Philosophie zoologique* in 1809, and his *Histoire des animaux sans vertèbres* in 1815–20. Lamarck broke with the old notion of species, sought to explain their transformation and the evolution of the animal world, and prepared the way for the now accepted theory of descent.

What mattered was his belief that human beings had descended from primitive ancestors, and that they had therefore inherited instinctive impulses which had to be restrained and domesticated in order to meet the demands of civilised coexistence. In the light of this idea Freud began to visualise the unconscious as a custodial institution, a mental province in which otherwise disruptive instincts could be confined and silenced. In other words the unconscious mind was not simply a mental reservoir into which thoughts and ideas lapsed by default. For Freud it was a psychological establishment maintained by expensive forms of repression.

Clinicians continue to disagree about the scientific status of such an idea, and there are many psychiatrists who claim that the successful treatment of neurotic patients can be accomplished without having to take Freud's so-called 'metapsychology' into account. But apart from its scientific credibility, Freud's notion of the unconscious mind raises philosophical problems which are just as interesting as the clinical ones. Does it, for example, make sense to talk about an unconscious idea? What is the logical status of a thought of which the thinker is unaware? The argumentative techniques which have been developed by philosophers in the last twenty-five years have made it possible and profitable to ask questions of this sort, and Professor Hampshire, Warden of Wadham College, Oxford University, brings to this discussion an elegant finesse which is seen at its best in his distinguished book, *Thought and Action*.

DISCUSSION

MILLER Professor Miller implied that after a short period in which the mind, as it were, went into the wilderness and was not regarded as a negotiable item in psychological discourse, the idea of mental life returned on the back of the machine, and as a result of work which had been done in the Second World War with servo-mechanisms and signals and information theory, it became necessary to reintroduce the idea of mental representation in order to make certain psychological findings intelligible. And he said that the notion of conscious life was now an important ingredient in psychological discourse. He went on to imply that these mental representations weren't necessarily confined to conscious thought, and that we had to include the idea of an unconscious mental life in order to explain certain psychological findings. Now what I'd like to ask you first is whether you think that there is any consistency or coherence in the idea of unconscious thoughts.

HAMPSHIRE Yes, I certainly think there is. But we've got to distinguish from the beginning the unconscious and the preconscious, to use Freud's own terms, and say that the preconscious mind is involved in many of our thinking processes, particularly computational ones, and that we ought not to associate so strongly as we have in the past the idea of thinking and the idea of conscious awareness. A great deal of our thinking proceeds without conscious awareness. An example of this would be what I'm doing now, as I'm speaking; I'm choosing words and I'm thinking, but I'm not duplicating the process of speaking with a conscious awareness of my choice and the reasons for my choice. I choose a particular word, as all speakers do, as the appropriate word, and this choice issues from a process of thought, but not one of which I am at the time consciously aware. I might be able to reconstruct the thought later, but it's not a 'shadow' process, parallel with the actual speaking. Because of the influence of English empiricist philosophers, we have in the past made too close an association between thinking and conscious thinking. Some thinking is conscious thinking – when we're very consciously arguing a point – but in the exercise of the use of language itself and in many of our skills, we are thinking preconsciously, working things out without knowing how we work them out, or by what steps we've arrived at a conclusion.

There's a rather good example, which is given by a modern philosopher. He points out that it's quite natural if we trip coming downstairs, to say: 'Well, I thought there was another step.' The implication is that the process of walking downstairs is governed by thought and belief. And a great variety of such thoughts and beliefs are at a preconscious level, not formulated and not worked out articulately. Once one realises that thought is often separate from conscious awareness, one is prepared to look on the notion of the unconscious – which is distinct from the notion of the preconscious – with more charity. Unconscious thoughts, in the history of philosophy, have played a large part in the sense that philosophers have noted that our thinking, particularly imaginative thought, takes non-logical forms.

Nonetheless, Freud took an absolutely decisive step, peculiar to himself, when he spoke of the unconscious mind as introduced by the process of repression. Repression is a process which he thinks takes place in all civilised, thinking men, irrespective of what the social conditions may be – whether we're living in a very free, impulsive, liberated society or not. We need, as we grow up and as we learn, to control instinctual forces by repression, and repression normally makes our unconscious thinking inaccessible to us. There's a barrier which is very hard to lift and which cuts off our conscious reflective mind from our unconscious thinking. The claim is that this unconscious thinking follows an order which is not like the logical order of an argumentative conscious mind, but that it proceeds according to an order of its own; and this order is ordinarily best explained by an association, for example, through experiences in the past, by puns, by verbal associations, or by what Freud calls 'condensation', when we choose one particular idea to represent a whole number of separate ideas which have occurred together in our past experience.

His therapeutic aim was to cure neurosis, which he saw as a general condition of man, and the method was to gain access to the unconscious mind, partly through interpretation of dreams, partly through free association, which would lift this barrier of primary repression. You thereby gain some access to the unconscious mind. And when you gain that access, you discover that what you are dealing with is an association of thought which can be traced back to a childhood situation, the situation which he characterised as the 'family romance'. Freud describes what he considered to be the ordinary stages of the family romance that you pass through – for example, for boys competitive relations with your father, your father as a punishing figure, rivalry between brothers, and a desire for unpermitted love and some intense relationship with your mother. I don't think, from the point of general philosophy, that the details of this are of very great significance. But what is of significance, I think, is the revelation of an unconscious mind which has a coherence which is imaginative and non-rational. That was the really important step. I think that there's some misunderstanding about it, because very often the suggestion is made that the unconscious mind represents raw instinct and that Freud is just one more thinker who represents consciousness as controlling instinct, and somehow superimposed on instinct. That is not the case. The doctrine is really about thought. In fact one of the most powerful criticisms that can be made of Freud is precisely that he doesn't give a characterisation of emotion, of its part in our conscious life and its origins in the unconscious mind; rather he offers an account of thought, representing much of our conscious purposes and our conscious attitude to the world and to our friends and our family, as 'masking thoughts' – characteristically called 'phantasies' – which at a deeper level explain our behaviour and our reactions.

MILLER   Nevertheless, wouldn't Freud and his supporters wish to say that the phantasies themselves, albeit cast in the form of thoughts, were propelled at least by emotions, by emotional attachments, by passions directed towards the mother and by sexual feelings which can be characterised as emotions?

HAMPSHIRE   Yes, but I think the difficulty is to see what is meant by unfelt emotions – that is, emotions of which we're not consciously aware. In general, his theory of emotion, the theory of affect, as it usually appears in his translated writings, affirms that we are excited by input stimuli, and they build up a reaction inside us, a mounting of emotional pressure, which has to be discharged. The organism is aiming at a state of equilibrium and at the discharge of emotion. This is the standard Freudian account. There's no suggestion that emotion serves some valuable purpose from a biological point of view, that it's a valuable self-originated power; that isn't in any way suggested.

MILLER   You mean, for humans, emotions are nothing other than excitations which build up in the nervous system and simply seek discharge regardless of the use to which they might be put.

HAMPSHIRE   Yes. I think he's driven to that because I find it almost impossible to think what an emotion of which you're not aware would be. I can understand the notion of a desire that you're not aware of, but precisely when we use the stormy term emotion, which suggests strong affect, a perturbation, then we seem to be speaking of something of which we *are* aware. But, against the background of what we've just been saying about the preconscious mind, I find no difficulty whatever in the idea of thought as being below the level of conscious awareness – if below is the right metaphor.

MILLER   Can you say why there is more logical consistency in the idea of an unconsciously thought 'thought', as opposed to an unconsciously felt emotion?

HAMPSHIRE   I think that 'felt' feeling positively suggests that of which we are aware, while the thought of a pianist who is playing, or a violinist who is playing, or an actor who is acting, isn't something of which he is concurrently, or perhaps at any time, aware. He's thinking, and his fingers are acting. But if we say he is suffused with emotion as he plays (which I suspect is not the case with pianists usually) then I think we refer to something of which he is at that time vividly aware, and which might have this or that dynamic effect on his fingers, while the thought issues directly in the performance.

MILLER   Well, I've often wondered whether it was necessary to characterise the processes which go on in the brain, which determine the *outcome* of conscious thoughts, as thoughts. Why couldn't they be written out as cerebral processes which are antecedent to conscious thought, but don't have to be characterised as thoughts themselves?

HAMPSHIRE   You're now speaking of the brain, which is a physical object. This is the machine or the instrument with which we think. But when I was speaking of the unconscious mind, I wasn't thinking of an instrument, the brain, the literal physical thing, but of an assembly of habits and dispositions, and also performances, to which we don't have access except under very special conditions. And I think part of the greatness of Freud is to have laid bare in free association the nature of that thinking, and to have made it accessible to us – at any rate indirectly.

If you study ritual, or you study literature, or you study abnormal states of mind, you see echoes of the processes of the unconscious mind as described by Freud; and you might attribute the discovery to him without believing in the general picture of the mind that he gives, particularly of the stages through which we develop the Oedipus complex, for example.

If I start to ask myself the coarse question 'do I actually believe Freud?' then I find that there are discoveries he made which it seems to me one has to accept. First, about infantile sexuality. One may or may not subscribe to the detailed picture Freud gives of separate phases of infantile sexual development, in which sensual or libidinal wishes are focused on various parts of the body; but I think that the evidence is very strong that children, at an age when they don't have the concepts, do have thoughts of a very dynamic kind about their relationships to other members of the family. The whole story concerning children and their preconceptual thinking seems to me to at least be very plausible.

MILLER   Is that plausibility based on the experience of observing children, or is it derived from psychoanalytic patients?

HAMPSHIRE   I think looking back on the past, in literature and history, you see evidences of it, though not in a very definite form. I think it also arises out of psychoanalytical experience – that you do find these rather childish images of a very concrete kind. They hang around in the mind, in a rather farcical way, and can govern behaviour in an absurd, essentially comic way; that is another source of evidence. And I think that the experience of psychiatrists such as Bowlby[1] in dealing with children, seems to indicate that this is a useful way of thinking about infant thought. I'm not saying it's exclusive or that no progress will be made elsewhere, but this does seem to me to be a definite discovery, which has profoundly influenced the way people actually treat children.

MILLER   Can we go back, just for a moment, to the original distinction between preconscious and unconscious thought, and expand it a little? Presumably by preconscious we simply mean those thoughts which are not present in consciousness but to which we can have access without much difficulty. They can re-enter consciousness without apparently having to overcome obstacles.

HAMPSHIRE   Yes. A very interesting case of preconscious thinking is simultaneous translation, when speech is rendered extremely rapidly into another language. If you ask, 'why did you choose that word as a translation rather than that?' an interpreter can probably tell you, though his telling you would not be a matter of his recapturing what he said to himself at the time. Nonetheless interpreters can recall the occasion, and they can reconstruct their thinking, this question having been asked. But they didn't need to have that reason present in their mind in order to make that choice. And in explaining their choice of word, they don't meet any special barrier with an emotional association, with an emotional charge attached to it, as we do when we are trying to penetrate the unconscious mind.

Repression serves a purpose for all of us; you're able to cope with your life because you dismiss and keep below the hatches – to use a slave-ship metaphor – certain thoughts you have which are incongruent with your conscious goals and desires. You feel threatened in your ordinary life if these thoughts are dug up and the irrational basis of your conduct is revealed. Not simply because it's irrational, but because you are expending a great deal of energy keeping these disagreeable, and obviously rather absurd, thoughts, out of consciousness. That is the big difference.

MILLER   So one would distinguish the preconscious from the unconscious on the basis of relative accessibility. In the preconscious there is some degree of accessibility. But nevertheless, one would want to distinguish between two different types of inaccessibility, in the unconscious as conceived by someone like Chomsky[2], and the unconscious as conceived by Freud. Because Chomsky, when talking about the unconscious mental structures which predispose one to speak creatively, and hear and understand

[1]Bowlby. See p. 177.
[2]See footnote on page 91.

sentences which one has never heard before, would nevertheless say that the structure which allowed one to do this was radically inaccessible to consciousness and could not be retrieved. But not because there was a bar to doing so. Not because it's repressed.

HAMPSHIRE   I'm not quite confident about what Chomsky means, but certainly there is a distinction. He has said that the patterns and forms which enable us to construct new sentences and to identify what is said to us, to make all the minute discriminations we have to make in order to understand, that this capacity is in some way built in, literally, to the brain, not only to the mind; that it's physically programmed rather in the way in which, say, a bird's mating procedures are presumably physically programmed into the organism. He certainly used to think that, and it, of course, wouldn't follow that we have an internal representation of these programmes to which we can have access merely by reflection.

MILLER   And it's not the same as a person who is unfamiliar with the terms of English grammar being unable to print out kinds of grammar, as it were. It's something more radically inaccessible than that, isn't it?

HAMPSHIRE   Yes, I think Chomsky thinks – unlike Freud – that this is a matter of the intrinsic complexity and elaboration of these rules, which are not easily arrived at. But I don't feel confident about that. I'm not quite sure how it should be interpreted, but I agree, it's another kind of unconscious from Freud's.

MILLER   But one which doesn't have that active repressed feeling, which, of course, is the characteristic of Freud's idea of the unconscious.

HAMPSHIRE   No. According to Freud, there's an emotional investment in keeping out of sight and out of mind the absurd concatenation of thoughts which have a tremendous effect on our behaviour. I think it's important to note that the unconscious mind as described by Freud – unlike the preconscious mind – isn't in any way continuous with the conscious mind. The preconscious mind has a rational structure, though it may not be the neat rational structure that logicians talk about. But it has a concatenation which is a matter of going from reason to conclusion, in some form or other, while the unconscious mind has an absurd structure, the structure of dreams; in some of its activities, it is uncontrolled by the sense of reality, by the reality principle; it contains a high element of wish, a high element of merely surreal or arbitrary association, and it's highly concrete.

MILLER   It contains, as you say, this high element of wish, and yet you find it quite difficult to conceive of or see as intelligible the notion of a wish which is strongly felt and yet not experienced.

HAMPSHIRE   I don't see what is meant by 'strongly felt' except in terms of how the thought issues in action. Imagine a child in a highly excited state. (The convenience of taking a child is simply that it's easier to see how conceptual thinking might be pushed on one side.) The child might be in a highly excited state, and there would be phantasies or thoughts of some form of attack that's going to be made on him or her; these thoughts originated in its mind, because of some sort of association between either a word or an image or an object, and this thought of attack and of threat. The intense feeling would be something, I would say, the child was aware of, otherwise I don't see what is meant by intense feeling. I'm speaking as an academic philosopher. I don't see what can be meant by intensity, except in relation to consciousness or action.

MILLER Yes. Well in spite of the differences between Chomsky's conception of the unconscious, and Freud's active repressive notion of an unconscious, there does seem to be an overlap at least in this area. Chomsky talks about some sort of deep structure which determines and organises the actual expression of a performance in speech, and the comprehension of the speech that one's hearing. There is something comparable, is there not, in Freud's idea of unconscious urges and wishes which undergo transformation through the agency of a censor, and then issue in the manifest content of a dream. Now although there obviously are profound differences between these two, there is something very similar in their conceptions of a deep underlying form, which has a manifest content.

HAMPSHIRE Yes, and I think that the idea of manifest content and deep underlying form has been vastly influential. Whether we should attribute it all to Freud, I don't know, but it's been vastly influential in interpreting human behaviour in everyday life, by undermining the idea that in any emotional matter you can take what people say as their reason for a particular emotional attitude, without asking yourself the question, 'What do they *really* mean?' This has affected not only the way we talk about people individually, and our reluctance to write testimonials and to attribute to them very stable characteristics, but has affected interpretation in anthropology and in history, interpretation of ritual features of behaviour, and interpretation of literature as a whole, I think. The opposition between manifest content and latent meaning, the idea that you've got to unmask, including unmasking yourself, that you can look through to needs of the person which he hasn't formulated, and that these can be inferred from his mistakes or his idiosyncrasies, or the nervous tics in behaviour, or the idiosyncrasy of style, or the movement of a brushstroke – that all these things reveal an individual, and reveal a world which is private in a radical sense, even to the individual – most of this is attributable to Freud. Chomsky is a different case, I think.

The concept of a universal language goes back at least to the seventeenth century. In fact the first proponent of it in England, or the most influential, was a warden of Wadham College, Oxford, called Wilkins, who had this idea that the different languages must have a common base, because there must be what we would now call a biological singularity of the species which enabled us to learn language in the way that we do; and it would be a great advantage if we got down to this base from which the historical languages would be deviations. Even before that, there was the Adamic conception of language, the idea that there was a basic language – Adam speech – from which all other languages had developed. But there must be an underlying capacity in the species to have in mind the grammatical forms which are common to all languages. Otherwise how do we learn? This idea was formulated long before Freud. People who've speculated on language have often thought that. There does, therefore, seem to be a radical difference between this and Freud's idea of the unconscious mind. Although the latter exhibits features which are supposed to be general, nonetheless the point in gaining access to it is to gain access to something highly particular – as it were to an individual trace, like a thumbprint. You try to find a private world of phantasy which is governing, say, a hysterical paralysis, and you arrive at certain thoughts which have produced this effect. That seems to be different from the Chomskyan idea that underlying all our symbolic behaviour there must be something biologically common. In fact Freud didn't really think enough about what is biologically common.

MILLER   And yet Freud liked to characterise his enterprise as something which was biologically founded.

HAMPSHIRE   Yes, I know, but are you convinced by that? I am not, because I don't think he asks a biological question, or if he asks it, he doesn't allow the answer to determine his proceedings. He does not ask: 'What is the advantage conferred on the species, from the point of view of Darwinian natural selection, of these mental arrangements I have discovered?' For example, what really is the advantage of repression?

There is the suggestion, occasionally in Freud, that human beings are diseased animals; the disease being caused by long periods of nursing and long periods of being brought up in the peculiar institution – if it is an institution – of the family. There's some ambiguity whether the family is a biological institution or a social one; but at any rate, it is distinctive of human beings. They then develop repression, and hence neurosis, as a necessary part of becoming adult, conscious, self-directed, humans. But why, exactly? What's the advantage?

MILLER   Well, couldn't Freud account for that in Darwinian terms by saying that one of the ways in which the human species had achieved its success was by the nurturing of intelligence in the protective enclave of a long infancy, which allowed the individual to learn through language. And that one of the sacrifices which had to be made in undergoing this tuition was the repression of otherwise disruptive instincts, which would blow apart the family and destroy its tuitional function.

HAMPSHIRE   Yes, I think that's in part absolutely right. He certainly thought that you paid a price, that there was a cost attached to culture.

And that repression drew a kind of boundary around culture, and thus round science and art; and he was extremely pious about both science and art. But he also retained the idea that the real energies of men – it's an old idea – come from the imaginative forces which are repressed. You would shift mankind in a good direction if you enabled it to gain access to those thoughts which are pre-logical and are in the unconscious mind, and deflected their energies from the act of repression; that there was, so to speak, in this instinctual type of thinking, a source of energy which is etiolated, thinned out, in culture.

On the other hand, he was always, throughout his life, extremely pessimistic. He became more so the longer he lived. He thought that there was a strict limit to the degree to which human beings could be liberated by self-knowledge or by access to the unconscious mind. I think he was very sceptical about any radical liberation, and he's greatly misunderstood by many popular thinkers, who believe he was in favour of some kind of Californian self-expression, which is very much not the sort of thing that he thought either possible or desirable. He said: 'Much will be gained if we succeed in transforming hysterical misery into common unhappiness.' That you can do by his sort of technique. But he didn't think that there was any possible form of civilised society which dispensed with repression, and hence dispensed with neurosis. You might lessen it, but not much more than that.

MILLER But nevertheless, this could be adequately described as a biologically advantageous arrangement – for all the penalties of neurosis and so on, which are inflicted upon the individual who has to undergo it – if it produces an intelligent, resourceful, tool-using creature.

HAMPSHIRE Yes, I suppose my real complaint is the complaint I would also make about Spinoza – that the stress is so predominantly, in Freud, not, as might be thought, on sexual impulse and its gratification and the ills of postponing its gratification, but on thought; he seems to think that human beings are at their best when they're thinkers. Which may be true, but I think from the natural history point of view it is a little hard to work out. If you put that view together with the lack of a theory of emotion, except at the conscious level where we have this rather primitive theory of discharge of affect, this gives an unduly pessimistic view of the survival of the race. One would hope that the account he gives of the unconscious mind would leave a larger place for the value of the emotions, for the actual value of them, as ensuring not only the survival of the individual but the survival of the species. There isn't really an account of that, it seems to me. His theory of love, for example, is rather thin, although there's a marvellous essay on love. There's an even more marvellous paper on mourning, and on certain fundamental issues like that. They are wonderful papers, but they're not intellectually convincing to me because of this lack of a view of emotional expression as being part of the primary endowment.

MILLER Yes, and although one can see the selective advantage of repression at a deeper level, I find the biological model which he uses very implausible. The idea of the discharge of excitation, and the idea of an organism which seeks some sort of null state of excitation, is something which I can't quite make sense of. Not in terms of what we now know about the nervous system.

HAMPSHIRE Yes. It is a devaluation of impulse and of emotion; you aim at an equilibrium where the organism is, so to speak, fitting in to its environment in a static and peaceful fashion. But not acting and reacting with it; not drawing on intrinsic emotional and desiring sources of its own. The theory of instinct can't be a substitute for an account of the emotions and permanent attitudes, such as fear and love.

MILLER One gets the impression in reading, for example, the essay, 'The Instincts and their Vicissitudes', and the paper, 'Narcissism', that the emotions are almost inconvenient epiphenomena of the mind, which are seeking self-extinction in order to produce some state of nirvana or calm. And this I find implausible.

HAMPSHIRE It *can't* be plausible if you think of human beings as animals. It just makes them too discontinuous with the rest of the biosphere, the living world, or whatever you call it.

MILLER And so we have this rather paradoxical situation of a theory whose logical and biological foundations seem so shaky and implausible in many respects, but which, at the same time, has had such a profound effect upon the way in which we visualise each other in everyday life. How can a theory which is so shaky in so many of its logical structures have had such far-reaching effects?

HAMPSHIRE I think so far from that being exceptional, it's the usual case in the history of thought – just as in the case of individuals, you can say that their virtues are exaggerations, in a positive direction, of their vices, and their vices are an exaggeration, in a negative direction, of their virtues. If you think of Plato or Kant or Descartes or any other great thinker who has contributed some vivid, convincing new picture of the mind which then enters common speech and common thought, you realise that at the same time what's enabled him to get there is a kind of craziness at the periphery.

That's certainly true of Plato, for example. You couldn't possibly say that the substantive positions taken by Plato are plausible. The same goes for Hume, who's had a profound influence on most British thinkers. He says that our experience consists of ideas and impressions, which succeed each other with inconceivable rapidity, and expects you to believe that, when it's obviously not true in a literal sense. So I don't think it's quite the right question to ask how Freud can be so implausible, logically speaking, and yet transform our thought in the way he has because I think this is often the case. The position is made rather tantalising and awkward, though, by the fact that his theory has a clinical or therapeutic setting, and you naturally don't want to treat patients in a Platonic way, or in a Cartesian way. You don't want to treat people along the lines of a theory which is not founded in logic and in experimental confirmation; and certainly Freudian theory is not, and it is admitted that it is not.

So you demand rather more of Freud than you would of a philosopher, and he of course despised philosophy and wished to be considered a scientist. But I myself think that he really stands among the rank of philosophers, in one sense of the word 'philosophers'. You can't use Freudian theory as a blueprint for action on human beings, in the way you can use physiology or discoveries that might be made about chemical processes causing insanity.

MILLER   And yet it's precisely as a blueprint for action that he's had his most profound influence. His theories have profoundly altered the way in which we visualise practical relationships with one another, if only that we are led to suspect one another's motives in various ways. And this has had a profound practical effect on ordinary social life, in a way that surely Plato has not.

HAMPSHIRE   Yes, but if you're involved in controversy about clinical psychiatry or clinical psychology, and you talk about Freud, you're asked: 'Do you think that the claims made by Freud and by Freudians can be treated in the same way as the claims made in pharmaceutical psychiatry, for example, where there are presumably verifiable connections between certain mental states and physical bases?' Then I think you have to say: 'No, it's not that kind of theory; it can't be used with that degree of precision and definiteness.'

MILLER   I sometimes feel that the behaviourists who attack Freud precisely on this point – that you can't actually characterise the criteria by which you decide whether Freudian analysis has been effective or ineffective as a treatment, that there's no way of falsifying or proving the theory in terms of the clinical outcome – sometimes misconceive the sort of negotiation that is going on in psychoanalysis. There are subtle transformations of experience which simply cannot be written down in a form which would satisfy a statistician, or an ordinary natural scientist but which nevertheless do affect the outcome as far as the patient who undergoes the experience of psychoanalysis is concerned.

HAMPSHIRE   Yes, but any thinker who transforms the way in which people talk to each other, and perhaps more important still, the way in which they think of themselves, and the way in which they think that they possess or lack self-knowledge – any thinker who does that obviously has a huge effect on human life. But it's not the same as saying that he gives you, as it were, a drawing of the human mind which you can operate with, in order to identify a particular neurosis and suggest its origin and its cure. If there were a chemical discovery of the cause of schizophrenia, you could say: 'We now know that the lack or presence of this chemical agent will produce such-and-such symptoms, and if we vary the levels of this agent in the brain, we vary the symptoms.' There is nothing of this kind in Freud. That is not to say that you can't enter into extremely fruitful discussions with psychoanalysts or that psychoanalysis itself might not have an important social role. I think it might, but that's rather different from saying that the theory is grounded in logic and experiment, as other scientific theories are. Freudian theory isn't so grounded.

MILLER   Indeed, but nevertheless this fruitfulness arises from the peculiar character of the model of the mind with which psychoanalysts operate.

HAMPSHIRE   Yes. If you were to abandon the notions of repression and the unconscious mind and the family romance and the methodology of access through free association, dream interpretation, parapraxis or mistakes and so on – if all that were to be abandoned, then the theory would be abandoned. But I don't think it should be abandoned. If you ask the true or false question and say, 'isn't it paradoxical that you don't really believe the substantive assertions but have a great reverence for the theory and think it's had great effects?' then I think one's applying the judgement 'true or false' to distinct propositions. I do not believe severally that the evidence supports the separate propositions which attribute neurosis to this, that or the other feature of the Oedipus complex, for example. I don't think that the evidence supports that. But then I don't think you ought to think of the story of the Oedipus complex in quite such a precise way.

MILLER   So one could say that Freud's contribution is as a creative moralist rather than as a natural scientist.

HAMPSHIRE   I don't accept that dichotomy. I think there are a lot of other things that fall between what you can properly call science and what you can't; for example, I think some kinds of anthropology have that intermediate status. Imaginative accounts of the working of a society have been given by many different anthropologists, each having different pictures of how society works, but you can't exactly say that they are scientific, in the sense which a textbook on scientific method defines. And I would say there are a number of very valuable human enquiries which fall between science and ethics.

   Of course, Freud himself would have hated to be thought of as a moralist, but I think he might have been patient with the thought of himself as in an interstice – a kind of gap between purely imaginative enquiries, and scientific ones. In this gap you would find certain sorts of historical enquiry, anthropological research of a certain kind, studies of ritual and myth, for example. All these are not scientific in the narrow sense, but they may have a transforming effect on the way we look at people, and they make a claim to be true, but true in a sense which doesn't reduce to a set of proven evidenced propositions.

MILLER   And you don't feel, as some social scientists would, that these are truths of a provisional nature which are awaiting the sort of hard evidence which will eventually allow Freud to be incorporated into the truly scientific? You're saying that it is constitutive of the Freudian enterprise that it will always be interstitial.

HAMPSHIRE   Yes. I believe that if it were scientific, it would be physics or biology, and not a characterisation of thought. Freud, of course, hoped that his metapsychology – his theory of the mind – would be shown to have a physical basis, and that when that physical basis was discovered, you could discard his theory of the mind. He was a reductionist.

MILLER   In fact he made an abortive effort to do that in his 'Scientific Project'.

HAMPSHIRE   Yes. The 'Scientific Project' was an attempt to show, as a materialist such as Freud should show, that his account of the mind mirrored or was a shadow of the real substance – the real substance being the material processes going on in the body. I think that had a bad effect on his theory of psychology, because he modelled it on these mechanical metaphors, hoping the physical details would be discovered later. He produced a sort of abstract drawing which was going to be filled in, and this made the theory, in some respects, very unreal as a picture of the mental. At the same time I think that that kind of reductive approach is much too simple-minded, philosophically speaking. But that's a large question.

7

dialogue with
Norman Geschwind

The Organisation Of The Living Brain

INTRODUCTION

For a creature like man, who prides himself on the spontaneity of his own thoughts and actions, there is something disturbing about the idea that whatever he thinks and does can be traced back to neurological events of which he is unaware. In fact it's quite difficult even to make sense of the idea. As I frame this thought and move my hands in the effort to put it down on paper, I can find no evidence to support the claim that what I am doing is dictated by nervous events going on inside my head. I get no impression that what moves my hands is happening in one part of my brain, or that what enables me to form sentences is happening somewhere else. All that I am aware of is the indivisible unity of the effort to make myself understood.

But it only takes a small injury to shatter this indivisible unity. If one of the blood vessels inside my brain were to clot or break, I might lose the power of movement on one side of my body and yet retain the ability to speak and understand. If the injury was somewhere else in the brain I might lose the ability to recognise objects placed in my hands whilst retaining the ability to recognise them when held in front of my eyes, and so on.

By studying the brains of those who have suffered such injuries, neurologists have begun to recognise consistent clinical patterns from which it has become apparent that there is a complicated division of labour within the human brain.

Of course the belief that mental functions can be mapped on to cerebral structures is almost as old as the study of anatomy itself. But until neurologists began to study the clinical effects of localised brain damage, the traditional picture was speculative rather than scientific. The mind was visualised as a confederation of mental faculties – will, memory, foresight, perception and so forth. And each of these faculties was identified with its own part of the brain. The problem is that the way in which the mind visualises its own functions, that is to say the categories in terms of which it represents its own activities, do not necessarily correspond to the way in which the brain elaborates mental processes, and the faculties which have been mapped on to the anatomical structure of the brain are as artificial and as arbitrary as the political frontiers drawn on the geological map of the globe. The effort to reconcile mental faculties with cerebral anatomy was brought to its absurd climax in the fashionable pseudo-science of phrenology, which flourished in the early years of the nineteenth century, and until it was superseded by clinical analysis phrenology virtually paralysed the scientific study of cerebral localisation. In the last quarter of this century clinical neurologists have renewed their efforts to study the division of labour within the human brain. And with the benefit of more sophisticated anatomical techniques they are beginning to build up an even subtler picture of the relationship between mind and brain. I discussed some of these results with Norman Geschwind whose work as

Professor of Neurology at the Harvard Medical School has established him as one of the leading authorities on the organisation of the human brain.

DISCUSSION

MILLER   Most people feel intuitively that the mind is in the head. Perhaps that's because they know the brain is in the head, and that the brain has got some sort of connection with the mind. But people also feel that the mind is a unit, an indivisible whole. I believe I am right in saying that nowadays this view is beginning to change and scientists now regard the nervous system as something in the nature of a federal institution, in which the unity is achieved, rather than given. When did scientists first begin to get the idea that the brain was divided up into parts responsible for separate functions?

GESCHWIND   That is, of course, a very good question. The idea that the brain has something to do with thinking is a very old one. When scientists began to look at the anatomy of the nervous system, they really had very little notion of how this organ was put together. I believe that the origin of the idea, if you want to use modern terminology, that the brain is a collection of different kinds of computers, which are connected to each other, really goes back to Meynert. His name is mostly familiar to many people because he was Freud's teacher. Meynert was probably the first person to develop the idea that you could begin to understand what was going on in the nervous system by not only observing where certain structures were located, but also by learning the patterns of connections of these structures. There is a German saying that it was Meynert who endowed the brain with a mind.

MILLER   Meynert thus made it clear that the brain is not just a homogeneous jelly, but is instead a structure whose parts are connected by individual fibres. Furthermore, the clinical neurological observation of patients who had sustained brain damage made it clear that the anatomical structure was related to the organisation of separate functions.

GESCHWIND   Meynert set the stage for this approach, since he was the first to classify the different types of connection. For example, he used the word 'commissure' to describe the large connections such as the corpus callosum between the two sides of the brain. The awareness of these connections between the two cerebral hemispheres led some of his students to speculate as to what functions they might have. As early as the 1880s the prediction had been made that damage to the corpus callosum could lead to separation of the functions of the left and right sides of the brain. These predictions were confirmed in the early 1900s, when a German neurologist named Hugo Liepmann first described what happened when there was extensive damage to the corpus callosum so that the two halves of the brain became disconnected from each other. In this picture of a section of the brain (fig. 1) you can see the large white bundle which acts as a connection between the two sides of the brain. Since nerve fibres carry impulses in

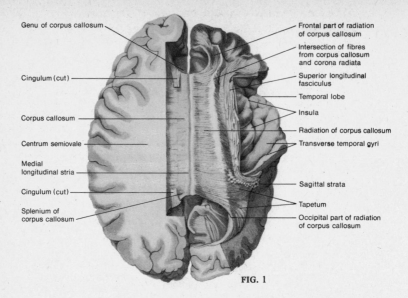

Genu of corpus callosum

Cingulum (cut)

Corpus callosum

Centrum semiovale

Medial
longitudinal stria

Cingulum (cut)

Splenium of
corpus callosum

Frontal part of radiation
of corpus callosum

Intersection of fibres
from corpus callosum
and corona radiata

Superior longitudinal
fasciculus

Temporal lobe

Insula

Radiation of corpus callosum

Transverse temporal gyri

Sagittal strata

Tapetum

Occipital part of radiation
of corpus callosum

FIG. 1

only one direction, the corpus callosum contains one large group of nerve fibres transmitting information from the left side of the brain to the right side. There is, of course, a reciprocal set of connections travelling in the opposite direction, from the right side of the brain to the left. Although each fibre is a one-way street, traffic flows in both directions.

There are other bundles of connections between the two sides of the brain but in mammals, including humans, this is the largest one. In some animals, it is missing. A kangaroo does not have a corpus callosum, nor do any of the other marsupials, which depend on another group of fibres called the anterior commissure, which is also present in humans in addition to the corpus callosum.

One of the most dramatic early examples of the effect of destroying the corpus callosum was published in 1908 by another neurologist named Kurt Goldstein. He described a woman who had been taken to a hospital because of her bizarre behaviour. Her left hand would come up to her own neck and would start to choke her. She would pull the left hand away with her right hand and would sit on it. She complained that her left hand was bad and beyond her control. While in bed, she would throw the pillows on the floor and tear the bedclothes – but *only* with her left hand. Asked why she was doing that, she would again insist that her left hand was beyond her control.

This behaviour was, of course, bizarre, and suggested that she had delusions of control from the outside. Goldstein, however, concluded, on the basis of his examination, that she had suffered damage to the corpus callosum, and that the two sides of her brain had thus been disconnected from each other. This conclusion was confirmed after her death when direct examination of the brain showed the predicted damage in the corpus callosum.

The behaviour of this patient was, of course, astonishing, and most people would obviously wonder how someone could actually attempt to self-strangulate. Yet once you think of the fact that the two sides of the brain had been separated from each other, the mechanism becomes clear although still surprising, since it runs counter to all our normal intuitions about behaviour. The possibility that, after the damage, each side of the brain was experiencing different emotions is astonishing. Yet accepting this makes it possible to understand that the two sides of the brain might behave differently and that they could in fact behave hostilely to each other.

Since the time of that original description, similar phenomena have been demonstrated repeatedly.

I find it fascinating that in every case that I know of in which bizarre or unpleasant behaviour is carried out by one hand of a patient with callosal damage it is the left hand which produces the strange or unacceptable actions, although I cannot rule out the possibility of occasional exceptions. This suggests that the fundamental emotional tone on the right side of the brain is different in a more or less consistent way from that on the left. Recent findings that the right hemisphere may be especially involved in some forms of depression are consistent with this idea.

MILLER I wonder if I can ask an awkward question. In which side of the brain was this lady resident? You quoted her as saying: 'The side of me which is doing that is bad.' This gives one the impression that she herself, the intact her that she would claim to be herself, was somehow on the other side of the brain, and that she was repudiating the mischievous side. Couldn't the disconnected mischievous side have been saying: Well the other side is lazy and inert.

GESCHWIND You have put your finger on an important problem and one of the hardest to deal with. Someone could object that the woman insisted that she had no control over the curious behaviour of her left hand. Why couldn't this behaviour be regarded as something like an epileptic fit beyond the control of the individual? If you think about it for a moment, however, you suddenly realise that it was not the whole woman who was talking. Rather, it was the left side of the brain which was talking. Since it was disconnected from the right side, the left side could not give a correct account of what the right was thinking or feeling. We know that, in the overwhelming majority of people, the left side is the one that is important for speech, and the right side usually has very limited language abilities. Therefore, if the two halves of the brain are separated, when the patient says: 'I don't know why my left hand is behaving in that way,' it is not the whole patient who is talking to you, but only the left side. The right side of the brain almost certainly has a very rich mental life, but because it does not speak, one is easily deluded into thinking that it is not active when in fact it is every bit as alert, attentive, and active as the left side. The right hemisphere almost certainly has its own emotional responses to the behaviour of the left but, since it has no verbal output, it can express its views only through actions.

MILLER   Do you mean that if the speech were distributed symmetrically on both sides, there might even be an argument between the two sides? It's only because one side has got a spokesman that it's able to look as if it's one person talking.

GESCHWIND   Exactly. Of course the right side of the patient was really expressing its views, but since it lacked words it did this in a different way. It certainly expressed its opinions very actively, by having a battle with the other side of the brain. It is an intriguing fact that, in nearly all similar cases which have been reported, the left half of the brain apparently does not start the arguments with the other side. It nearly always seems to be the *right* half which acts aggressively toward the *left* half. That may be no accident, since we know from other kinds of evidence that the parts of the cortex (in other words, the outer surface of the brain) which have control over emotion are located to a greater extent on the right side than on the left. It follows that emotion is not really a property of the whole person or of the whole brain.

We have several kinds of evidence which show the special importance of the right side for emotion. Take, for example, patients who suffer from epileptic seizures which start in a given location. You can picture this as a situation in which there is a small electrical storm starting in one particular place in the brain and which disrupts the functions of that region. With epileptic seizures which begin in certain places on the right side of the brain, the patient will very commonly describe the sudden awareness of curious and eerie sorts of emotions, such as strange fears, and he may also describe other-worldly feelings. These phenomena are more common with seizures beginning on the right side than with those beginning on the left.

Secondly, we know that patients who have suffered severe damage to the right side are often quite unconcerned even when they have gross physical disabilities such as severe paralysis of the left side of the body. Some of these patients will very airily tell you at first that there is nothing wrong with them. If you then press them a bit further, they may then say: 'Oh, of course, my left side is all dead, but that's okay, you guys will take care of it.'

By contrast, the patient who has suffered extensive damage on the *left* side of the brain, and is paralysed on the right side of the body, usually shows the appropriate depressive response.

The patient with damage on the left side of the brain can show normal depression because the brain areas which are necessary for the expression of this emotion are intact. But once there is destruction of those regions in the right half of the brain which are responsible for that kind of emotion, then the patient no longer expresses depression and appears to have emotions which are really quite alien and surprising to most people.

MILLER   Well now, this raises a problem about the integration of the two sides. In this lady that you mentioned at the beginning, who was beginning to strangle herself on one side, why was it that simply separating one half from the other half released what seemed to be a devilishly aggressive person on that side. Can you be implying that we are, in fact, two people, one of whom is bad and one of whom is good?

I know that there is a popular view that there's a good half of the brain and a bad half of the brain. What is actually going on when separation occurs and this woman's aggressive hand comes up and strangles her?

GESCHWIND   A curious fact regarding the popular notion about the functions of the two brain halves is that it is often exactly the opposite of the true situation. Those people who complain that we are not educating the right hemisphere and are therefore destroying the emotional lives of our students seem to neglect the fact that it is usually the right hemisphere which is the source of the unpleasant behaviour in the patients with disconnected hemispheres.

I think that we should not speak about good and bad in describing the brain, however appropriate those terms are in other situations. It is more reasonable to say that the human has a brain which is a very complicated apparatus, which has to be designed to be able to handle a tremendous variety of environmental circumstances. The brain is endowed biologically with the ability to use different inborn capacities in different situations so that human beings can live in different kinds of societies. The boy raised in ancient Sparta was trained to acquire a different set of talents from those of a modern English child.

The inborn ability to adapt depends on the possession by the brain of a large number of capacities. The question is often raised as to whether human beings are or are not innately aggressive. In some species, the repertoire of emotional states is limited. It is difficult to turn a rabbit into a very aggressive animal. Humans can, however, often be turned into very aggressive beings, which means that there must be in most people an innate capacity for aggression. Humans are innately aggressive, but they are also innately loving, and they are also innately placid, although the inborn level of each of these traits differs from person to person so that the ease with which someone can be moulded to his society will vary.

These inborn states, which are capable of being expressed in different situations, will in general depend on different locations in the brain. It is obviously impossible to build any kind of machine in which everything is located in the same place. A result of this physical limitation on design is that even in the normal brain, different events are taking place in different locations, and even a normal human is not a unity.

I know that many people will object to the belief that even normal brains are not unitary, but let me suggest that it may be precisely this fact which produces the distinctive character of consciousness. We are most likely to be fully conscious when we are aware that there are multiple tendencies pulling in different directions, and that very complicated decisions have to be made about which one of those directions is going to be followed. You will not be in this situation if you are a very simple animal which really is unitary – but you will be in it frequently if you are a human.

MILLER In the case of this woman, why should the separation of one half of the brain from the other have released, of all the various things which it might have released, this violent self-punishing activity? After all, it is very hard to imagine a society in which strangling yourself could be useful on any occasion.

GESCHWIND I think that that is true. In order to understand fully what is going on you have to remember that damage to the nervous system is not exactly like the effect of cutting the wires in a radio – and it is worth thinking for a moment about why it is different.

If you cut the wires in a radio and simply leave it on the shelf, a year later the structure of that radio will not have changed. On the other hand, after damage to the brain in the human and other animals a whole complex of changes takes place and changes may continue to occur throughout life. There are many chemical changes, so that, for example, some nerve cells may become more sensitive to certain substances. This can result in the exaggeration of certain pre-existing tendencies. Yet this is only one of a large number of structural and chemical alterations. It is a common error which is often made even by sophisticated researchers to assume that when the brain is damaged the forms of behaviours that remain are just as they were in the normal state. The changes in the brain which occur make research difficult, but they cannot be ignored.

In the normal state, people perform reasonably well in controlling these conflicting tendencies. I say 'reasonably well' because the acquisition of this control is often hard and the results are almost never perfect. Think for a moment about the process of socialisation of a child. What are the parents' main teaching activities in the first six years of life? No one teaches a child how to talk and no one really teaches a child how to walk, and most people do not teach their children how to read. In that case, how are the parents spending their time? What they are doing most of the time is teaching the child how to respond to all sorts of emotional impulses – teaching him not to bite the dentist, or to wolf his food, or to kick his sister. This kind of education is often very difficult, as most parents can tell you, and although many years are spent at it, the success rate is often moderate, but rarely perfect. The difficulty arises because the parent is trying to bring the many parts of the system under some kind of reasonable control without destroying the pieces, which would obviously be counterproductive. After destruction of many interconnections, such as occurred in the patient we have been talking about, the controls can no longer operate successfully and the system goes haywire.

The point to stress here is that the events which go on after brain damage demonstrate the surprising fact that thinking may be going on in different places, and that each of the different regions may not be aware of what is going on in the others. In the same way, you may have emotions going on in several different places in the brain, each of which may not be directly aware of the emotions at the other locations. Once you realise that concept, you should go back and look carefully at the normal. I believe that the odds are that disunity is present in normals, although we have overlooked it. When someone tells us that he is of two minds about something, he may not realise that this apparent metaphor may be an unwitting statement of fact.

There is powerful evidence from animal experiments, in which certain studies can be carried out in a controlled way that is usually not possible with humans, that different emotions can be present in different parts of the brain. It was shown some years ago that, after appropriate surgery on its brain, a monkey with one eye covered was very tame in response to what he saw, but, when the opposite eye was covered, he was very aggressive and behaved like a normal monkey in response to these visual stimuli. When both eyes were uncovered, the monkey, depending on which eye was actually seeing something, responded aggressively or placidly. Furthermore the monkey, who was visually tame when the appropriate eye was covered, would still respond with anger when touched. It is clear that many kinds of unexpected dissociations can exist.

Can similar phenomena exist in normals? Let me give you one example of a situation in which certain actions which are not connected to each other go on in normals. It is well known that when a photographer says 'Smile', most people produce a terrible grimace. This is not necessarily, as is often thought, an effect of embarrassment, since most people will find that they cannot smile well before a mirror in the privacy of their own homes. It is true that a few people can smile well to command, but in response to the command to laugh almost everyone fails and even professional actors find it difficult to respond with a 'normal' laugh. And yet, everybody has laughed thousands and thousands of times. Let me try to explain this curious failure of people to carry out on command something they have done so often.

When someone gives you the command to laugh, you try to control the many muscles of the face from the so-called 'face area' of the motor cortex on both sides of the brain. You have, in fact, never acquired the program for controlling these regions in the act of laughing, and you behave as you do whenever you attempt a poorly learned skill. As a result, the individual muscles do not participate to the proper extent and with the proper timing. The effect is a very poor laugh.

On the other hand, an amusing event or a funny story leads to stimulation of structures deep in the brain in the so-called limbic system[1] which is very important for emotional responses. When nerve cells in the

[1] The limbic system is a part of the brain which has become chiefly associated with the physical and psychological processes concerned with emotional arousal.

limbic system fire, they in turn stimulate another group of nerve cells which are not in the surface (the cortex) but in the depths of the brain. That group of nerve cells has built into it the whole program for laughing which is exactly right – you now produce the normal laugh. Yet you cannot directly stimulate that region in the depths from the parts of the cortex which understand language, and thus language cannot trip off the response of laughing. The response to a funny story is roundabout; it leads to activation of part of the limbic system which then in turn triggers the normal preprogrammed act of laughing.

MILLER   So there are parts of ourself, parts of our brains, to which we don't have conscious access, although we regard those parts as parts of ourself. After all, we regard smiling as part of our repertoire. But we don't consciously have access to spontaneous smiles.

GESCHWIND   No, we do not have access to it. There is another aspect of our behaviour which we cannot appreciate until we look carefully at the brain mechanisms involved. Consider some situations in which you move your arm. You move it in throwing a ball, and in yawning. When walking, you swing one arm forward when the opposite leg moves forward. Most people would assume that in every case the movement of the arm is controlled by the same system. In fact, we know that the movement of the arm can be controlled from many different locations and that, after damage to one part of the brain, some types of movement of the arm may be lost while others are preserved. Take, for example, the patient who has had a stroke (in other words, damage to the brain by blockage of a blood vessel), which has led to paralysis of the right arm. The patient finds it relatively easy to bring the arm in to the side with the elbow and wrist bent and with the fingers clenched. By contrast, it is very difficult, often impossible, for the patient to hold the arm fully outstretched to the side. Yet that patient may yawn, and, to his own astonishment, the 'paralysed' arm may rise and produce exactly the 'impossible' movement. When this happens, the family may become excited by this apparent sign of a preserved capacity to move. Yet it is probably a mistaken hope since the movement, as part of the process of yawning, does not arise from the higher parts of the brain. It probably originates in another group of nerve cells in the medulla (the part of the brain just above the spinal cord in which control of respiration is located). This region presumably has its own special program for activating that movement of the arm as part of the process of yawning, but not in any other situation.

MILLER   One might have thought that a movement of an arm would play no significant part in respiration. How does it come about that deepened respiration is associated with a big movement of the arm, and it is all apparently located in one centre of the brain?

GESCHWIND   I am no expert on yawning, and I don't know whether anyone has advanced a good explanation of its functions. My own guess is that raising the arm tends to lift the chest wall and helps to achieve maximum expansion of the lungs. But I could be wrong about that.

MILLER We can observe the same sort of thing in patients who've had strokes, and half of their face is paralysed. You ask them to smile, and they can't. But if their sense of humour is stimulated, they will in fact smile on that side of the face.

GESCHWIND That is, of course, another example of the point I have been making. It is also related to what I said earlier about the existence of a region in the depths of the brain which contains the innate program for smiling. If we ask a patient who has suffered paralysis of one half of the face after a stroke to smile, he cannot produce even a poor smile on one side since the face area of the cortex has been destroyed on the opposite side of the brain. Yet when something amuses the patient, the region in the depths is still intact and produces a smile. Even more strange, you can observe patients who show the reverse phenomenon, who have suffered damage in the depths on one side, but not on the surface. When you ask the patient to smile, he does it with both sides of his face. Yet when you tell him a joke, he will laugh with only one side of his face. So you can get complete reversal. Yet most people would suppose that every time you moved your face, you were using the same system. But instead, in fact, there are multiple systems and these different systems are often at a distance from each other and under quite different kinds of control. This is an important point, because it is not just the layman who believes that there is a single centre for controlling the hand. The same error is often made by researchers in the field of behaviour. For example, some investigators will carry out experiments on emotional expression in which they *ask* the subject to smile or frown, often with the underlying presumption that they are tapping the same system which is used when these movements are produced in response to emotional stimuli. They may, however, be tapping different systems. What we have learned is that the brain really is a kind of federation and, furthermore, a loose federation; it is not perfectly connected. The extent of the disunity varies from person to person. In any case, there does not appear to be a central prime mover overseeing all behaviour.

MILLER It's a commonsense idea, that our actions issue from some central authority.

GESCHWIND The assumption, that the self is unitary, is, of course, often built into discussions by philosophers, psychologists, linguists and even workers in neurological areas. Many phenomena which occur in behaviour are misinterpreted because of this presupposition.

The error of that particular assumption does not only cover simple things like moving the hand or the face. It probably also applies to much more complex kinds of behaviour. For example, the automatic assumption of most people would be that the system for the production of language is unitary. It is instructive, however, to look at examples of patients who have suffered damage to the language systems. These systems, which are usually on the left side of the brain, are built into humans and enable them to acquire language. Patients who have suffered damage in those systems are technically called aphasic. The term aphasia means disturbances in language resulting from brain damage and aphasic patients will make errors in grammar or in word choice.

MILLER   These are errors of *language* as opposed to errors of *speech*.

GESCHWIND   Yes, that is an important distinction. It is not correct, as one might first assume, that these patients are paralysed and cannot move their speech organs correctly and therefore produce slurred speech. The important point is that they will produce incorrect words or will make grammatical errors depending on the exact site of the damage. Some patients will make predominantly grammatical errors while other patients will in fact speak grammatically but have a great deal of difficulty in finding the precise words.

Aphasic patients typically exhibit a large number of surprising phenomena. For example, some of them will use real words incorrectly; they may even use words which do not exist. A patient who is a native English speaker and who is asked about his job may say with perfectly clear articulation: 'Well, you know, I used to fleaber the sodent.' Obviously some of the words are not English. Where did they come from? You cannot argue that they were parts of a private vocabulary which have suddenly appeared since such errors will typically appear in large numbers in many patients. We are thus left with the question of their origin.

An assumption that is often made is that the errors made by the patient reveal the method of operation of the remaining normal parts of the system, but that may not be true at all. What may in fact be going on is that after damage other parts of the brain are being used for a function in which they have not previously been involved.

MILLER   All right then, what authority is redistributing the functions? Who or what is deciding that there is a deficit and is therefore redistributing the function to another area which is not accustomed to perform that particular function?

GESCHWIND   It does sound mysterious at first. Your question expresses the natural mystification of most people when faced with this idea. But if you think about it, you will realise that it is not necessary to assume the existence of some mysterious entity which redistributes functions. Consider a simple example from ordinary life. Suppose that you look down the hall and see a friend of yours walking there. You notice that he is tilted to one side. You discover that he has been skiing and has fractured his leg. Why is he leaning to one side? The answer is obvious: one leg is in a cast and in order to restore his balance he redistributes his weight. He does not, of course, perform that act consciously, but his nervous system is designed to make the readjustment automatically. It would be a naïve error to presume that the bones of the broken leg contain the programs for the control of the posture of the other side of the body!

After damage in the nervous system, what the patient does may be an expression of similar processes. The redistribution is the result of the many processes which go on after injury. We might think for a moment about some of them.

In the first place, you have to remember that nerve cells can be of two kinds. There are nerve cells which when stimulated cause other nerve cells to fire, and these are called excitatory nerve cells. But you can also have inhibitory nerve cells which when stimulated will prevent another nerve cell from firing. If a group of inhibitory nerve cells are destroyed, there may be an increase in the activity of those nerve cells which had been suppressed. Let me go back to the woman who was strangling herself. We know that when physiologists have studied the corpus callosum they have found that a large number of the fibres in that structure are actually carrying impulses which inhibit rather than facilitate. When the corpus callosum is destroyed, it is likely some of the effects will be the result of release of previously inhibited systems on the other side.

There are other types of change which follow damage. Suppose that, as a result of damage to nerve fibres, a nerve cell loses many of its inputs. In that situation, there are often chemical changes in the nerve cell which make it increasingly sensitive to the chemicals that would have been released by the nerve fibres which have been destroyed. As a result, the nerve cell now responds to small amounts of those chemicals to which it has become sensitive and which may be floating around in the bloodstream or coming in through other intact nerve fibres. The nerve cell is now active but in a totally different way from what it was in the normal situation.

Most of the redirections which follow injury occur in an almost automatic fashion. What makes the situation even more complicated is they do not occur in every patient who has suffered the same damage. This should not trouble us since we know that all brains are not the same. In my own research, we have looked at large numbers of human brains. Once you start looking methodically you realise very quickly that brains differ from person to person, just like hair colour, height, the pattern of the facial bones and the proteins in the blood. Therefore, we have every reason to believe that not all brains are going to respond in the same way.

MILLER   This account explains away the apparent anomaly of someone having a self-strangling part of the brain. Simply because one separates one part of the brain from another, and therefore disinhibits that part of the brain, one hasn't got to assume that one is disinhibiting a previously controlled strangling section of the brain, but that some disordered and caricaturing function has been released which, in the intact brain, would never be involved in strangling – but would in fact be doing something else.

GESCHWIND   I would like to stress that that case is a very dramatic example and therefore the notion that the behaviour is a caricature of the normal situation comes easily. There are many cases, however, in which it is not easy to be aware that some behaviour produced by the patient is in fact a caricature since it may apparently have enough features in common with the normal function to prevent you realising that the observed behaviour is being carried out by another mechanism.

As I said earlier, there are phenomena observed in aphasia which appear to be very curious. There are, for example, some aphasic patients who will read words aloud in a rather strange fashion. They may look at the printed word 'symphony' and read it aloud as 'orchestra'. That cannot be an error based on physical resemblance between the two words, but it does appear to be based on similarity in *meaning*. The same patient may read 'daffodil' as 'flower'. Why does that happen? One type of theory would argue that in the normal reading process we read in different ways. If an English word is spelled in a regular fashion, we can sound it out syllable by syllable. This theory would argue that some words and, in particular, irregularly spelled words, are treated as almost direct symbols of the things they represent so that one might proceed directly from the printed form to the meaning. One could then postulate that in this case the brain damage has revealed to us some portion of the normal reading process which has remained intact after destruction of the other normal process involved in the sounding out of words. Since the patient can no longer sound out words, he will therefore use only the other system which connects the printed words directly to the things that they represent.

MILLER So the fact that he reads *orchestra* in place of 'symphony' implies that there is an intact level at which he is still recognising the similarity or at least the association between symphony and orchestra.

GESCHWIND Exactly. But is this interpretation correct? There is another possibility, which is that in these patients reading aloud is occurring by means of mechanisms which are not used in normal reading. One possibility is that all the normal mechanisms for reading are inoperative and that the patient is now reading by the stringing together of a series of mechanisms not used in the normal process of reading aloud. Thus, the sight of the word 'symphony' might arouse an internal image which is then named. That is probably not a way in which we normally read aloud. But consider now how this will alter reading aloud. The printed word 'prime minister' might easily arouse an image of Disraeli or Thatcher, just as it might in a normal. The normal can, however, still read 'prime minister' aloud correctly, but since this patient cannot read aloud by the normal route, he is forced to name the picture. In that case, the spoken response 'Disraeli' or 'Thatcher' to the printed word 'prime minister' becomes easily comprehensible. This is not a normal process of reading aloud and one might easily draw an incorrect conclusion about the normal process from the effects of damage. It is even possible that this roundabout process takes place occasionally in normals but is a source of *errors*, not a normal process of correct reading.

MILLER So they'd been forced, as it were, to use an understudy method of reading.

GESCHWIND Yes, but this method will never be accurate because the system being used after damage is a roundabout route which is not normally used.

The situation is analogous to what happens after severe injuries to the spinal cord. We know that patients in whom the spinal cord is effectively completely severed do not have bladder control since the brain is no longer connected to the nerves leading to the bladder. Therefore, you expect that those patients are going to have no control over their bladders. Yet every once in a while, a patient is seen who is apparently capable of controlling very well the regular emptying of his bladder. That fact led to some ingenious theories to explain the apparent preservation of bladder function. The most likely explanation is that these patients have learned, sometimes unconsciously, a particular trick, i.e. that exerting pressure on the bladder may trigger reflex emptying. It is even possible, although I am not certain of this, that in some cases the pressure may not even be exerted by the hand. It is conceivable, especially when the damage to the cord is not in the upper levels, that the act of taking a deep breath and then bearing down very forcefully might exert enough pressure to set off the reflex.

There are many examples in neurology of 'trick' movements by which a patient duplicates remarkably effectively the action of a muscle which is completely paralysed, although he usually has no awareness of the clever strategy he has employed. In any case, one should not confuse such highly useful tricks with preservation of the normal mechanism. This kind of mechanism can take place at any level of the nervous system. Let me give you another example at a completely different level of the nervous system. Several years ago, I saw a patient who had had surgery carried out on his corpus callosum. Splitting of this structure is sometimes carried out on patients who have severe, widespread, and uncontrollable epileptic seizures. Exactly why this works is not altogether clear, but it does work in many patients. The patient whom I saw had undergone this operation and thus the two sides of his brain were disconnected. There was, however, a surprising finding. If you asked him to do something with either his right or his left hand, he would carry out the command. That he successfully carried out verbal commands with the right hand presented no problem, but the successful performance with the left hand was perplexing. Let me explain why. Since the left side of the brain, which is the speech side, was intact in this patient, and since the left side of the brain usually controls the right hand, it was no surprise that he responded correctly if you asked him to show how he would throw a ball with his right hand. Movements with the left hand are usually controlled from the right side of the brain. Since the right brain has poor language capacities, one would not expect it to understand a command and therefore would not expect it to respond to a command to use the left hand. This is not a problem in normals since the left hemisphere will understand the command and will transmit the instructions to the right side of the brain. But since the patient's hemispheres were disconnected, the left hemisphere could not fulfil this function. Why then did he carry out verbal commands with the left hand?

Some observers had drawn the conclusion that the right hemisphere of that patient did in fact understand the commands. But careful observation showed that his successful performance was based on a completely different mechanism. When I asked the patient to show me how he would salute with the left hand, he would say: 'I know just what you want me to do. You want me to do *that* with my left hand,' and simultaneously with the utterance of the last phrase, he first saluted with his right hand and *then* saluted with his left hand. Obviously, a normal who is asked to salute with the left hand does not usually carry out the movement first with the right hand. A few minutes later, I again asked him to salute with his left hand, but I held his right hand in order to prevent him from carrying out the movement first with that hand. As long as I held the *right* hand, he could not carry out the command with the *left* hand. When the right hand was released, he saluted with it and only then did he salute with the left hand. Somehow, this patient's left hemisphere had learned, I suspect unconsciously, that it could signal to his right hemisphere non-verbally and thus get it to carry out some act. In other words, his left hemisphere was treating his right hemisphere as though the right hemisphere was a foreigner who did not understand English, but who responded correctly to gestures. When he saluted with the right hand, the right side of the brain could see the movement, and although it had not understood the verbal command, it could now produce the movement by imitating what it had seen on the other side.

Clearly, this mechanism is not the same as the comprehension of language by the right side of the brain. It is another ingenious 'trick' mechanism.

MILLER   But was it essential for him to see the other side doing it? What happened, for example, if you put some sort of screen halfway down so that he was unable to see what he was expecting himself to mimic? Would the *feeling* of saluting with one hand be enough to induce obedient saluting with the other?

GESCHWIND   I can't answer that question because I was seeing this patient under circumstances which were not suitable for detailed testing. But I hope to try out your suggestion in the future.

I also want to stress that a common response to this sort of story is that what has been described is an isolated curiosity. But phenomena of this kind are not bizarre curiosities. These stories are dramatic and therefore informative examples of phenomena which are extremely common in patients with brain injuries. In fact, the phenomenon that I have just described to you, in which a patient signals to the other side of the nervous system which does not understand language, is something that I have now seen hundreds of times. It is a phenomenon seen in patients with ordinary, common disturbances of the brain such as strokes.

You often need one of these very clean-cut and dramatic examples in order to arouse your consciousness and your awareness. You then realise

that the same type of phenomenon is occurring in many other circumstances and that it is indeed a very routine effect of damage to the nervous
system. The existence of all these substitute methods, which mimic
normal behaviour more or less accurately, makes it clear that actions which
appear remarkably similar may sometimes be capable of elicitation from
more than one location in the brain. The nervous system often has many
different ways of carrying out actions which at first look similar. A major
reason for the existence of all these special mechanisms is simply greater
efficiency. If, for example, when you walked you had to bother to think
about controlling with your cortex all of the leg muscles on both sides,
walking would become an impossible task. (Of course there was a
politician of whom it was said that he could not walk and chew gum at the
same time!) In the course of evolution, animals have developed systems in
the lower levels of the nervous system in which the entire act of walking is
represented, so that triggering one of these systems can set off the entire
built-in process.

Obviously that process is very different from what goes on when a new
recruit is being taught how to march. The drill sergeant explains that at the
word 'March' the recruit is to step forward smartly with his left foot and to
swing the right arm forward at the same time. Yet when the command is
given, some recruits will step forward with the left foot and swing the left
arm forward. But although all of these men have always walked by putting
the left foot forward and the right arm forward, some of them still find it
difficult to respond to the verbal command in order to produce a
movement that they have done in response to other types of stimuli, every
day of their lives many times.

The reason for the difficulty is that they are now trying to control their
walking at a very different level. They are now attempting the very difficult
task of co-ordinating the motor cortex on both sides of the brain instead of
simply triggering the normal preprogrammed system at a lower level.

MILLER So it's a totally different activity when they're relearning it in that way.

GESCHWIND It is useful to think of an analogy with genetics. One of the great advances
in that field was the distinction between phenotype and genotype. The
genotype of a living thing consists of the genes it carries. The phenotype is
the set of observable characteristics. If a flower is red, you cannot
necessarily predict its genetic endowment. We know that a flower which is
red might carry two genes for redness, or it might have only one gene for
redness. The distinction between the phenotype, i.e. what you see on the
surface, and the genotype, i.e. the underlying genetic structure, is essential
to any real understanding. Thus, the uninitiated may be surprised to find
that two dark-haired people can have a blond child. Yet, a dark-haired
person may be carrying one gene for light hair, which can be transmitted to
the offspring. If each dark-haired parent is carrying such a gene and passes
it on, the offspring will be blond. In a very similar way, the behaviours that
we observe may be thought of as similar to phenotypes, and apparently

similar behaviours may result from underlying brain mechanisms which may be quite different from each other. If you fail to realise that, you are likely to make serious errors analysing the mechanisms of behaviour and in analysing how minds work. The great problem is the hidden assumption that similar behaviours always depend on similar mechanisms. The hidden assumptions are the most dangerous ones since they are often not expressed explicitly. I have no doubt that bringing this kind of assumption to awareness will accelerate our understanding of the neurological mechanisms of the mind.

8

dialogue with
George Mandler

THE NATURE
OF EMOTION

INTRODUCTION

It is difficult to imagine what life would be like in the absence of emotion. An existence which was undisturbed by such feelings, disagreeable though some of them are, would scarcely count as living, and people who lose the capacity to experience rage, jealousy, joy and terror often refer to themselves as if they were dead. Conversely, when we meet someone who consistently fails to display emotion we tend to regard them as robots or zombies. Something less than human. Karel Capek created just such a character in a play which Janáĉeck turned into a better known opera. *The Makropoulos Case* tells the story of a woman who accidentally tried out an elixir of life in the sixteenth century. At the beginning of the opera she has outlived all those for whom she once cared, and longs for death as the only acceptable alternative to an emotionally meaningless existence.

What are these feelings without which it is so difficult to imagine a tolerable existence? How do emotions arise and in what sort of physiological processes are they grounded? These are the sorts of questions which students of human nature have repeatedly asked themselves, but until the twentieth century the descriptions provided by playwrights and novelists were much more satisfactory than anything supplied by the scientist. The problem is that although emotions are no more subjective than perceptions are, it's much harder to characterise and measure the factors which give rise to them. It is a relatively simple matter to standardise the visual stimulus which is responsible for the sensation of scarlet, but it's not nearly so easy to identify, let alone reproduce, the events which make someone 'see red'. A situation which makes one person angry can amuse someone else and *vice versa*. But the relationship is not altogether haphazard, and as long as we make an allowance for individual differences we can safely predict the *sort* of things which will make someone angry, jealous or terrified. Otherwise social life would be impossible. Just as it would be if we were unable to detect emotions in others. Anger, jealousy and fear are usually accompanied by observable changes in behaviour, not to mention noticeable alterations in complexion and blood flow, and although these are also subject to personal variation the patterns are consistent enough to enable us to tell when someone is furious or frightened.

Psychologists have tried with varying degrees of success to translate these somewhat informal intuitions into scientifically acceptable generalisations, and in his research on the relationship between situations and emotions George Mandler, Professor of Psychology of the University of California, has begun to identify what it is that makes us reassuringly different from the tragically bored heroine of *The Makropoulos Case*.

DISCUSSION

MILLER As we're going to talk about the rather personal question of human emotion, I wonder if we can start with a rather personal note, perhaps rather an autobiographical note. I spend a lot of time as a theatre producer working with actors, and trying to get from them a convincing expression of emotion.

Now a lot of the traditional ideas about this subject spring from the notion that there is a fixed repertoire or a stock of nameable emotions, which can be expressed or conveyed in a more or less convincing way. And this has led to a lot of obvious logical troubles, and I believe that you have a more manageable way of handling this difficult problem. I wonder if you could tell us about it.

MANDLER Starting off with acting, and the ability to exhibit many emotions and hundreds of nuances, leads directly to the question of the mental mechanisms that make it possible. Traditionally one thinks of two kinds of actors – the ones who when asked to produce a particular emotion just do so; and the ones who need to experience, to feel an emotion in order to portray it. That distinction illustrates the two components that produce emotions. One component consists of evaluative cognitions, which are the valuations that characterise our world, that reflect how we see the world as good or bad in all its varieties; these values represent the 'cold' aspect of emotion. The other component represents arousal – the visceral component of emotion. Given that any one emotional experience is a product of these two components, a multitude of emotions becomes possible, essentially an infinite number. The actor who produces emotions at will depends primarily on the cognitive content. The actor who needs to 'feel' adds the arousal to the mental content.

The repertoire or stock of emotions that you mentioned are categories of emotions and the category-names label collections of situations and mental states. The fears and anxieties, and the joys and the loves. Just to give you an example – we think of love as a single emotion, and yet, I can love a chocolate mousse, I love my wife, I can love a dog, I can love the way a symphony is played. All these are very positive events, but the way they are experienced depends on the particular situations. What characterises this collection of situations and feelings that we call 'loves', what holds them all together, is that they are all positive, that they all somehow involve our selves in relation to the loved person or object.

But let me first discuss the hot part, the arousal part of emotion. That comes primarily from the activation of the autonomic nervous system. The human nervous system – the mammalian nervous system – has two parts to it: one of them is the somatic, the other one is the autonomic nervous system. The somatic nervous system has to do with our senses, with the reception of information, the conduction of the information from our senses to the central nervous system. In other words, it takes in information from the world, and it acts on the world; mostly through the voluntary muscles, whose contractions move our limbs and makes it possible for us to act on the world around us. That's the somatic nervous system.

The autonomic nervous system has more to do with internal factors; with our viscera, our gut responses. And as in any kind of internal economy, there are two parts to it. There are the spenders and the savers. The sympathetic nervous system is primarily concerned with the expenditure of energy, and the parasympathetic nervous system is concerned with the conservation and the storage of energy. Broadly speaking, the sympathetic nervous system causes the blood vessels to constrict, the blood flows faster, the heart beats faster, and the stomach and intestinal activity slow down. The sympathetic nervous system is responsible for the body's emergency reaction. It makes the body ready to act with all the available energy.

MILLER   This is the flight and fight system.

MANDLER   That's right. The parasympathetic nervous system, on the other hand, makes the blood vessels dilate; the stomach and intestines start to work: energy is stored.

It is autonomic arousal that produces the hot quality, the intensity aspect of emotion. We're primarily concerned with the sympathetic nervous system – with the flushes and the heart racing and the pulse going up. While this is a highly complex system, the available evidence suggests that what we actually experience is a very general feeling of arousal, or intensity.

There are some variations. For example, there are emotional states that have very specific peripheral physiological states – we call these peripheral to contrast them with central physiological states in the brain. Sexual arousal, lust, clearly involves a more localised system; the experiences are localised in sexual organs, and in sexually sensitive areas of the body. But generally speaking, things like joy and love and fear and anxiety, all seem to have the same global feeling of arousal to them.

The one problem that has classically been apparent with respect to arousal is that there is no real consistent account about what it is that gets the autonomic nervous system going. If you look at the textbooks, and try to find out what is supposed to start up sympathetic nervous system reaction, what you will find is a list of things: threat, danger, tissue injury, the necessity for flight or fight. What I have tried to do during the past twenty years is to find some general principle that tells us when and why autonomic arousal will occur. The answer I have come up with is embodied in what I have called interruption theory. Interruption has an unfortunate ring to it, because it sounds rather negative – interruptions seem to be 'bad'. What I mean by it is a very neutral sort of thing. Another way of describing this phenomenon is in terms of a discrepancy between one's expectations and the actual evidence from the world.

Whenever an expectation is interrupted, whenever an action cannot be brought to completion, whenever a plan is not quite brought to its end, or to its goal, arousal seems to occur. To convey something less negative and more neutral, consider the interruption of an expectation. For example, when I expect somebody to offer me a particular salary, say £100, I walk into that situation and say to myself that £100 is what I'm going to get paid. If I get £80, that's an interruption. If I get £120, that's also an interruption. In other words, anything that deviates from an expectation is a discrepancy from the modal way in which we look at the world. The evidence is fairly clear-cut that any kind of interruption, any deviation from the expected, any discrepancy produces arousal.

Let me give you another example: to move away from the rational cognitive aspect. You walk down a flight of stairs, and all of a sudden the last step that you expected is missing. Now you didn't expect it in the sense that you said: Well, there are fifteen steps; I am now on step fourteen, the fifteenth is coming up. The body is automatically acting in response to that stairway. That last step is not there. You step into the void; loss of support occurs, and immediately the autonomic nervous system, the sympathetic nervous system, reacts. It is an emergency reaction in Cannon's sense. Something is different.

From an evolutionary point of view, it makes very good sense to construct an organism that reacts significantly and distinctively when the world is not the way it has been in the past. And in that sense the autonomic nervous system doesn't just have an internal function, it also alerts the organism to something important going on; the world is not the way it was. We do not need access to some specific knowledge for the arousal to occur, and we certainly don't have to have any conscious knowledge that the world is different. The autonomic nervous system will be triggered whenever these interruptions occur. That kind of reaction is the second adaptive function of the autonomic nervous system, in addition to its role in maintaining the internal economy of the body.

MILLER So in other words, one of the functions of the autonomic nervous system is to keep the smooth running of the internal economy going. It manages the home affairs, as it were, whereas the somatic nervous system is a sort of foreign affairs department, dealing with our relationships with the outside world. Nevertheless, the efficiency with which we handle the outside world is to some extent dependent on the smooth running of the interior, and therefore the autonomic nervous system has got to be in contact with the outside world and able to scale up its efficiency if there is an emergency.

MANDLER That's right. To take your metaphor a bit further, if our internal economy isn't working right, our foreign affairs suffer. Whenever there is visceral upset there is likely to be interference with the way we handle our relationship with the environment.

Let's discuss next the other component of the emotional system. You will recall that evaluation must be there in addition to arousal. The evaluative part of the emotions is much more varied, more complex than the arousal part. There are three sources of evaluation, and as a first approximation one can think of these values as arrayed on a continuum of good things and bad things. The first are innate, genetically established sources of value. These are selected by the evolutionary process, and they are good and bad events that have been identified as such in the history of the species. Then there are the values that are culturally acquired, which we learn about as a result of growing up in our culture and society. The third kind of value is derived from the structural aspects of events, of the way we perceive and have become used to their internal structure. Let me illustrate all three of them.

At the innate level, we're all born with a liking for sweet and dislike of the bitter. You can take a newborn child and it will suck happily on a sweet substance and will reject a bitter substance. Similarly, we don't like looming objects. Little children already shy away from large looming objects coming at them. Pain, or tissue injury, is another instance. All of these values are part of our makeup, they exist because we are the kind of organism we are. However, even these values seem to be amenable to change, to cultural influences, and we seem to be able to learn how to restructure even some of those.

MILLER   But there's an obvious advantage in having a built-in ability to discriminate good and bad. There's obviously some sort of selective advantage . . .

MANDLER   That's right. The important things in the world are built-in, because that's the way we survive; that's the way the organism has adapted.

The second kind of value includes a huge array of things. We learn that they are good and bad, without ever having had any experience of them. My favourite example is that the French know practically from birth (or rather from the time the culture is transmitted) that one doesn't eat what you call maize — what the Americans call corn. That's pig food for the French. Americans eat it all the time. Maize is good in America; it is bad in France. In fact, it's good in most countries in Europe and in the Western hemisphere, and the French seem to be unique. That's a culturally learned dislike. It's a culturally learned evaluative cognition. There's nothing about a three- or four-year-old that needs any experience with maize to teach him or her that this is a bad substance. It's the culture that teaches it. That may sound like a peculiar example, but actually we are immersed in cultural values. They determine many of our attitudes towards foods and clothes, they determine what are good manners and what are bad. Cultural values even teach us how far you're supposed to be from people when you talk to them – the Italians can be close; the Swedes have to be further apart from each other. All of these likes and dislikes represent culturally acquired values.

The third kind of value is the one that I really find the most interesting, because less is known about it and it is less well described. It is based on internal structure. Let me give you an example.

Categorically I know what a horse is, and you know what a horse is, because it has certain features, and certain relationships among those features. Horses are sort of medium-sized to large animals that have four legs, that have manes, have tails, a restricted range of colours, and so on. Everybody knows what features are relevant to the identification of a horse. But what's a beautiful horse, and what's an ugly horse? It's a very different kind of a question. The same features are involved, but it's the relationship among those features that make you decide that it is a good horse or a bad horse, a beautiful horse or an ugly horse.

MILLER   But that of course overlaps with the cultural determination.

MANDLER   Yes, actually our culture determines what objects and events we will encounter and how they will be structured. In that sense the culture determines what we will experience and what particular structures of objects and events we will consider to be acceptable, familiar, and comprehensible. We need experience with an object in order to be able to understand it. An example is our cultural (structural) definition of what is acceptable in music. When Beethoven first appeared on the scene, it wasn't that he used different notes or used different orchestras (though in a sense he did), but it was rather the relationships among the chords he used, and the particular chords he used, that made his music sound very strange. It was the structural aspect of his music that was different, just as Schoenberg in the twentieth century produced a structurally different music. Both Beethoven's and Schoenberg's music produced discrepancy in the listener. And in this case the discrepancy also produced negative emotional reactions. The discrepant thing can be, but is not always, seen as different, as unusual, strange, and unpleasant. In a funny sense it is a reverse use of the notion that 'I like what I know, and I know what I like.' In this context we are fundamentally conservative toward our environment. We like to see the things we know; we like to see the things that are constructed in the way they ought to be constructed, which means in the way they have been constructed in the past. When they deviate then there is some sort of evaluation about this new structure. But since the discrepancy is an interruption, there's also arousal. And the combination of the two produces an active negative emotional reaction.

It may sound somewhat strange when I talk about arousal and evaluation; it sounds as if emotions are just those two things, and that one actually ought to feel arousal and evaluation; but of course we don't. We feel real joy as a singular experience: the same with love, anxiety, fear and whatever.

What happens is that in consciousness, in our phenomenological[1] experience, these are constructed as a single experience. Just as I don't look at you and say: those eyes and that nose and that mouth, if I put them all together, they make Jonathan Miller. I experience Jonathan Miller in terms of the same process by which our consciousness constructs our

[1]Phenomenology. The systematic investigation of conscious experience as experience, regarded by some as the true method of approach to psychology.

world in order to make maximal sense out of it. In the same way consciousness constructs a single emotional unit. What's the result? The result is that there are a multitude of emotions, depending on the particular evaluations of the moment.

There are, of course, classes or categories of emotions. Things that are potentially physically harmful produce evaluations that we call fears. Things that we want to be with, want to spend some time with, incorporate into our world, are the things that we call loves. Anxiety is a little different. The subjective experience of anxiety, at least in Western culture, seems to occur when the evaluation is: I don't know what to do next. A certain sense of helplessness, plus arousal. In anxiety the cognitive evaluation seems to be: I'm helpless, I don't know what to do. At the same time there is, of course, some amount of arousal because helplessness does in fact interrupt our normal course of dealing with the world. This particular analysis of anxiety may hold only for Western culture, because what we call anxiety occurs in very different forms in some other cultures, as for example in some South Pacific cultures where anthropologists have provided us with specific analyses of different ways of experiencing emotions.

MILLER   I can understand how this analysis can handle situations which one could describe as crude emergencies. Sudden interruptions of one's expectations could produce flushes of fear, anxiety or alarm, and that would alert one to deal with the situation perhaps more efficiently. But how does this analysis deal with some of the feelings which people might describe as the more common emotions? I mean, although we *do* have fears and alarms, they're – in a sense – unrepresentative feelings. They don't constitute what people regard as their emotional life. The loves, the expanding senses of joy, of satisfaction, or such peculiar and negative feelings as jealousy or envy for example. How can they actually be fitted into this analysis?

MANDLER   All right, having made a crude distinction, let me be more specific about the ongoing experiences.

First of all, we always experience some degree of arousal. In other words, I do not want to give the impression that people are either in a state of zero arousal or in a state of increasing arousal. All the evidence we have suggests that the evaluation of how aroused you are is made against the previous level of arousal. So that arousal is judged in terms of how much more aroused I am now than I was before, how much more sympathetic nervous system activity is going on. So there is a continuous level of activation which potentiates whatever evaluations we make about the world.

At the same time, we also evaluate the world continuously; we are continuously trying to make sense of the world and commenting on it and on our behaviour: this is a good situation, this is bad; I like this, I don't like that; I'm late, I'm early; I wish I were with her, I wish I were not with him. All these kinds of conscious and unconscious thoughts go on all the time. So that the kind of analysis I've given is not best illustrated by the punctate great emotions, but rather by a continuous flow of changing levels of arousal, changing levels of degree of emotional involvement, and changing evaluations. For example, take the case of mood, which probably best exemplifies the sort of question you were raising.

MILLER   Yes, I was going to ask you to distinguish between mood and emotion.

MANDLER   What we usually mean by mood is a continuing state of arousal plus evaluation, in which the evaluation stays fairly constant. What do we typically mean when we say 'mood'? I am a little reluctant to enter into an analysis of the common language, because it is so vague and sometimes opaque to analysis. But I think what we mean by mood is that somebody's in a state of persisting low level emotion. We don't say that somebody was in a bad mood for thirty seconds. We tend to say: 'Why was he in such a bad mood all day yesterday?' Or: 'My God, you're in a good mood today.'

What happens is that for some reason or another, you have a negative evaluation of the world in one case and a positive one in the other, because of something that has happened, that you're continuously reminded of, and that persists throughout the day, typically at a low level. We don't think of moods as being outbursts. But it's the background evaluation that we carry with us. For example, let's say that I arrive in a town for a visit and the airline loses my suitcase, so that for two days I am not only without toothbrush and shirts, but also without all my papers, and yet I have to carry on. There's a background of being continuously reminded of that terrible thing that happened to me – which really isn't that terrible – but it impinges on my life during the ensuing twenty-four – forty-eight hours. And if somebody asks: 'Why were you in such a bad mood during your visit?' I might say: 'Well, because I lost my suitcase.'

Or somebody meets you at the airport whom you haven't seen in ten years. You're absolutely delighted to see him. You say: 'My God, isn't it wonderful that I found John after all these years in this town'. The good mood persists. The interesting part is that given the arousal, due to the lost luggage or the found friend, the result is a generally raised arousal level. And I'm very impressed by the fact that raised arousal levels potentiate any other emotions that happen to come along.

MILLER   In what sense?

MANDLER   People who are aroused, for whatever reason, will react more strongly to a particular evaluative situation than they would otherwise. Let me give you a personal example that happened many years ago. I usually don't eat much during the day, and I usually only eat one main meal – dinner, so that I get pretty hungry. That means my expectations at dinner time are very high, and easily interrupted; and when interruptions occur there is, of course, a high degree of arousal.

We have a telephone right next to the table where we eat dinner, and just as I was about to eat, the telephone rings: somebody wants to sell me a magazine. And I had an unbelievably nasty, rage reaction. I practically shouted: 'How dare you bother me.' When I sat down Jean said: 'Well, you know, the poor woman would just like to sell you a magazine. Did you have to be that angry?' I was unusually, irrationally angry. Here was a case of arousal. A particular situation, the telephone call, interrupted me, kept me from starting my dinner.

About a week later, the same situation occurred; it was practically identical, except for one big difference. We were at dinner and the telephone rang; it was somebody whom I had not seen for three or four years who happened to be in town. He was not a particularly close friend, but somebody I liked, an acquaintance. I had a very positive overreaction to this person. Again, a high degree of arousal. Inappropriate affect because of the high degree of arousal, but it was positive because I liked that particular person. So that the background interruption, the background degree of arousal, tells you how much intensity will accompany the emotional reaction to some other event or person.

The other example concerns athletes. It turns out that even something as non-emotional as athletic exertion, which drives up the autonomic nervous system, can produce excessive emotional reaction. The example is supported both by anecdotal evidence and by some interesting current research. If an athlete, for example, is presented after he's run a mile, with some good or bad news, irrelevant to the race he's just run, the reaction tends to be what we call irrational, it is more intense than is usual or would be appropriate.

To come back to the example of background mood. If I am already aroused, if I'm already in the state of negative evaluation, I'm likely to react more strongly to a negative event than I would otherwise. But I might even react more strongly to a positive event. It's the well-known story: 'Don't tell him that today, he's in a bad mood.' The explanation is that you're already aroused, already in a negative state of evaluation, and another one simply potentiates the state more than it would in another context.

MILLER   What you're saying would seem to imply that the instrument upon which these feelings or these experiences play is the body, and particularly the viscera, the guts and so on. Now, if this *is* the case, one would expect to find that people with, say, broken necks lead a poorer emotional life than normal people. Is that so?

MANDLER   There have been two or three studies of people who have had spinal injuries, that essentially cut off all sensation from the part of the body that is below the point at which the spine is severed. These studies show that the more extensive the part of the body that does not feed back information to the central nervous system, the more extensive the loss of reported feeling. The question that was asked was: 'Compared to the way you used to feel before you were injured, do you feel less or more intense in your emotions?' The replies are scaleable with the level of the injury. The lower the injury, that is the more body feedback that is still available, the less there is a loss of feeling; the higher the injury, all the way to the level of the neck, the greater is the loss of feeling. The subjective sense – the intensity of feeling has gone.

MILLER But nevertheless, once having had a physique, isn't it perhaps possible to conjure up *memories* of what these bodily feelings were like?

MANDLER There is a kind of reminiscent imagery about one's autonomic system just as there is, for example, in vision. We have autonomic memories just as we have visual memories and auditory memories; shadowy reminiscences of what these things are really like. I can have a visual memory of the Taj Mahal, for example, but that's not as good as seeing the Taj Mahal. It is an echo of the actual perception, and in the same sense people can have memories of autonomic arousal.

MILLER So you could say that these people are having disembodied reminiscences of what is was once like to have been an embodied person. It's what we imagine the experience of the dead might be like.

MANDLER Yes. I think one ought to do much more work with these unfortunate people because they could tell us much more about a variety of things, about body image and the general idea of how we construct who we are.

MILLER So in a paradoxical sense, these are prematurely posthumous experiences that they are undergoing.

MANDLER There's some interesting work that was done with animals some years ago. If you decouple the sympathetic nervous system, sympathectomise these animals, the sympathectomised animals cannot – or have great difficulty – learning to avoid shock, because there is no feedback from the body to tell them this is a nasty feeling. However, if you teach an animal – these animals were dogs – to avoid a shock to a signal, then when the signal goes on, he knows the shock will come in thirty seconds, and he jumps away or does whatever is needed to escape from the shock. If you perform the sympathectomy after the animal has learned this response, the animal maintains the avoidance reactions. In other words, you need it in order to establish the feeling, but in some sense – and unfortunately we don't know how the dogs feel – he remembers that prior experience and the lack of the sympathetic nervous system does not prevent him from still executing the escape response.

MILLER So in that case, those unfortunate patients who have suffered paralysis or the loss of sensation below the neck, have got, through reminiscence, *some* experience. If they are in a situation, a totally evaluative cognitive situation which they would judge to be bad or favourable, they would as it were go through a phantom rehearsal of what they once had actually undergone.

MANDLER I don't have the evidence on that. I would assume that would happen – but all I know is that when you do present them with emotionally tinged situations, and ask 'Do you think you feel worse or better than you did before you had the injury?' they will report their current feelings to be much weaker than they were before they were injured.

MILLER But nevertheless analogous in character – it's simply a weaker form.

MANDLER Oh, yes. They know what it feels like to be afraid, only they don't feel *as*

afraid or *as* loving as they used to. And by the way, they report they wish
they could.

MILLER That in itself is rather an interesting paradox.

There's one objection which I'd like to put up, and I'd like to hear you
answer this. So far, the description that you've given of emotional states,
which result from arousal, which in its turn results from evaluations of the
world, seem to arrange our experiences on a scale, which goes from
negative at one end to positive at the other. But people don't necessarily
arrange their various emotions on a scale arranged horizontally like that.
Although they would classify some as favourable and some as un-
favourable, they would in fact discriminate between them as being very
distinctive in their own right; the sense of envy or resentment or jealousy
has got a characteristic emotional tone, which makes it absolutely
distinctive.

MANDLER I do not wish to give the impression that emotions are based just on a single
dimension of good and bad. I use it simply for expository purposes. The
point I want to make is that at the simplest level, at the level of lower
animals, and possibly at the level of the newborn, cognitive evaluations are
relatively simple. They may be just: 'this is good, that's bad'; 'I want this, I
don't want that'; 'I want to be in this situation, I don't want to be in that
situation'.

I certainly do not think that the experiences of emotions can be arrayed
on a simple continuum. Actually, of course, one could ask people to array
joy, ecstasy, jealousy, fear, on some scale. But that's a psychologist's game
I don't particularly want to play. Just because you can scale something
doesn't mean it's interesting, which is sort of the converse of the belief that
if you can't scale it, it isn't interesting, which used to be a psychological
maxim. Rather, I want to talk about the specific experiences, past and
present, that go into a particular emotion. Jealousy is a good example.

Jealousy involves a whole host of current evaluations, about one's own
image, one's own self-esteem, as well as evaluations about the other person
– one's partner, some image of the other person, one's estimation of that
other person's value. And then a third person walks into the picture, and
you compare that person with yourself. Presumably one is rarely jealous of
somebody whom one values as much less competent – relative to the loved
object – than oneself. In other words, is one jealous of somebody who just
happens to be nice to one's love partner? No. One is jealous of somebody
when one thinks there is a potential relationship between those two people.
But that already involves a very complex schema of structuring the world
among the three of them. In other words, the various values involved in a
case of jealousy make it a much more complex phenomenon than just a
point on a continuum of good and bad.

The various values and evaluations that occur in the process of
constructing one's jealousy could, of course, be arrayed on the good-bad
continuum, if for no other reason than the fact that people can simplify and

assign numbers and values to practically any experience or action. But that doesn't mean that the underlying experience or mechanism is simple. The quality of the emotion that is experienced is a complex result of many different evaluations of people and situations, and the interaction of these evaluations with different levels and occasions of arousal.

The outcome happens to be not particularly pleasant for most people, though there are people who enjoy being jealous, and if they're not and if they're not challenged by some threat to their relationship, they seek that threat.

MILLER   I was going to raise that point. You see, it seems that in the case of jealousy, and I'm sure this applies to many other emotions, what is experienced and what is undergone is not necessarily the result of a discrepancy between what you expect and what the world actually hands out to you. One of the characters in Othello actually says: 'They are not jealous for the cause, they are jealous because they are jealous.' Jealousy can arise without there being an actual objective discrepancy between what you feel about the world and what actually happens, because the jealousy can simply arise by a phantasy that you project onto the world. Now how does *that* work?

MANDLER   I don't want to make a strict distinction between the real world and the world of the head, because in the long run we're all talking about the world that we construct in our own heads. It was Kant who taught us that the real world is essentially unknowable, that we construct it, and I think that's fundamentally true. We live in a constructed world. The distinction can be made, however, between the world of immediate experience, which depends on the current 'reality', and the world of our memories, expectations, and phantasies.

In other words, there is a world that is very much dependent on the evidence out there, but there's also another world which has relatively little evidence to feed into it. In the case of the paranoid, the 'external' evidence is slight; but we all are a little bit paranoid, and we all can, for example, carry a disembodied jealousy with us. And I think what you're saying in the case of jealousy, though Othello may not be the right example, is that there are people who go around looking for rivals, and anybody can be an imaginary rival. They don't need any evidence in the world of rivalry. They are carrying possible rivalry in their head.

MILLER   But in that case, what interruption could be said to have taken place such that arousal has occurred?

MANDLER   What probably lies behind the occasions when people construct an imaginary rivalry is the need, the desire, the hope that you will achieve whatever you want. If, in addition, one sees anybody at all as a potential rival, then all these people are a threat to the completion of the general goal of achieving one's wants. If I don't see anyone as a threat to what I want to do, then there's no interruption. If I see everybody as a threat to what I want to do, which is this abstract generalised rivalry, then I'm continuously interrupted and continually in a state of rage. The person who is continuously in a state of rage on a bus, because he thinks he is always in competition with somebody wanting to take the next available seat, is being interrupted because somebody wants his seat. Every seat is his seat, every potential possibly open seat is his seat. And the person who lives in a continuous rage of jealousy, has a sense of 'anybody could take my loved one away from me'. That's the interruption.

MILLER   I see, so the interruption can in fact be synthesised from within.

MANDLER   Absolutely.

MILLER   And that will create the emotion.

MANDLER   The question is always what it is that your mind expects, not what the external, objective world says it is reasonable to expect. And the trouble is, of course, that our expectations and what the world tells us to expect are often very different.

MILLER   Well then, could I propose an alternative argument and say that far from such a phantasy actually bringing about the emotion of jealousy, the propensity to experience the phantasy that all people are potential sexual rivals, is in itself a constitutive part of the emotion of jealousy?

MANDLER   Yes. As long as there is behind it, this need to possess all women, to be irresistible. If I have a phantasy that every woman really basically wants *me* and nobody else, then the world constitutes a continuous potential for jealousy. All other men are potential rivals, though there is no rhyme to this reasoning, because if I am really irresistible then all women would be flocking to me, regardless of the attractiveness of other men. But what's behind it is the need to possess. If I say: 'I'm not interested in women', then no man is a rival. But again, we need to keep in mind that this is one possible constellation of jealousy and other values and needs will enter into jealousy under other conditions, and particularly in other cultures.

MILLER   But in that case one would have to say that in this case the emotion was created in advance of the actual response; that the emotion is part of what you wish, what you desire. As far as I can tell, your analysis has been a reactive one, in that you imply that emotion arises as a *result* of something that happens.

MANDLER   We carry the wishes, hopes, fears, and the interruptions with us. After all, one can fly into a rage without anything objectively happening in the world, because one happens to think of a potential situation. You're quite right – we carry the plan, the interruption, and the occasions for its interruptions in our heads with us, and very often we don't want the world to tell us about 'reality'. What we call irrational behaviour very often is behaviour that is very little dependent on external evidence of the kind that those of us who are 'rational' are willing to abide by. In other words, if I am rational I know that it is not the case that all women desperately want me and nobody else.

MILLER   So there are states of mind which one would simply have to say were character features rather than emotions. There are people who don't necessarily *feel* envious but they *are* envious.

MANDLER   Absolutely. Emotions are not something that people 'have,' they are constituted of people's states, values and arousals.

MILLER   And there may or may not be characteristic episodes of feeling, accompanied by certain critical experiences.

MANDLER   Fear may be a better example – people who are characteristically fearful because of some past history. They carry the fear with them, they are anxious.

MILLER   So in that case, interruption is built in because they already carry a phantasy of . . .

MANDLER   Of what they want and what could happen.

MILLER   I see, so the more one internalises all the possibilities of the world, the more one carries with one all the possibilities of interruption that the world has to offer.

MANDLER   Yes, and conversely if you think of a very simple animal that doesn't have many phantasies, for example, a lower mammal, I would assume that these animals don't have a rich phantasy life, and therefore have a simpler emotional life. Jealousy would be a very complicated issue, probably an impossible emotion, for a cat. Though people try to read jealousy into their pets.

MILLER   What about those people who seek situations in which there are often dramatic interruptions, for the sake of simply having strong feelings, good or bad?

MANDLER   Some years ago I looked at some research findings on people that are variously called psychopaths, sociopaths or juvenile delinquents. There seems to be some evidence that some of these people have a high, interestingly high, autonomic nervous system response. As a result there may be very few situations in the world that give them the autonomic jag, that is an increase in autonomic activity. Most of us achieve a perceptible level of arousal from exposure to rather common situations. These people *also* want to feel something, and in order to feel it, they need to put themselves into danger situations that the rest of us don't need in order to have an autonomic nervous system response over and above the base level. And it seems to be the case that the sociopaths, to the extent that they are thrill seekers, put themselves into situations where it is more likely that they will be in danger of death or injury. It is in those situations that they will be more likely to experience a noticeable level of arousal and therefore will be able to experience something like normal feelings. They are very often people who are described as emotionally impoverished because they can't find situations that give them enough of an autonomic response in order to feel the depth or the heights of emotions.

MILLER   Well, I'd like to ask you a rather awkward question about that, and it goes back to what you were saying about our carrying potential images of interruption inside our head, which can supply emotions even when the world doesn't justify them. If such people do have a need for interruption – and presumably therefore have got the capacity to reconstruct in phantasy the interruptions that they require on such an exorbitant scale that it's doubtful that the world could ever come up to such a level – why do they actually have to go out into the world to seek a danger which could probably never match the danger which they could phantasise?

MANDLER Because what we can do in our heads is typically not as potent as what the world can really do to us. The world – the evidence of our senses – overrides the power of our phantasy most of the time. I can imagine all sorts of things, but I can't imagine with the intensity with which they really happen.

I remember, for example, during the Second World War, the best training that was given to people was the most realistic training. Just telling people what a situation is going to be like isn't enough, and it isn't good enough training when you encounter the real situation. For example, I was trained for prisoner-of-war interrogations and during training we interrogated training personnel who were playing prisoners-of-war. And what impressed me very much was that when I was doing real PW interrogation, that's the way it really was, just like in training. In contrast people who hadn't gone through that training could only fall back on their imaginary constructions and they frequently had difficulty in handling the interrogations and didn't know what to do. In other words, there is a real world out there and it is thankfully more powerful than our phantasies.

MILLER And it *is* thankfully more powerful because the experience of the physical senses is actually more powerful than anything that the brain can construct from inside, and also because the world can come up with unexpected versions of interruption – things that you couldn't perhaps imagine in your wildest dreams.

MANDLER Both of these cases probably happen. It's an interesting question because the power of the real world may be true by definition. If I tried to imagine an interruption, it is clearly some interruption that must be within my ken because creativity must draw from existing knowledge. So you're quite right. The world is both more joyful and more cruel than our imaginings.

MILLER I see. Well, I'd like to pick up a question about the way in which we can transform our emotions as a result of the dramatic situations in which they occur. I'm thinking here of masochism. The emotional experience of pain can be transformed by the ritual situation in which it occurs. Now does this mean that the experience of pain as such has been changed by what happens?

MANDLER First of all, I don't think so, but I don't really want to call it the emotion of pain. We know that pain itself is already a very complex phenomenon, subject to external gating[1]. For example, pain can be swamped by a very high level of auditory input. There was a dentist in Cambridge, Massachusetts, some twenty years ago, who developed what he called the audio-analgesiac. You put on earphones and heard music at very loud

[1]External gating – the variations in the subjective experience of, in this context, pain, caused by the presence of an independent non-painful stimulus.

sound levels, ranging from 85 up to bursts of 115 decibels. He would drill your teeth without any other pain killer, and you didn't feel any pain.

So pain by itself is manageable. The fact that pain is 'painful', is an interesting problem because in some cases of lobotomy, for example, one can differentiate between the pain experienced in the emotional sense of the pain experience, and pain experienced as an unemotional, merely sensory quality.

MILLER   Isn't it possible for a patient who's had a lobotomy to say: 'Yes, I'm in agony and I don't mind.'

MANDLER   That's right, or rather: 'I am in *pain* and I don't mind.' And I think that what happens in the masochistic case, is that what is painful – the pain *qua* pain – becomes incorporated into what is generally a very pleasurable, positive, usually sexual, scenario. It is not a means to an end but an end in itself.

MILLER   But not to the point where the feeling of pain is reclassified as pleasure?

MANDLER   No. I think it is reclassified in a sense similar to the lobotomy patient. In one case the patient says: 'I feel the pain but it is not agonising'; in the other case the experience seems to be: 'I feel the pain, but I also feel great.'

MILLER   But could we discriminate a little bit more closely. Concerning the patient who had a lobotomy and who said about pain that it was great, wouldn't it be fair to say that that was rather different from a patient who, in fact, sexually enjoyed the experience of pain? The latter wouldn't say that the pain was great, he would say that the total experience within which the pain was occurring was great. But that he was still having horrible pain. And in fact, if the pain were not horrible, the masochist experience wouldn't be realised.

MANDLER   The quality of the experience seems to consist of pain together with some other positive, usually sexual, experiences and values. But it is not felt as being decomposed, it is a single unique emotional experience. In that way masochism illustrates what we discussed earlier, the way in which several different values and arousal are combined into a single felt emotion.

9

dialogue with
Rom Harré

AN ANALYSIS
OF SOCIAL
ACTIVITY

INTRODUCTION

In 1872 Darwin published a companion volume to his book *The Descent of Man*, in which he dealt with the biology of facial expression. The recognition that human beings and living apes had descended from a common ancestor had led him to the conclusion that a comparative study of facial expression would throw considerable light on the origin and development of social behaviour. Darwin's book was a popular success, but the methods which he used were too anecdotal to yield any systematic generalisations, and until the second half of the twentieth century the comparative study of non-verbal communication remained at a standstill. With the development of more sophisticated methods, the analysis of primate behaviour produced valuable insights about the social function of human expression, and psychologists were able to identify a whole set of expressive mechanisms which man had inherited from his ape-like ancestors. But the success of this method had regrettable results, for it led some psychologists to assume that human behaviour was a thinly disguised version of the territorial and reproductive strife that was to be found in primate communities. These misleading conclusions were widely publicised in a series of best-selling popularisations, and the reading public was given the false impression that biologists had identified in the human species an incorrigible tendency towards aggression and territorial ambition. Fortunately this has been counterbalanced by social psychologists who emphasise the distinctively cultural aspects of human interaction, and without denying the existence of instinctive imperatives, such workers stress the overwhelming importance of institutions created and maintained by man's unique gift of language. For although it would be foolish to deny that human beings are prompted by biological impulses which resemble the ones displayed by their animal relatives, it would be even more foolish to overlook the extent to which this heritage has been transformed by the peculiar institutions of a culture based on language. The point is that language creates a domain which has no counterpart in the animal world – an elaborate system of rules and norms, rights and duties without which it is impossible to visualise, let alone describe, the realities of human existence. It is only inside this framework that concepts such as shame, pride, honour, embarrassment and humiliation have any meaning. And according to psychologists such as Rom Harré it is these considerations which determine the conduct of life.

DISCUSSION

MILLER   I was struck by a slogan in one of your books, to the effect that for scientific purposes we ought to treat people as human beings. I wonder what the force of that slogan is?

HARRÉ   I was trying to say two things: something about the proper foundations of the study of human psychology and something about the nature of science itself. The surface meaning was the thought that psychologists ought to draw upon the knowledge people have of the way they live their own lives. This should be a kind of basic resource for understanding human life. I mean that people know they have plans, they deliberately formulate projects, they scheme, they talk about their past and present efforts, they strive to get themselves off the hooks they realise they have impaled themselves upon. They land themselves in predicaments, realise they have done so; in consequence they are embarrassed, angry or despondent. Sometimes they privately glory in the wonderful way in which they exemplify paradigms of their society. This presupposes a vast amount of native understanding which ought to be available to us as students of human life, as part of our apparatus of understanding how that life is created by the co-ordinated actions and particularly the talk of intelligent social beings.

MILLER   Is it possible to be scientific about such intuitions?

HARRÉ   A great deal depends upon what one thinks of as a scientific enterprise. When psychologists first began to try to be scientists they were like a young man setting off to be a novelist who grows a beard, buys a typewriter, who dresses up and adopts the superficial manners of the literary world as he imagines them. Psychologists talked like physical scientists, they called their results 'measures', they decorated their learned papers with tables of numbers, and they even tried their hand at a little rather simple mathematics. It was just dressing up. Somehow the essence of the scientific enterprise eluded them. If one looks at the work of a great scientist like Darwin, who recorded his halting progress in great detail, one can see that what it is to be scientific is not just a matter of observing, measuring and predicting. First, one must have a way of controlling the abstraction of patterns from the complex and enigmatic world of our experience. Not everything that happens on some occasion is going to appear in a scientist's description of the events in question. On the other hand, one must have some way of explaining in a plausible and powerful way, what these patterns really are and how they came about.

Scientific observation is never performed just by looking. The world is far too complicated. Darwin thought of his plants and animals as if they were families, rather like the Darwins and the Wedgwoods. He traced lines of descent, grouping creatures not only by reference to how they look now, but from which ancestors they might be presumed to have descended. This is to think in terms of a model or analogue. Then he thought of the process by which successive generations are reproduced, as if it were like the way a gardener selects the plants whose seeds he will sow for next year. Natural selection is modelled on domestic selection. So on the one hand you need an 'as if' to look at the world; on the other you need an 'as if' to explain the world.

Now if you ask, 'how can we make psychology truly scientific and not just a pseudo-science dressed up in the rhetoric of the physical sciences?' then my slogan really recommends us to take for our 'as if' the knowledge we already have of certain ways of life, institutional patterns, social practices, and so on. For example, we could look at the things that are happening around us as if life were a play written by a dramatist and staged by actors and producers, as if it were a game played by people concerned to win or lose, but abiding by rules and conventions, as if it were a kind of jousting – a ritualised battle in the search for honour. The significance of descriptions in our experience of people and their behaviour comes through only if we are quite explicit about the model 'through which' we abstract the pattern.

On the other hand, to explain the patterns of human interaction we must use another, preferably co-ordinate set of models, thinking of people as if they were active agents following rules, as if they were actors following scripts. All these 'as ifs' or scientific models come from our commonsense understanding of social events we already know how to analyse and to explain.

MILLER Now if we take this 'as if' assumption as a model which shapes our vision and makes us look at the thing in a different way, it puts forward the idea that human life is characteristically and distinctively rule-bound and determined by conventions and constitutions. This immediately sets it aside from what one would strictly call the natural world; it would be something which could not be explained in terms of the brute facts of biological nature – although there are many psychologists who have as their ambition the idea of reducing it to animal facts.

HARRÉ In the last three million years we have laid over the animal facts of our existence not only Marx's social order of production, but a whole world of ceremonial and ritual, and particularly the world of talk. We have used talk and other symbolic devices to transform the basic biological facts into something which does not have a biological, but a cultural, identity. It has become customary to talk of this as the production of meaning. Let me illustrate this with an example. If we were to shake hands, someone strolling by might ask: 'Now what are they up to?' The mere grasping of paws is something which perhaps is a biological inheritance, but as people we could be sealing a bet, or greeting each other, I could be congratulating you, we could be preparing for a boxing match. There are umpteen things people can be doing when they do the one biological behavioural thing 'touch paws'. Handshakes are psychologically effective in so far as they are interpreted. It is those interpretations out of which we create a fragment of social order, and in the end create the social world.

MILLER And those facts are irreducible to biological ones; although they may require a foundation of muscular action, there's no way in which they could be satisfactorily described as *simply* muscular action?

HARRÉ It is easy to prove that the biological and behavioural levels of analysis cannot deal with the psychology of human interactions. These interactions exemplify conventions. In different societies different conventions obtain. So if you believe that among human beings, let us say, greeting is a fundamental social interaction, then the fact that some people greet each other by kissing on both cheeks, embarrassed Oxford dons by holding out their hands limply and hoping they won't be taken, and Indians by each steepling his or her own hands, this shows that greeting is not a behavioural phenomenon, but is a variety of possible physical movements, by means of which the common thread, the meaningful interaction of acknowledging and respecting one another, is performed. Some of these movements have not yet been used, some possibilities may never be.

MILLER And these facts are not ones which can simply be interpreted in the way that zoologists for example, like Desmond Morris, have done, as a list of signs which you can simply read off like a dictionary.

HARRÉ No, because they hang together into systems, they create worlds, they stand for further and more complex social and psychological matters than just their immediate interpretation. They may, for example, subtly endorse a certain way of interpreting relations between the sexes. We put them together into a continuous and ever-onward moving, flowing construction of conventionally constrained activities through which we live, and so we have to think of the flow of human social activity as occurring somehow as a whole. An image I like is to think of social life as a kind of conversation. All our actions, not only our gestures, and our talk, are creating a kind of conversation, an endless conversation into which individuals enter, make their contribution to the common discourse, and eventually fall silent, though some may go on contributing to the conversations of mankind long after they are dead, by writing books, becoming legendary, and so on. Babies are immersed in this conversation. We perhaps might come back to talk about that important fact later. We construct our worlds in talk of various kinds. Every exchanging of symbolic objects is a kind of extension of that conversation, I believe. So we have, as philosophers, or psychologists, or sociologists, to look at the properties of talk , the form of conversations, if we want really to get to the heart of what it is to be a human being, engaging with other people in constructing a social world.

MILLER So that the basic predisposing institution which sets this up for us is the existence of language within which we can do more than merely make appeasing signs at one another.

HARRÉ Exactly. But the study of 'world creating' aspects of language is a subtle and complex matter. When they first looked at recorded language, frozen onto the page by writing, for instance, the thing that struck the first investigators of speech, the Greek and Roman commentators on language, was the presence of logical and grammatical forms. They were interested in how words strung themselves together into distinctive patterns or sentences. For almost two millennia the study of language was devoted to looking for, and analysing, those structural properties we call grammar and logic. Really it was the structural properties of frozen speech, speech that was written down or recorded, that became the object of study.

But if one looks at real human interactions achieved with speech, one of the first things that strikes one is that the things that we mean are by no means intercorrelated with the grammatical forms of what we say. If a child responds to 'why don't you eat up your spinach?' with 'well, I don't like it', it is not regarded as a proper response. The sentence was in interrogative form, that is, it was a question, but as a speech-act it was used to convey an order, or, at the very least, a request.

MILLER Which means that one can't express the meaning of a sentence merely by parsing it grammatically.

HARRÉ Exactly. So that even the quasi-physical form that it takes is a limited tool for understanding the significance in the human conversation. We have to see it as it is used. We have to ask our speakers 'what are you *doing*?' with these sentences.

MILLER In other words, every sentence or paragraph or at least every utterance is a speech act. And one is doing something *with* the sentence, rather than simply meaning something by the grammatical form of it.

HARRÉ But one is doing something very complicated. One might, for example, be intent on insulting somebody. One might use a word which has a literal meaning in another context. One exclaims, for example, 'Stupid bitch'. Said in a dog kennels it would be an entirely different kind of speech from saying it at the kitchen table. Context tells us how to read the performative forces, as they are called, of speeches. There are even occasions when the performative force is so vivid and powerful that we don't even need to know what the language used literally means.

Let me sketch in an event that occurs every so often in Oxford during term time. Imagine one is in the Sheldonian Theatre. It is full of proud parents, the vice-chancellor, proctors, and college deans are all there gorgeously apparelled. As each dean comes up to present his candidates he says, grasping the hand of the nearest of his flock, '*Insignissime vice-cancellarie, vosque egregii procuratores, praesento vobis . . .*' and so on, and the vice-chancellor replies in kind.

Few, perhaps, and on some occasions none, of those proud parents have the faintest idea what this language literally means. Indeed, some of the deans don't understand it too well either. And yet everybody understands that when all these things have been said a degree has been conferred. It's the communal talking, as speech-acts, that does it.

Just think of the amazing power of talk. A group of people turn up on Saturday afternoon in a church. They talk together for twenty minutes or so. By a kind of miracle the future has been pre-empted. The marriage has been performed. To untangle the knot requires an enormous amount more talk at another place. Think of all the emotional, economic and other consequences which flow from twenty minutes of a peculiar kind of talk.

MILLER So in other words, a Martian who was gifted merely with English speech could not arrive at a parish church on one Saturday afternoon and by parsing the sentences which passed between the vicar and the couple at the altar understand that a marriage had occurred. He might simply think that a description of an event had been made, that a commentary had been issued by the vicar.

HARRÉ Should he have turned up on Friday evening when the rehearsal was on, even had he known that 'I will' was a way of committing oneself to a person for the rest of one's life, he would have failed to grasp the proper significance of the event. He needs the contextual understanding. He needs to see this as part of a culture. That is, he has to understand the idea that there are both weddings and rehearsals for weddings.

MILLER He needs more than merely the context of the occasion itself. He needs the whole context of the social institution within which marriage has a place.

HARRÉ Of course, it's the institution that calls for the talk, and it is the talk which, as it were, creates the institution.

MILLER Otherwise, our Martian might be led to think that when the bridegroom said 'I will', that the bridegroom was in fact issuing some sort of vague prediction about his future behaviour. Whereas in fact it actually constitutes the act of getting married.

HARRÉ Right. Notice something very peculiar about talk, which has this performative force. It has a peculiar relationship to time. This is one of the ways in which the social world constructed out of talk and the physical world constructed out of things, differ. In the physical world, if something has happened it is 'in the past'. It is fixed, and as a human actor one is stuck with it. If you have inherited a bunch of genes, that's it. You finish up with such and such a nose, or with hair turning prematurely grey. You cannot choose your parents, they say. The past cannot be remedied. One can influence the future a bit, by one's grasp of the rather unsatisfactory and problematic principles we call natural laws. But even the best engineers are liable to find that fractures occur in their most cherished structures. But social talk as social action has a quite different relationship to time. You can create the future by making promises, commitments, contracts, which will reverberate down the corridors of time, rigidly defining what should happen. Unlike the equations of probabilistic quantum mechanics, a contract is not just a probabilistic force affecting the future. It determines how the future should be. One can be held to account for failure to fulfil one's commitments. Contracts pre-empt the future in a way which nothing in the physical world does. It is, however, the 'shoulds' they determine, not the 'wills'.

The other marvellous thing about talk is that it can be used to recreate the past. The social past is not a fixed object like the physical past. A skilled social talker can recreate the past. The simplest way is to say: 'Well, I'm terribly sorry, I didn't mean it quite like that'. And if the other members of one's social circle accept that apology and the redefinition of the event, suddenly something in the past has changed. Its consequences for the present and future are now different from those of the event which it had been thought occurred.

MILLER   So if someone blunders into the room, trips up and overturns the table, and says sorry, the fact that the table was overturned has not been altered by the statement, 'I am sorry', but it *has* altered the social significance of what happened.

HARRÉ   Exactly. And so the power of speech to alter consequences is something which in a way mocks causality.

MILLER   So what is the performative force of an apology; what is someone doing with an apology?

HARRÉ   An apology works at two different levels. On one level it alters the performative force of something which has already happened. So, for example, when someone first blunders into your time by being late for your party, or into your space by approaching too close to your table, your first interpretation of their act is that it is a violation. Then, by apologising, the violation (actual or potential) is corrected, and a new social meaning has come into the world which now consequentially affects the present and the future. But justifying, excusing, accounting generally, also says something about the speaker. It displays him or her as a person of a certain kind, a proper, knowledgeable, reasonable, even rational being, and certainly morally worthy. What is more, it displays a person whose space or time or other rights have been violated as someone morally worthy too.

MILLER   In what way exactly?

HARRÉ   If I don't give a damn about your ownership of a particular time, if I regard you as a person of no consequence, I might just blunder in when I like and leave when I like, treating you with a kind of temporal contempt. But if I value you, I value too the time that you specify is yours by inviting me. One of my ways of valuing you is to show that I am contrite, for having violated something of yours, the sanctity of the time which you have laid claim to. By doing so I have shown that I am the right sort of person, because I am the kind of person who knows that you're the kind of person who ought to be valued by the kind of person who I am.

MILLER   These acts of contrition and so forth are unaccountable in terms of signs and signals and gestures of appeasement.

HARRÉ   There is something quite deep in coming to see just why the analysis of apologising as signals of appeasement won't do. Imagine the old man-watcher himself, or judging from Desmond Morris's illustrations, the 'girl-watcher', laid back on his park bench watching people come and go. No doubt gestures of appeasement from a biological repertoire do occur, when someone accidentally bumps into someone else. When a couple of girls wander down the park showing themselves to interested but anonymous bystanders, about all we can do is note their sexuality. But the world described in terms of that kind of approach is the world of accidents, of uncertain meetings, outside social frameworks. It is an anonymous world where nobody knows anybody else. There are no autobiographies at stake where there is no institutional framework. All we have got to go on in the anomic human playground of the London parks or the Naples promenade, is our biological inheritance. That is all that is left when you have washed away the fine fabric of social life. Regent's Park on a summer's afternoon is a place where there are no institutions and consequently we are left with the most elementary forms of human interaction. The same is true of old-fashioned psychology laboratories.

MILLER   Which is where the naked-ape picture of social reality arises. The one where you see people simply as accidentally dressed up, issuing signs and signals to play off aggression or to entice sexual advances or whatever.

HARRÉ   Yes, just to keep a little fragment of reality ticking over at the lowest possible level. Of course, very rarely do human beings live in those kinds of conditions. Mostly they know each other very well. Amongst other things they are constructing biographies and autobiographies of each other. They are living in very tight-knit communities. They have a delicately balanced system of performative utterances with which they construct the future and reconstruct the past. They do not live together by 'happen' chance. People from infancy are already living in institutions, where there are roles to be fulfilled. Most importantly of all, there are rules by which high-grade social performances are specified. The rules are cultural artefacts, I believe, which act as the ultimate control of all sorts of institutional activities.

MILLER   So presumably in a comparatively anonymous ambience, like a park in which many of the people don't know each other, even the ignoring of one another is an elaborate institutional act which could not be understood in terms of hives and packs.

HARRÉ   Certainly, if that ignoring is being read as having some kind of higher order social meaning. For example, one might ignore someone because to notice them would show that that kind of person was not the sort of person that it would be proper to take account of. For example, a beggar might be elaborately ignored, not just to avoid pushing five pence into his hand, but in order to avoid the possible interpretation that one would be the kind of person, not being Francis of Assisi, who would be willing to engage such an individual in a man-to-man conversation.

MILLER   Or that it would only be possible to engage in intimate and visible conversation with a beggar, if you were ostentatiously dressed up as Francis of Assisi, and therefore reaccounted for yourself as being that sort of person. And one might do that as a Saturday-afternoon entertainment. And this might be going on often without language, because in fact one is constantly presenting a sort of picture or portrait of oneself to others, even in fact, to anonymous others.

HARRÉ   It is worth emphasising that language and other kinds of symbolic actions do not constitute two distinctive ways of interacting, but human action is all of a piece. In many cases we can substitute a linguistic form for a gestural one. I could cock-a-snook to insult somebody, or I could say: 'You stupid clot'. Either would do. I might choose to adopt a particular style of dress as the mode in which I demonstrate the sort of person I am. On the other hand I might choose an accent or vocabulary.

I want to see the creation of social order as a kind of seamless web of meaningful activity and this is why, in the last analysis, it is so important to distinguish grammatical analysis of language from its performative analysis. Grammatically, language is a very peculiar and idiosyncratic thing. It isn't continuous with the other action activities of human beings in the social world.

MILLER What you're saying is that we can't even begin to arrive at a satisfactory analysis of what we mean, either by sentences or gestures, until we consider the entire institutional and uniquely human framework within which such meanings are actually delivered.

HARRÉ Exactly. Once one opens up the topic of the psychology of institutions, the systems of rules become a central area of research interest. Institutions exist day by day and year by year. It is curious, isn't it, that there might be a night on which every member of Oxford University was fast asleep, yet the next day up we get and a recognisably similar institution exists again. I think that we ought to be amazed that this kind of thing is possible. How can it be that we recreate an institution over and over again, surviving wars and pestilence, kings' commissioners, and innumerable changes of personnel? There must be something that outlasts all the changes. These are the overlapping systems of rules, or something approximating to them, some normative entity that is like a system of rules. This idea is the central 'as if', the one I take to be crucial to the scientific study of the human mind in action.

MILLER By 'institution', we don't necessarily mean something which is formally written down and constituted in a charter of some sort. There may be other sorts of institutions which are much more mobile and much more intuitive, but nevertheless, just as binding.

HARRÉ Certainly. And that's why one needs this concept of something by which we direct our actions, as if it were a system of rules. I was talking earlier about using models and analogies for explanation. Now what makes the kind of linguistic psychology I am describing scientific, amongst other things, is its use of the concept of a system of rules as an 'as if' explanatory device. When one is playing a game for the first time or repairing one's bicycle using that marvellous little book *How to Repair a Bicycle*, there are rules to follow in the literal sense. One does things step by step by following the rules. They are written down. We can have recourse to them. We explain the orderliness of our activities by reference to the efficacy of what are quite literally *the* rules.

When we are looking at more ephemeral and informal institutional activities, such as family conversations, the behaviour of football fans, and so on, then, as in any study worthy to be called a science, we must construct an explanatory apparatus with an 'as if'. We say: 'Let us look at these folk as if they were following something which was 'as if' it were a system of rules. These people know something and what they know is something like the system of rules. With that idea in mind we will search their talk for representations of some things that are like rules.'

MILLER   And in recognising such institutions, they are capable of recognising *violations* of the rules.

HARRÉ   Right. One of the social activities that we have found most illuminating in trying to understand informal institutions is the practice of giving excuses and justifications, of blaming people for doing things wrong and praising them for doing things well. In that kind of talk, which we call accounting, there is displayed for all to see what was previously informally known. If someone is accused of a violation then he can come back and ask for the grounds of the accusation and one might say something like, 'well, you're not supposed to run across the grass', 'beat a child so savagely', etc., or words to that effect. And thus you display the rule, be the sin venial or mortal.

MILLER   In other words, even for these informal unwritten laws, ignorance is no excuse. So that although there's no statute saying: Thou shalt not pick thy nose, there are in fact intuitive rules which define a violation of that sort, which leads to apologetic behaviour if you're caught at it.

HARRÉ   But one must go a step further to get away from the idea that it is particularly individuals who know the rules. One of the quarrels between the old psychology and, if I might say so, the advancing front, is on the issue of where the rules are located, where the thought takes place, where knowledge is.

There is a growing tendency to say something like this: that practical and social knowledge, the rules of proper action, the actual processes of thought, might not be in an individual's possession at all. All these things might be properties of the social-collective of the human group. In so far as the group has a social structure, so does the system of rules, so does the body of knowledge. A person having a certain location in the social structure, a certain role in an institution, has the right to display certain pieces of knowledge. In some cases the knowledge is apportioned out, and a totality necessary for action is created only by the whole collective, the institution as such.

MILLER   And people recognise or know who has got the different parts of the knowledge, so that there is a division of labour in upholding this institution.

HARRÉ   Continental psychologists and sociologists have been working on this idea for a considerable time, but we have been a little slow to take it up in the Anglo-American world. People have made detailed studies of the locations, so to speak, of medical knowledge. It is distributed through the medical system and it is differentially displayed by people depending upon their right to display it. A general practitioner may know how to cure a patient of a particular condition, but he may not have the right to display that knowledge. He may have to pass the patient on to somebody else, who also knows the cure, but has the right to perform it, so displaying his knowledge. We call such people consultants. Medical knowledge is socially structured in the same way as the medical profession is structured.

Knowledge is never stationary. There is a kind of seepage. Knowledge is moving through society all the time. If we think of knowledge as socially located, it can start its social journey in highly technical institutions, as esoteric knowledge known only to a few. But soon it begins to leak away and permeate the whole of society. The French psychologist, Moscovici, has done some most interesting work on how Freudian ideas have filtered through French society. Following Durkheim he calls these popular notions *réprésentations sociales* – social representations. French people have come to accept the Freudian way of thinking as part of the ordinary ways they think about human life – as the social representation of how the human mind is supposed to be. And so, of course, by virtue of this set of beliefs, the French, and everyone else, have become just that little bit more Freudian.

MILLER   Well I wonder if I can come back to the way in which the wisdom of psychology starts to alter the data of psychology. Can I return to a point which plays a very prominent part in what you write. You seem to be saying that the upholding of honour is really the principal impulse behind our behaviour, one to another. The maintaining of the best image of ourselves in the face of others.

HARRÉ   Yes, I think that's right, though we should be extraordinarily cautious about uttering universal statements about the psychology of the human race. Let us put it this way. From what one knows about cultures of the past and remote cultures of the present, from history and anthropology, the search for honour and the humiliation occasioned by the loss of it seems to be a recurring, dominant, human theme; the institutions that subserve this, the ritual devices by which honour is lost or gained, the rituals by which such losses and gains are publicly acknowledged to have been achieved, these are the institutions which one finds in almost every culture, however inverted, subverted or perverted they may be.

If one takes the idea of the search for honour as the guide, and looks at institutions and activities which in our society have sometimes seemed to be mysterious, or even perhaps not social at all, then one can sometimes get a glimpse of something quite exciting behind the façade of apparent meaninglessness. When psychologists of the new persuasion began looking at football 'violence' – I refer particularly to the work of my colleague Peter Marsh – the then current view about football fans was that they were resorting to, or reverting to, some sort of animal behaviour. Hooliganism was presented as a kind of breakdown of civilised constraints as the result of biological forces. The adrenalin was running high. The higher faculties had been abandoned. The choice of language reflected this view very strongly. 'Violence erupts at the London Road end'. 'Fans run riot!' etc.

MILLER   These were people stripped of civilisation.

HARRÉ   The implication was that they were behaving in the most primitive fashion and were under the control of something either genetic or hormonal. When Peter Marsh began to penetrate the social world of the fans, it turned out that a great many of these mysterious and allegedly subhuman activities were best understood as if they were a modern kind of jousting. The key to understanding their activities was to see that honour was at stake. Within these pathetic little prancings which in those days stood metonymically for fights, was a criterion proclaiming certain sorts of *moral* worth. Groups of fans had their own moral orders in which people gained status and honour and resisted humiliation by passing up the scale of respect in very much the same way as medieval knights had gained honour by jousting. Whatever else people may do, the search for honour is a very central activity. It may even predominate over the maintenance of life itself.

MILLER   Well, this seems to be a much more constructive and fruitful way of looking at what goes on in society. I've always been depressed myself by the way in which these things have been described as outbursts of the animal side of man, as if we were watching apes or lions. Whereas your analysis offers us a way of seeing it as yet another development of human institutions.

HARRÉ   A further level of complication needs to be added to the picture we have sketched so far. Institutions are in many ways officially sanctioned. I mean there are institutions which the state or church has set up deliberately, or institutions which have grown up from informal practices which have become officially controlled and defined, like hospitals, police forces, educational systems, and so on. These institutions have an official role and they have an official rhetoric which describes and prescribes their proper activities. They have an official role of honour. After a while an institution tends to ritualise these official and practical activities, to treat them as a kind of formal routine. Another kind of institution, an unofficial one, grows up inside the original. In the underlife, the search for honour is found in activities which are not officially sanctioned. In hospitals there is not only the official business of falling ill and getting cured, there is also the unofficial business of moving through the wards. Certain wards, and indeed certain diseases, have a more honorific status than others. Surgeons do not do operations just to cure people, but also to improve their standing in their courts of honour. In almost every institution of importance there is a double, or maybe a treble, social world. Once one has the idea of a search for honour as one of the central human preoccupations, one can see institutions containing other institutions, containing other institutions, and so on.

MILLER   Yes. And this happens even at the most informal and apparently non-institutional level, when, say, simply passing each other in the corridor and so forth.

HARRÉ   Indeed, the correlative of this is that activity which demeans is somehow something that has to be dealt with, remedied so to speak. At a communal table one cannot just reach over and grab the salt. One has to say, 'I wonder if you would mind passing me the salt?' Why this elaborate way of speaking? If one's fellow diner says, as schoolboys are inclined to do, 'yes, I would mind' he has misunderstood the purport of my ritual formula. I am showing him respect by offering him the opportunity to refuse me, knowing that he is obliged to reciprocate that respect by complying with my request.

MILLER But the schoolboy who takes the grammatical form of such a request literally is in fact playing a game which indicates and implies that he actually recognises the institutional significance of such a phrase.

HARRÉ Indeed, he knows that a potential violation is being remedied by acting in advance of doing it. In looking for an understanding of why certain sorts of performative force are present in everyday language in which we conduct our endless human conversations, we need only to remember that we must sustain the honour of each other.

MILLER The reason why I find this a much more optimistic view of ourselves than the purely reductive one, is that it introduces something which does not occur in the animal world, namely moral considerations. Although there are people who would say of their pets, 'oh, he knows when he's done wrong'. Now I believe you have a view about the way in which animals can themselves be drawn into the moral sphere, by being moralised.

HARRÉ If we can draw babies into the moral sphere, we can and do draw animals in to a certain extent.

MILLER But in the case of babies, we're drawing them into the moral sphere because we are actually training them to be moral because we believe that they have the capacity to become as moral as we are.

HARRÉ One has to make that point very carefully. When mothers talk to babies they continually embed their babies in a conversation in which the baby is treated as if it had a full complement of moral and intellectual qualities. 'Diddums want his bottle?' 'Isn't she happy'. 'He's Mummy's naughty little boy'. These are the sorts of things that are said. Recent careful studies of mother-infant interactions have shown that the mother does not react to the baby as to a kind of empty vessel. She reacts to the infant as if he or she has been transformed and psychologically supplemented by this conversational gambit. She treats the infant as if it had the moral and psychological attributes which she has ascribed to it in her talk. Bruner has suggested that mothers have theories about how human beings should be and what they are trying to do is to fulfil the theory in the person of their infant. The way to do this is to anticipate the full panoply of social and psychological competence. It really is a vastly complex psychology and moral sensibility that they are ascribing to their infants. They do not talk *about* their infants' intentions; they provide them with them, and then they react to the infant as if it had them.

What the infant does – so it is thought by people subscribing to this point of view – is to appropriate slowly from out of that conversational matrix those ways of talking for its own purposes, so gradually it learns to do intention-ascribing talk for itself, of itself.

MILLER Well this presumably in some senses corresponds to Freud's view of the introjection – to use his barbarous phrase – of morality. It becomes internalised as a result of these conversational nexuses.

HARRÉ Unfortunately, Freud never told us in detail how it does so. One of the great advances in recent years was the introduction of the concept of psychological symbiosis, quite a nice technical phrase. It describes the way the mother creates a complete psychological being by supplementing the inadequacies of her infant by her talk. Introjection, then, is not so much something being introjected, like force-feeding a pigeon; rather it's Vygotsky's[1] idea of appropriation, taking what is required for the job at hand from the public conversation. It is not just a matter of a growing skill, but also gradually coming to understand what rights one has to use this or that conversational gambit for oneself. Now animals live in families in a conversational milieu, just as infants do, for example, the cat, the dog, even the cows, are living in a kind of conversation. They have names, they are addressed as psychological beings, the state of their tails and ears are treated as conversational elements. But unlike human infants, cats and dogs don't, on the whole, appropriate all that much from the family conversation for their own purposes. They exist as psychological beings almost wholly in psychological symbiosis.

MILLER In other words they can't live up to the moral expectations of their owners.

HARRÉ But their owners consistently treat them in the same way as mothers treat infants, namely as having a morality.

MILLER But this is one of the encouraging aspects of human life – although often looked on in a very condescending way. People often say of owners who speak of their cats in this way, oh, that's just sentimental. But it seems, in the light of your analysis, that it reflects and expresses one of the most fruitful aspects of our personality.

HARRÉ Everything that moves, be it mechanical or animal, gets sucked in. When one, then, looks back again at the question with which we began: 'what is scientific about psychology that places talking and meaning and the moral order in the centre of the study?', we have to be very careful about the generalisations we come up with. Including the moral dimension in our study means that people, even infants (symbiotically), can be called to account for what they have been up to. If it is characteristic of humans to live in a world of moral orders maintained by systems of rules, which people can obey or disobey, we must allow for the fact that people must know or fail to know them. The generalities we are talking about in describing forms of life are not laws of nature, which describe the inevitable workings of causal mechanisms. Rather they are matters to

[1]See footnote on page 41.

which something like a metaphor of choice is appropriate. It would not do to suggest that people are often literally choosing directly this or that way, but we treat people as if they were. A metaphor of choice is an appropriate way of emphasising that families, offices, nations, and so on, are above all, moral orders. We must always be ready to talk our way out of trouble, to give an account of our activities. Those accounts contain, I believe, the research material that makes the kind of psycholinguistic enterprise I have been talking about more truly scientific than much which passes for science in psychology only by reason of its dress. By analysing accounts we get a first grasp on what the implicit moral order is, in which people are being presumed by other people to live. Account analysis is a first step which must be supplemented by more directed studies such as Kelly's repertory grid[1] system.

MILLER   Well, I sometimes wonder why it should be necessary to apply the term 'science' in order to give this sort of analysis respectability.

HARRÉ   In psychological and social studies one must always apply a theory to itself and to its rivals. If one asks, 'why do students of the social world, let us say, dress their activities up in these false beards, talking inappropriately of measures, laws, causes, etc?' it is because they have a certain conception of honourable activity. One can see the social psychology of traditional, social psychology as an exemplar of a life of honour, being lived by people in accordance with, in my view, mistaken ideas about what the honourable thing to do is. It is as if one had borrowed a moral order from some strange tribe, let's say the Tierra del Fuegans, and used it on odd occasions in England. The same sort of thing happened in psychology. They borrowed the moral order of physics and began to use it to construct social psychology as a life form without asking: 'Is this the appropriate garb? Is this the right way to be an honourable and honest investigator of human thought and action?'

In fact, a purely behavioural psychology, if anyone had ever without self-deception practised such a thing, would strictly explain nothing. The passion for understanding, for explanation, is what I would regard as the heart of the scientific enterprise. It was just that which, in borrowing the rhetoric of the physical sciences, without any real grasp of their methods, experimental psychologists simply left out of account.

MILLER   But of course natural scientists would insist that in order to qualify as a respectable explanation, a theory must yield predictions or it would not count as an explanation. Now on your account this would not necessarily be required of a satisfactory social explanation.

HARRÉ   In the long run the predictive power criterion must fail. Whatever we now think we know, we are likely to be overtaken by events. I do not believe that human psychology is a stable and fixed piece of mental machinery. We know that human social orders are unstable and are continually being

[1]George Kelly, an American psychologist who devised the repertory grid which is a written test for assessing personality.

replaced by very different modes of social organisation. Even if we follow the Marxist analysis we would find that different modes of production engendered different superstructures, different classes, different religions, and so on. So we would expect sociology to be continually chasing its own tail. And the same would be true of psychology.

MILLER   Well this in fact goes back to that point that I postponed deliberately, and that is that the facts of psychology can themselves be fed back into the system so that they actually alter the observable facts themselves. You were mentioning the way in which the knowledge of Freudian psychology has altered the way in which people behave. And it's certainly happened in, say, sexual psychology.

HARRÉ   Yes. I think this happens in two different ways. One way is where the psychological theory becomes part of the theorising with which ordinary people will order their own lives and if one believes, as I do, that the main way the human mind comes into being is by virtue of people holding theories about themselves, then of course, there is a very potent effect. For instance, if you believe that deep in your unconscious you have an apparatus of repression, that your mind is the triumvirate of id, superego and ego, then that belief will have an enormous influence on how you order your life. You will organise your experience in those terms. That this happens has been well established by the French students of social representations.

But there is another, and more subtle, influence that I think one can observe. It has somehow to do with the method rather than the content of psychological studies. If you believe that you can take a human being or two, put them into a laboratory, surround them by recording apparatus, and by manipulating 'variables' cause them to act, then you are picking on just those aspects of human life which are most automatic, which are in some ways the least human.

If the psychological experiment is successful and really does pick up something universal, it is very unlikely to be a cultural matter. It may be how the gaze drops to mark a shift of attention, how sexual signals are picked up, but these are, by virtue of their universality, of minor psychological significance and socially both trivial and banal. But if you can promulgate the results of this kind of experimentation as *the* laws of human psychology, in which people are treated as automata, then you offer people a vision of human psychological functioning which is that of humans reduced to automata.

MILLER   And they might even start to conform to it.

HARRÉ   Exactly. I do think that the influence of Skinnerian behaviourism in the United States can actually be discerned in certain fragments of American life. Most people in the United States believe that they have to be trained to do things (even to make love), and then being trained they must wait for the appropriate conditions to be realised. Then, like automata, they will routinely produce the necessary actions. Renting a car in the United States is a fascinating example of this. The beautifully trained Avis girl says the same thing from coast to coast, talking exactly like some automaton from *Dr Who*, and one can see somehow that that person deeply believes that this is the way the human psyche should function. The idea of doing the thing a little bit differently each time, perhaps instead of saying 'take care how you go now, do you hear', saying something else instead, even outside the exigencies of a job, would threaten the kind of routinisation in American social interchanges that goes well beyond the ritual of custom. I think one of the elements in this is an assumption of scientism that has somehow filtered down through the teachers' colleges, through the business schools — a legacy of the idea of humans as fit subjects for experimentation, that simple or complicated they are ultimately automata. That I think is not a scientific principle, but a moral view which I would wish to repudiate.

dialogue with
Robert Hinde

THE
STUDY OF
INTERPERSONAL
RELATIONSHIPS

INTRODUCTION

In 1952, when I went up to Cambridge to sit for a scholarship in Natural Science, the candidates were going through the familiar rigmarole of laying odds on the questions which were likely to come up in the zoology paper. It was generally agreed that if our excited reaction to Niko Tinbergen's recently published *Study of Instinct* was anything to go by, there was almost bound to be an essay on animal behaviour. I can still remember my exhilaration on turning over the exam paper to find that the eagerly awaited question had been set just as we expected. Apart from my relief at getting a question for which I was well prepared, the fact that such a topic had been included at all confirmed my suspicion that the publication of Tinbergen's book was widely regarded as a significant event, and that if I was successful in the examination it would not be difficult to find teachers eager to discuss its far-reaching implications.

Many of the ideas contained in Tinbergen's book were based on work which had been initiated during the thirties by the great German naturalist Konrad Lorenz, who reinstated the observation of animals in their natural setting. Lorenz and Tinbergen's method represented a dramatic departure from the laboratory research which had been carried out in the earlier part of the twentieth century. According to Lorenz it was necessary to become emotionally involved to the point of 'falling in love' with the group of animals in question. 'Were it not for the unaccountable gloating pleasure some of us take in watching "our" animals, not even a person endowed with the supernatural patience of a yogi could bring himself to stare at a fish, a bird or an ape with the unremitting perseverance which is necessary in order to perceive the governing principles prevailing in the behaviour of an animal.'[1] But this was not just sentimental natural history. Lorenz and his colleagues insisted on a comparative method in the effort to elucidate the evolutionary processes by which living creatures had developed their characteristic habits.

By 1953 the new science of ethology had established itself at Cambridge and distinguished work was being conducted by W. H. Thorpe and by Robert Hinde. I was delighted therefore to discover that Robert Hinde was a Fellow of the college I was about to enter, St John's, and although animal behaviour was not a part of the medical curriculum I asked him if I could take a course of weekly supervision in the hope of finding out something about human nature from the facts which he was helping to discover about the psychology of animals. I remember those weekly sessions with great nostalgia, and when I knew I was going to do these interviews I was eager to recapture some of that early enthusiasm. I had overlooked the fact that scientific interests move on, and that although Professor Hinde had established an international reputation in the field of animal behaviour, his curiosity had by now led him to the study of human relationships, and it was this topic which we found ourselves discussing.

[1] Konrad Lorenz, *Studies in Animal and Human Behaviour*.

DISCUSSION

MILLER   When I first came to you as a student in the fifties to study animal
behaviour, there was the implied assumption that as a medical student I
was going to learn something about human conduct from studying animal
psychology. And I suppose this came from the acceptance of the theory of
evolution; that we were not just simply placed in nature above the animals
and apart from them but because we were relatives and descendants of
them we had inherited some measure of our behavioural repertoire from
them.

Now in your own development as a psychologist you've moved from
animals to human beings. Is there any sense in which you would say that
your own commitment to the theory of evolution has actually led
inevitably to your climbing back up your own evolutionary tree from
birds, through hamsters and monkeys, to the study of human
relationships?

HINDE   Let me say first that in those curious discussions that you and I used to
have together such a long time ago, and which I used to enjoy very much, I
hope I never implied that man was just like the animals, or that there were
necessarily many fertile *direct* parallels to be drawn between animal and
man. I think I have always maintained that the study of animal behaviour
was sometimes useful for understanding human behaviour, not so much
by direct parallels between the one and the other, but by virtue of the
principles which it threw up, principles whose applicability to the human
case could subsequently be assessed.

When you deal with the behaviour of babies, for instance, there are very
obvious parallels that can be made with animal behaviour. But as soon as
you start dealing with the behaviour of adult human beings, the
complexities that are specific to the human case become more important
than the parallels in many ways. It's for that reason that I want to lay the
emphasis on principles and not on direct parallels.

MILLER   There are many people who've stayed strictly within the province of
animal behaviour and find that a completely satisfactory domain. What
was it that led you to move from animals to man?

HINDE   Well I suppose that I've always been more interested in the causation of
behaviour than in the evolution of behaviour. If you're interested in the
role of behaviour in evolution or in how behaviour evolved, or in how
species evolved, then you're likely to stay within the animal realm. But if
you're interested in the causation of behaviour, and if in any case you
always have an interest in what it is that makes human beings tick, then I
should imagine that you're very likely to move in the direction in which I
have moved.

I originally studied bird behaviour. I moved from birds to monkeys for
a specific reason, namely that I had been interested in the parent-offspring
relationship in birds. I came into contact with a very remarkable London
psychiatrist, John Bowlby, who was interested in the problem of whether a

brief separation experience between a child and its mother could produce long-term effects on the child's personality development. At that time Bowlby had only retrospective evidence to go on; experimental evidence with man was impossible to obtain, so we decided to set up a monkey colony and to study this particular topic experimentally with monkeys. And I was involved because I'd been working with parent-offspring relationships in birds and there was nobody else around at that time who was interested in these topics.

We found first that a baby monkey shows many of the same symptoms as a human child shows when it's separated from its mother for a while – symptoms of protest and despair and so on. Second, that even a brief separation of a week or so could have, under certain special circumstances, long-term effects on 'personality' development. One has to be very careful how one says that, because it doesn't imply that all monkeys, let alone all children, who are separated from their mothers for a while incur long-term effects on their personality. It *can* happen in certain circumstances.

MILLER   Well in the case of monkeys, was it invariable that separation produced long-term effects, and that it was only in man that it was more variable?

HINDE   No, in monkeys it was, I would guess, just as variable as it is in man. It's one of the illusions that people have about animals, as well as about Chinamen, that all individuals are the same. Of course they're not. The individual variability in animals is every bit as great as it is in man. And the effects of separating one infant monkey from its mother are very different from the effects of separating another one.

MILLER   But underneath the variations, what were the first principles that you could identify which were common to both – other than the fact that separation sometimes produced a sort of long-lasting effect on the personality? Was there something more specific than that?

HINDE   The most important issue was finding that the best predictor of how upset a young monkey would be by a period of separation from its mother was the nature of the mother-infant relationship beforehand. Of course what's good about working with animals is that you can measure things rather more easily than you can with man, and we could measure certain aspects of the mother-infant relationship before separation. We found that in those mother-infant dyads in which the mother frequently rejected the infant's attempts to gain the nipple, and in which the infant had to work hard to stay near the mother when it was off her (that is where *she* didn't accommodate to *it* but *it* had to accommodate to *her*), the infant was most disturbed as a consequence of the separation experience. In other words, the more stressful the mother-infant relationship was, seen from the infant's point of view, the more upset the infant was liable to be as a consequence of the separation experience.

MILLER   Is it possible, by setting up several generations of such dyads, of such pairs, to see why it should be that any given mother-child relationship in primates should be stressful to begin with? Was there any sense in which you could have said that it was likely to be a stressful relationship because the mother herself was the result of a previously unsatisfactory relationship with *her* mother?

HINDE   That's exactly the sort of issue that we should like to get into. One of our main aims is to see how the mother's personality affects the mother-infant relationship, and how the mother-infant relationship affects the personality of the developing infant.

MILLER   And were you able to perpetuate problem families with monkeys?

HINDE   To establish that would take many years, so we can't say that we've done it yet. We've got cross-generational effects, and we can relate the 'personality', if you'll allow me to use that word about monkeys, of the offspring to that of the mother. And that's as far as we've got at the moment.

MILLER   Why are you so anxious to avoid the word personality?

HINDE   It's partly through talking to tedious people who label me as a biologist and say: 'Ah, he's just a naïve biologist who thinks that human beings aren't any different from animals.' That's why I chose my words carefully. But as we were saying earlier, there are, of course, major differences concerned with cognitive complexity in the way in which a human mother looks after her baby and the way a monkey rears her offspring. For instance, a human mother thinks about her relationship with her child and evaluates it according to cultural standards: so far as we know these issues simply don't arise in the monkey world.

MILLER   And yet some ethologists would have us believe that we are nothing other than complicated apes – naked apes, if you like. People find this view objectionable not only because it runs counter to their experience of human life, but because it seems to reduce the dignity of man.

HINDE   I have mixed views about this. So-called human ethology, which involves the application to man of principles and methods that have been developed for studying animals, has had some very good and useful results: for instance it has facilitated the development of objective methods for recording behaviour and so on. On the other hand it has involved, for instance, treating children as though they were fish. And children aren't fish; you need different methods to study children from those used to study fish, and there are things about children which are important that simply aren't relevant for fish. Fish don't have moral development, don't develop a growing moral capacity or anything of that sort. You can't talk about a fish's self-image; maybe it's very important to fish, but we're a long way from ever being able to find out about it.

MILLER   How does your procedure differ, then, in the light of the fact that you're confronting something human rather than animal?

HINDE   Well you've got one important tool which you haven't got with animals. You can talk to people, and that's very important – a fact that human ethologists, in my view, tend to neglect.

MILLER   It's not just a research advantage, though. Doesn't it alter the concept of the material you're looking at? The absence of language in an animal doesn't simply make them into dumb people.

HINDE   No, the human mother may be evaluating her relationship with her child and the results of her evaluation may influence her future conduct with the child. And one can key in on that, and learn something about what the mother feels about her relationship with the child, and about the child's behaviour. It may be that what the participants in a relationship *feel* about what's going on is as important for the prognosis of that relationship as what actually *goes* on.

MILLER   So language has a double role. It provides a research tool in that it enables you to ask questions of your subjects, which you can't do with monkeys, but it is also part of the constitutive characteristic of the creature you're looking at. Would you want to say that it was only through the medium of language that the values which guide a mother's relationship to her child are raised and built?

HINDE   The current climate of opinion is that language is a key issue. But there's no hard evidence one way or the other and, as I said just now, it's becoming apparent that monkeys are more complex than we thought they were, although they don't have language in the sense in which you and I are using the term language at this moment. But there can be little doubt that language is crucial.

MILLER   Because it creates and perpetuates the standards by which the participants in a relationship can judge their own performance.

HINDE   It may also be intrinsic to their judging of their performance. It may be that we can judge our interactions, by virtue of the fact that we have language, in a way in which we wouldn't be able to judge them if we did not have language. So it isn't just the act of judging but it's the capacity to judge.

MILLER   But isn't it even more far-reaching than that? Isn't it through language that we can remodel the standards and values, so that, unlike monkeys which have relatively invariable relationships one to another, we are capable of modifying from one generation to the next, and from one culture to the next? And it's only through language that this can happen.

HINDE   But it's very important to keep a proper balance. It's easy to go off on this tack and say human beings are enormously complicated and can build up traditions or norms from generation to generation and so on, and to get oneself into the position of saying: 'Well then it's no good – this animal stuff is totally irrelevant.' And I don't believe that either. For some research purposes, work on animals is better than work with people just *because* they're simple. Just *because* you can look at some issues unclouded by the complexity of the human case, you can get insights, through studying animals, into principles which *may* underlie human behaviour and whose relevance to man you can then assess.

MILLER   Given that the relationship between a monkey mother and her child is relatively simple compared to man's relationships, what principles can you derive from such a model system which enables you to study human beings' much more complicated situations?

HINDE Well one issue I've already mentioned is individual variation in the response to a separation experience. Another issue in which I would like to think that the monkey work has helped, though it was not the initiating factor in the change in opinion, is over who determines what in a relationship, and specifically in the mother-infant relationship. The question arises, as a child grows or as a monkey infant develops, are the changes in the mother-infant relationship simply due to the fact that the infant gets bigger and stronger and more interested in its environment and so on? To the naïve observer this seems clearly to be the case: the infant gets physically stronger and it can run off and leave its mother. And yet when you analyse the data in detail – and this could be done more easily with monkey data which is 'harder'[1] than human data – it becomes very clear that the rate at which the infant achieves independence is determined in large part by changes in the mother.

MILLER I'd just like to press you a little bit on the question of 'hard' data. What exactly is it that makes the data in the monkey so much recognisably harder than it is in human beings? Is it simply that you can interfere, whereas you're morally disqualified from doing that in a human situation?

HINDE Well, you can interfere in the sense that you can reduce the number of interfering variables; you can keep monkeys under relatively controlled conditions, and that's one issue. You can never control the vicissitudes of human life in quite the same way.

Second, everything happens much faster: monkeys grow up quicker. And so the effects do not require you to work over such a wide span of years. I have had students who work with elephants and they have a real problem because elephants live for a helluva long time. It's pretty bad when you're working with people, who live as long as you do, and good extended studies require really more than one generation of psychologists. With monkeys things happen faster, so that's another reason why their study can be revealing.

MILLER But there isn't any constitutive difference to make one say that the facts of animal psychology are intrinsically harder and therefore more scientific than the facts that we might be able to elucidate from the study of human beings? There are those who would claim that there is something *intrinsically* soft about the human sciences and they would even go so far as to say that it's a contradiction in terms to apply the term 'science' to the study of human nature.

HINDE Yes, I feel very strongly about this. I think it's part of the hierarchy of values that science brings with it. What is most respectable in science is what can be replicated in half a dozen laboratories, and although replicability is a very desirable aim, adherence to that dictum leads scientists away from problems that are important, just because they're

[1] Hard data depends on relatively few interacting variables and thus is more readily replicable.

complicated. That is a bad way to structure scientific values. Just because one can't *easily* achieve replicability, it doesn't mean to say that one should rule out whole areas of science as soft. Because every social situation is different from every other, studies in the social sciences will never be replicable in the same way as, say, experiments in physics are. What counts is the validity of the principles that emerge; they should have generality across situations.

MILLER   All right then. Given that there is a domain of human studies which has a reasonable claim to be considered as a science, what sort of intellectual apparatus does one bring in to the study of human psychology which can improve the chances of making it scientific?

HINDE   Well I'm a biologist by training, as you know, and I would feel that the first issue is an adequate descriptive base. Chemistry became a science with the periodic table for instance, and biology became a science with the natural classification of organisms. In the social sciences, a comparable descriptive base is something that we must look for. And that doesn't imply that I believe in pure description or any of the other things that you might say to me as a consequence of my saying that. But it does mean that description must be an important early goal.

    I think the second thing I would say is that one must be adequately aware of differences in levels of complexity. Within the human social sciences in particular, one is constantly dealing with a succession of levels of complexity, with emergent properties at each level. One of the great problems that social scientists constantly have to grapple with is the relation between these different levels of complexity.

MILLER   What criteria does one use in order to decide that this description rather than that description is a satisfactory one? What is going to count as a good description of a given stretch of human behaviour?

HINDE   Criteria of what is a good description are going to be, first of all: is it related to a problem, and I would say a real life problem and not just an academic problem; and second, does it help you push that problem forward? For instance, does it help you to state the limits of your generalisations? Relevance in other words.

MILLER   The question I'd like to press you on is this: how do you identify what is going to count as a good soluble problem? In physics, it's quite clear what the problems are, and they seem to be quite hard-edged. How have the problems emerged in the study of human relationships, and how do scientists determine the criteria of good description?

HINDE   I feel like doing what you did to me, and saying: 'What do you mean by hard-edged when you talk about the problems that come up in physics?' I doubt whether they're any more difficult to specify or any less difficult to specify than they are in psychology. And that it's only because you and I know less about physics than perhaps we know about psychology, that you say that.

MILLER   But in physics or chemistry the object of study does not have an opinion itself about what it's doing at the time when you're studying it; whereas participants in a human relationship may have opinions about what they're doing which may disagree with your own description of what is going on.

HINDE   Sure. And that's one, but not the only, criterion. Of course in the study of relationships the description must be related to what the participants think is going on. But that doesn't mean that what the participants think is going on is necessarily right. It's only one aspect.

MILLER   What happens when the participants give one account of what they are up to, and you as an observer give a different one? What is going to settle the dispute when there's this kind of conflict?

HINDE   The accounts can be different without conflict. They could both be true, and they could both have validity at different levels of interpretation. This is an example of what I said about making a clear distinction between different levels of complexity.

MILLER   Let's talk about your own work on the relationships between mothers and children, and try to identify the factors which you regard as being relevant to a good observation of such a relationship.

HINDE   Well what we tried to do initially was to sit down and consider which things about relationships in general matter. Not specifically mother-child relationships, but relationships in general. While we do not really know enough about relationships yet to be able to be absolutely specific, one can categorise the *sorts* of things that matter. We came up with a list (fig. 1) of eight categories of what matters about interpersonal relationships.

CATEGORIES OF DIMENSIONS

1 Content of Interactions

2 Diversity of Interactions

3 Qualities of Interactions

4 Relative Frequency and Patterning of Interactions

5 Reciprocity vs Complementarity

6 Intimacy

7 Interpersonal Perception

8 Commitment

FIG. 1

Roughly, these are what people do together; how many different sorts of things they do together; the qualities of their interactions; certain properties that emerge from the relative frequency and patterning of the interactions; the degree of reciprocity or complementarity in the interactions – does one boss the other or are they, as it were, equals; intimacy; interpersonal perception; and commitment. Now those are just categories of dimensions, they're pigeon-holes to help us put our thoughts in order. And, of course, they don't all matter in all relationships.

For instance, the baby's commitment is irrelevant in the mother-child relationship to take an extreme example. But I think these categories provide initial pigeon-holes into which we can put what's important about relationships.

MILLER Let's take some of these categories and consider them in the light of actual relationships. When you talk about the content of interaction – say between a husband and a wife – what are you thinking of?

HINDE Well in our society there are certain things which it is accepted that husband and wife do together, and if they don't do those things together, then we may speak of them as being married only in name. In other words the *content* of the interactions between husband and wife defines the husband-wife relationship. The content of the interactions comes first on the list of categories of dimensions because sociologically we usually distinguish different types of relationships according to what people do together. A mother-child and a teacher-pupil relationship for instance, are different by virtue of the sorts of things that mother and child and teacher and pupil do together. While in both cases the interactions are high in complementarity (i.e. the two partners play different roles), what the partners do differs between the two relationships.

MILLER Are you saying that the relationship is nothing other than the list of the actual interactions that take place?

HINDE Of course not. I'm saying that we differentiate husband-wife relationships from other relationships by virtue of the things that they do together.

MILLER Is there something over and above what they do together which allows us to say of any couple that they are husband and wife?

HINDE In our culture it is expected, for instance, that there are certain qualities of tenderness between husband and wife, that is, that the qualities of their interactions should be of a certain type. Now the extent to which that is a required characteristic of the marital relationship, or an expected characteristic, is a cultural issue which would vary from one culture to another.

Let's take another example. If a mother has her child adopted, you don't say that she has a mother-child relationship, because she doesn't do the things with the child that are intrinsic to the definition of a mother-child relationship. But I do not mean to imply that all socially recognised relationships are definable in terms of the content of the interactions – 'friendship', for instance, is not.

MILLER Let's move on to consider the dynamics of the relationship.

HINDE Well the most basic issue that I would want to emphasise is the necessity for coming to terms with the dialectic linking the relationship between two individuals and their personalities. Every relationship – the properties of every relationship – depend on the personalities of the individuals involved. But it's also true that the personalities of individuals depend upon the relationships they have experienced and are experiencing. There is a sense in which we *are* the people that we have loved and hated. That dialectic is, in my view, one of the crucial issues that psychology must come to terms with.

It's also true that every relationship is affected by the other relationships in which the individuals are involved, and by the social norms current in the culture in which they live. That network of relationships is determined in its turn by the relationships within it, and those social norms are transmitted and transmuted through the agency of dyadic relationships. So there's a dialectic between the social situation and the nature of dyadic relationships with which we must also come to terms (fig. 2).

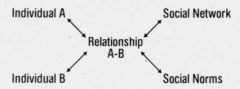

FIG. 2. The dialectics between the properties of a relationship, the personalities of the participants, and the social situation.

MILLER   But there must also be a sense in which what goes on between individual A and individual B and the relationship between their personalities, is not only determined by the relationships which individual A and B have with C and D respectively and so forth, but by the social norms which affect them individually before they enter into relationships one with another.

HINDE   Oh, that's absolutely true, but then it becomes a rather difficult matter of definition as to what you include in personality. The values and norms with which an individual enters a relationship are in a sense part of his personality. And this is also part of the intrinsic difficulty of putting into two dimensions a rather complicated situation that actually continues through time.

MILLER   But you wouldn't want to say, as some human ethologists do, that what is irreducible about individual B is what he inherits from his biological ancestry.

HINDE   You keep on harking back to this issue. I think that there are some very important influences that do not come from the individual's experience, like being male or female for instance. Again, being young or old, to use a less controversial issue, is largely a biological matter, and helps to determine how individuals behave, and how they relate to other people.

MILLER   But there must be features of an individual which one wouldn't want to include in his own personality; what he, as an individual, expects his society to expect of him, for instance.

HINDE   Well now you're getting on to the very interesting issue of how much personality is a constant from one situation to another. What one means by the personality of an individual and how far personality or behaviour is consistent in the context of different relationships, are crucial issues.

MILLER   This raises the whole question of people occupying different roles with respect to one another. But most people would intuitively say that although they occupy several different roles – husband on one occasion and boss on another and so on – they think of themselves as being the same person slipping into one of these roles after another. And that presumably constitutes what they think of as their irreducible personality. But that personality is nevertheless responding to what he identifies and recognises as being the things that are expected of him – (a) in his role (b) as a person. There are certain factors which he will identify in his social environment as being determinants of his own conduct. He would know that certain things were expected of him as a man, and certain things were expected of him as a husband, and so on, before he entered into a relationship with any specific person.

HINDE   Yes, I would agree with that. But I'm trying to look at it from the other point of view. Take another case. If you ask why little girls behave differently from little boys, let's say, it's partly because little girls are expected to behave differently from little boys, and therefore other people give them opportunities to behave in different ways, and elicit different behaviour from them; and it's partly because they are female, and have different hormonal build-ups.

MILLER   Well of course there are those who, at this particular moment in history, would actually find it very objectionable to hear such a claim made about biological differences.

HINDE   Well it doesn't mean to say that there is no overlap between the two sexes or anything of that sort. The ranges of practically every psychological characteristic in males and females overlap extensively. I'm talking about influences, and no more than that.

MILLER   Then, in your own work and in the work of those who study social relationships, there must be an enormous amount to be studied in the area of social norms and this must be done long before you get to the empirical study of how any two individuals respond to them. Because in order to see how two people might prosper or fail within their own relationships, you have to have some accurate description of the social norms themselves.

HINDE   Well I got into this because I believe that the study of interpersonal relationships is a neglected area in the human social sciences. If I can use the same diagram in a slightly different form, I think that one can see the social sciences as shown in fig. 3. Personality theory and much of what we now call psychology are concerned with individuals; while social psychology, sociology and anthropology are concerned primarily with the social network and social norms. The study of relationships is a neglected area in the middle. Developmental psychology and psychiatry are concerned with the two dialectics to which I referred – between personality and relationships on the one hand, and between relationships and the social situation on the other. And that's why I personally believe that we have a real need for a science of interpersonal relationships – not only because of its intrinsic interest but because it is important to every

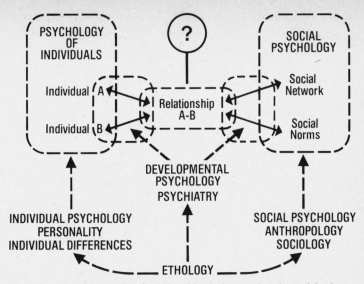

FIG. 3 The role of the study of relationships in integrating the social sciences.

one of us that our knowledge in that area should be increased. Also because it's a sort of necessary glue for the human social sciences.

MILLER   How do you proceed on a day-to-day basis in this neglected area?

HINDE   Well I can tell you specifically what we're trying to do. We're trying to see how the relationships that children have at home relate to what goes on in nursery school, and how it relates to their interaction with their teachers and with their peers. So we're looking at the mother-child relationship, and the child's personality, and then seeing how that personality relates to the relationships that he or she forms at school with teachers and peers. And we're not just watching. We use a variety of instruments to try and get at what the mother feels about her relationship with the child; what the mother feels about the child's relationships with the other members of the family; what the child feels about it all, insofar as it's possible to establish that with young children – and it's not easy – as well as what we can see about what they actually do. And what the teachers think about it all, which is also very important.

MILLER   In the home, then, in watching relationships inside a family, do you actually use the techniques which an animal behaviour student would have used – sitting in hides and watching – or are you in fact a known watching participant in the situation?

HINDE   Some of our techniques are very closely related to the ones that we used with monkeys, and that was a point that I made earlier, that this is one of the contributions that human ethologists have made – though of course psychologists were doing good observational work before ethologists came along. But the point is we're not doing *just* that, for to do simply that is where I feel the human ethologists err; we're trying to get at what the mother feels about the situation, and what the child feels about his relationships with his various family members and with people at school and so on.

MILLER   So in any given stretch of your observations in the home, you're not just a silent, unmentioned spectator of what goes on? You are known to be an interested investigating spectator of what's going on. Are you ever, simply because they grow used to you, something which can be regarded as an eye which is watching, so that the relationship is proceeding without your affecting it?

HINDE   You get the same naïve question, if I may say so, when one watches animals in cages. Do they behave normally? And of course they don't behave normally. And a mother and child with an observer present does not behave exactly as a mother and child without an observer present would do. I think, as a matter of fact, in school the behaviour is very little contaminated by the presence of the observer, but at home it certainly is. But the proof of the pudding is in the eating and the fact is that if there are relations between what goes on at home and what goes on at school, then one is picking up relevant differences between families which may involve also differences in the way in which they respond to the observer but which nevertheless are related to differences in the way that children behave in nursery school. One's not claiming that what one is getting is pure truth. One's teasing out the thing, and contaminating it a little in doing so. But, all the same, getting at real differences.

MILLER   I hope the question didn't arise from a sort of naïve appreciation of the situation. But it's obvious that one's presence as a human spectator in a human situation is not going to have merely a quantitative effect. A monkey does not recognise you as a moral spectator, but in the human situation your moral consideration of what's going on must have an effect on the outcome.

HINDE   You're suggesting that the mothers might be on their best behaviour that day, for instance, and there's a certain amount of evidence that they are, as a matter of fact.

MILLER   Is there a way of discounting the moral self-consciousness of the participants?

HINDE   There are two points here. First, we are concerned ultimately with differences – between families, between relationships, between children. Those differences may or may not arise from the presence of the observer. Those that do may themselves be of interest: how a mother acts in front of an observer may be an important key. However, we do try to minimise them. One approach that helps is to use a number of different instruments in parallel, of observation and interview and test and so on, and relate them to each other. Every approach that one has to studying human behaviour has some problems in it. All observations have some problems, have limitations. Interviews have problems and limitations. Tests have problems and limitations. By using them together and relating them to each other, one can hope to overcome some of these things. I want to be clear that I am not claiming unique success, but we try.

MILLER   Well you might want to claim that your very presence is actually part of what's going on. The reaction of the mother and the child to your moral scrutiny may be one of the things which you would want to observe.

HINDE   That's what I'm saying; it may be an important issue. That's exactly what I was getting at. Not that I wanted to discount it.

MILLER   Perhaps it was unwise of me to use the word 'discount', but what I'm driving at is this. By what criterion, in any given set of pairs that you're studying, are you able to differentiate the conduct that is intrinsic to the relationship, and the conduct that is due to your presence? By what criterion do you separate performances for you and performances between them?

HINDE   We can't separate them out ultimately, but we can get some sort of handle on them, by comparing the different instruments. So that if I find, for instance, that a mother who says her child is very unmalleable and will never do what he's told is also a mother who actually never tells a child not to do anything, I have a deep suspicion that she's not telling him not to do anything in my presence, or in the observer's presence, so that I won't see that child behaving badly.

MILLER   In other words there are consistent differences between pairs which enable you to say – regardless of the complication of your presence – that you could actually see what is going on.

HINDE   Well we can make some progress towards seeing what's going on. I'm not claiming clarity of vision, God knows. I mean if we could have clarity of vision, we'd be there. But one can make some progress towards teasing out these issues.

MILLER   In that case I'd like to ask what may be an even more irritating question. I think that when people are studying areas of biological science in the laboratory, they can foresee advances which might be the result of being able to introduce a certain instrument into the situation. Can you foresee that the progress of this area of science will be hastened by any advance other than a conceptual one? It sounds as if it's something – unlike any other science – where there will be a slow, regular development of its body of knowledge.

HINDE   I don't believe in paradigms displacing each other in this area of knowledge. And I think there's an awful lot of time wasted by people jousting with each other for the honour of their paradigms. What I see happening here is the different paradigms and principles having their areas of applicability defined, and what is needed is an awful lot of slow work. Can I give you an imaginary example? Suppose one finds that some children who have a rather stressful relationship with their mothers are very much oriented to the teacher in school, whereas other children with similarly difficult relationships at home are very much oriented away from the teacher and won't have anything to do with him or her. Then that poses the next question – what makes the difference between these two sets of children? And so one gradually goes on and teases the thing apart, as to the determinants of their different behaviour in school.

I don't believe in breakthroughs.

MILLER It makes a critical difference that you should say that about the area which you're studying, in comparison to the physical sciences, where breakthroughs in a sense are of the essence.

HINDE Well it may be that one day we shall have an $E = mc^2$ or something or other. But we don't, and I do not believe it will come in the foreseeable future. I think an awful lot of people have gone astray through making glib analogies between the social sciences and the physical sciences. They're very different. For one thing the human sciences are much more complicated than the physical sciences. The number of interacting factors is much greater in any problem that one's dealing with, and so complexity is intrinsically greater. In my view it's a matter of hard work and teasing things apart.

dialogue with
Clifford Geertz

NOTIONS OF PRIMITIVE THOUGHT

INTRODUCTION

In the sixteenth century, when European explorers sailed to the previously unknown worlds of Africa and America, they encountered human beings whose habits and customs were almost inconceivably different from the ones which were known in England, France and Spain. With the development of evolutionary theory the idea began to emerge that these people represented an arrested stage in human development, and that by studying the beliefs and practices of the so-called savage, it might be possible to reconstruct a picture of what came to be known as the primitive mind. According to armchair anthropologists who theorised on the basis of anecdotes supplied by missionaries and colonial administrators, tribal magic bore witness to the existence of a pre-scientific mode of thought, one which bore a striking resemblance to that of the civilised child. For someone like Sir James Frazer, author of the seminal *The Golden Bough*, magic beliefs expressed the attempt by a child-like mind to grasp the underlying principles of natural causality. But as anthropologists began to leave their studies and go out into the field, it soon became apparent that the idea of the primitive mind was a reflection on the primitive state of social science, and that there were much more fruitful ways of explaining the apparently simple-minded peculiarities of magic and ritual. Modern anthropologists no longer equate the savage mind with that of the child, nor do they regard tribal man as a fossil remnant of our primitive ancestors. Students who have spent their working life amongst so-called savages are invariably struck by the efficiency, subtlety and finesse with which these supposedly primitive people manage their lives in an unyielding and often hostile environment. Such observations are inconsistent with the belief that the tribal mind is a simpler and more incoherent version of our own, and from the reports of anthropologists such as Professor Clifford Geertz of the Institute for Advanced Study at Princeton who have shared the rapidly vanishing life of tribal man, it has become increasingly apparent that the magical practices which accompany the technical activities of pre-literate people express a different, but by no means primitive, attitude to the world around them.

DISCUSSION

MILLER   The theory of evolution had an irreversible effect on our view of the place of mind in nature, if only because it introduced the idea that mind had a history. I wonder if I could start by asking you what anthropologists now think about the emergence of the human mind?

GEERTZ   About three decades ago – as a result of a new fossil find in Africa – our views changed a good deal. Up to that time the notion had been that the animal that is man emerged as a sort of whole, complete and entire. Archaeologists began to find that different parts of *homo sapiens* evolved at different times. First the chest evolved into reasonably human form and later on the legs and finally the brain became 'more human'.

Fossils began to be found, the so-called australopithecines, which displayed an essentially modern body structure together with brain capacity sizes in the anthropoid ape range, that is to say, more or less the chimpanzee sort of size.

Then, in later fossils, those of the pleistocene – that is, the Ice Age – there was an enormous explosion of brain size. So the question no longer was posed as to what selected out the whole and complete animal. Rather, anthropologists began to reflect on the question of what specific features would, or anyway might, select for such an extraordinary explosion of brain size in what, in geological terms anyway, was a very short period of time; what features might have led, in Darwinian terms, to such a large brain. They began to think about what sorts of things could really have had an effect on that. And the answer became very clear when they began to realise that the brain is heavily involved with culture, that at least some of the selective factors were cultural.

So they began to construct theories about the way in which tools would, in those days, have had selective advantages for those who possessed them – for hunting perhaps; for fighting; whatever. Particularly for hunting, because there were, or so it seemed, tools associated with some of these earlier pre-human animals. So the notion developed that an animal who had a slightly larger brain and was thus able to make slightly better tools would have a selective advantage and that such a culture-nature interaction would snowball and bring on the rapid brain explosion. These days, the same general view is, I think, still held, but now our notion of the cultural factors involved has widened and somewhat changed. The 'man the hunter' sort of image, a sort of macho image of the pleistocene, has now been at least moderated. We know, or think we do, that these early peoples did a lot more gathering of food alongside hunting and that consequently women were rather more important in the whole process, as was co-operation between the sexes. The most recent work, still *sub judice*, seems to show the first example of food sharing and social behaviours of that sort. Social skills, the ability to share, the ability to feel what other animals feel, to react to such other animals with sensitivity, would have, again, a selective advantage in a group which was living and sharing food, in which some people were hunting, some people were gathering, and so on.

Thus, the notion now is that there is this feedback loop between cultural and biological development in the pleistocene (or perhaps even before) such that human culture and the human brain formed in an interactive system. In a sense the brain was selected by culture. It is not that the human brain came first and culture, or rather man's capacity for culture, emanated from it; and this carries the additional implication that the human brain probably could not effectively function outside of culture, that it would not work very well if indeed it would work at all. You get a notion, in short, rather different from what was thought previously when the idea was that there was this entire organism that, as a result of some specific genetic happening, at a certain point made a sudden change or leap to man – suddenly was totally human. Now, the conception is of a much more gradual, more complex mosaic notion of the way in which man's brain and therefore his mentality arose. Now there is no Rubicon to cross, there's no missing link to be found. What has sometimes been called the critical point theory of the emergence of man, in analogy to ice freezing all of a sudden or a plane becoming airborne at a particular instant, is no longer very plausible. The appointment-to-rank image, as it has also sometimes been called – up to now you have been an animal, now you're a man – has been displaced in favour of an image of transition, one proceeding through rapid (geologically speaking) and complex (biologically speaking) development by means of an interaction between culture and biological factors.

MILLER   Now, in the view of the growing development of the mind, anthropologists themselves have developed their own view of the way in which the mind develops, and there was at the end of the nineteenth century an idea that these early stages of the mind were somehow primitive, i.e. they were supposed to have certain characteristics which were very different from what they perhaps rather complacently called the civilised mind. I wonder if you could give some sort of outline of what it was that some of the earlier nineteenth-century anthropologists thought about these earlier stages and where they went wrong.

GEERTZ   Yes. Well they were, as of course almost everyone was at that time, at least in the English-speaking world, heavily dependent upon individualist, associationist psychology. So they thought that the evolution of mind was essentially an intellective business, especially in the first stages. And so, for example, E.B. Tylor[1], who is usually considered to be the founder of anthropology, the first professor at Oxford and so on, had the notion that primitive man saw or experienced things – shadows, dreams, all kinds of hallucinatory effects – which he was unable to explain. And like a very early version of a modern scientist, he then erected an hypothesis to explain these anomalies. He – that is the primitive – postulated the existence of a separable soul, which of course then could be used to account for death as well – when you die your soul leaves; or for trance – your soul departs momentarily. When you are dreaming your soul goes abroad. Tylor's theory was that primitives developed a kind of primitive science, that their attempt to explain the world was a primary driving force behind their thought processes.

Afterwards, Sir James Frazer[2] developed this line of reasoning further in his theory of magic. Frazer says that magic is an attempt by individual primitives to try to explain, and thus to control, the world, in the same way

[1] Sir Edward Burnett Tylor (1832–1917). British anthropologist.
[2] Sir James George Frazer (1854–1941). A British social anthropologist and folklorist. His *Totemism and Exogamy* (1910) developed out of *Totemism* (1887) and *The Golden Bough* (1890), his most famous work.

perhaps that a modern scientist does – only he gets it wrong. Frazer's main distinction, the one for which he is famous in this 'primitive mentality' area, is that between contagious and imitative magic. People developed the notion that if something was associated with something else, physically connected to it, it would have magical power over it. Or, contrariwise, if one thing resembled another it would have power over it. So, for example, if you dance like a deer, it will bring the deer – imitative magic; or, if you get the hair of somebody you can bewitch them, because it, the hair, was connected with them – contagious magic.

Let me give an example from my own fieldwork, which may perhaps make things a bit clearer. My landlord in Java was robbed which, as he was a very poor man, made him very unhappy. In any case, the thief left behind a small cap that he had been wearing. So my landlord took the cap and made it into an effigy of the robber, put it on a spit, and slowly turned it. When I asked him what he was doing and why, he said: 'The thief will have an enormous fever and he will know that I am "cooking" him. Therefore he will come to me for relief. That is, he will go to a curer and the curer will tell him to come here and give the stuff back if he wants to get well. If he doesn't the fever will never stop because I am going to keep turning this thing for as long as it takes,' which indeed my landlord did. That was both contagious magic, because the cap was connected to the man, and imitative magic, because of the effigy and the fever imagery.

So the earlier phases of anthropological thought about 'primitive thought' was essentially cognitive – the response of individual men, or women, faced with unknown aspects of the world, trying to explain and, as best as possible, control them. The trouble with such an approach, of course, is that most magical and religious ideas, such as those about spirits and souls are heavily affective – they are heavily marked with emotionality and passion. The cognitivist kind of theory about primitive thought makes 'primitives' sound like highly intellectual beings – more intellectual beings than any we know, indeed than we are ourselves. Further, it tries to account for all their beliefs in terms of error. That is, they are trying to do what we are doing . . .

MILLER   Only badly.

GEERTZ   . . . only badly. That's right. They are getting it wrong.

MILLER   But wasn't there also the belief, which was perhaps partly the result of evolutionary theory, that by looking at the mental processes of the savage or the primitive, that one was in some privileged way being allowed to look at the childhood of mankind?

GEERTZ   Yes. There was a conception of a childhood of the race, a childhood that was recapitulated in the childhood of civilised individuals. So in Frazer's case, for example, he thought there was an historical progression, an evolution, from magic to religion (which is not so much a matter of mechanical control in his view but more one of propitiating spirits) to science. And he sees that progression – or if he didn't, a number of other people influenced by him did – as being present in the child, who begins by being very magical in his thought, believing in what Freud called the omnipotence of thought, that he could control the world, his mother, or whatever, with his thoughts. Then the child becomes highly propitiative toward the world, trying by beseeching to get out of it what he cannot do by omnipotence of thought means. And then finally he becomes rational, 'scientific', like civilised adults are supposed to be.

In short, the idea was that an analogy could be drawn, really a three-way analogy, between the history of mankind – the phylogenetic history of mankind – the ontogenetic history of the individual – and then, as the third term in the analogy, psychotics and suchlike were considered to be regressive to earlier stages both ontogenetically and phylogenetically.

So in the same sense that there were survivals in culture that harked back to earlier stages – beliefs in spirits and so on – that you can still see today in superstitions, in psychosis you were getting a regression back to some earlier phase of individual psychological development.

Now the trouble with all this, among other things, is that there is virtually no evidence for it – either that these three processes are really parallel, or that the history of the race in fact went through these postulated stages. In fact I think almost no anthropologist now holds this view. The evidence is overwhelmingly against it, or anyway, overwhelmingly absent for it.

The earlier theorists were in fact drawing information from contemporary peoples and then reading it back in time. It was a kind of alchemy that turned space into time and it worked about as well as alchemy works in general. You look at the Australian aborigines for example and you say, well, they are like people of the Ice Age, and to do this is to make, of course, an elementary error. They are contemporaries of ours, not our ancestors, and they have been around just as long as we have, have as long a history and as much development as we have. So the whole 'primitive mind' view rather broke down, logically and evidentially, and besides was so individualistically and associationally based that it left out almost the whole social and affective nature of man.

MILLER   What was the next step then in redressing this error?

GEERTZ   Well, first there arose a concern with the social aspect of the matter. A French philosopher-cum-psychologist-cum-savant – Lévy-Bruhl[1] – said,

---

[1]Lucien Lévy-Bruhl (1857–1939). A philosopher whose study of the psychology of primitive peoples gave anthropology a new approach to understanding irrational factors in social thought and primitive religion and mythology. *Ethics and Moral Science* (1905), reflected the positivism of Auguste Comte. Contending that theoretical moralities cannot prevail, this book laid the groundwork for a pluralistic, relativistic sociology. Much of his subsequent attention was devoted to primitive mentality, which he first examined at length in *How Natives Think* (1926). From the French sociologist Emile Durkheim he adopted the concept of *representations collectives*, or group ideas, which account for differences in reasoning between primitive man and modern Western man. He suggested that primitive thought and perceptions are pervaded by mysticism and that primitive mentality, though not opposed to the laws of logic, is not governed exclusively by them.

'It's not how the *individual* thinks that matters, it's rather the thought patterns of the *entire society* – it is they that make "primitives" think as they do.' He made a very sharp distinction, which he was much abused for and took back a bit in later life, between 'primitive thought' (that is, again, what a *society* shows rather than an individual shows) and modern thought, also collective in this sense. He called the first pre-logical and the other logical. The pre-logical mentality – which is the 'primitive' one – consisted of thinking that things had mystical participations one with another, that you could have an effect on something by the sort of process I talked about in connection with Frazer; but which no longer was thought to grow out of an individual failure to understand, but rather out of a set of concepts, ideas current in the society in which the individual lives. So the whole question got turned around. Instead of saying the reason we have rational science and they do not is because we are rational and grown up and they are not, it's really the other way round. We have rational science therefore we can be rational, whereas 'primitives' cannot because all they have are these odd religious doctrines concerning mystical participations and so on.

As I say, this view too was sharply criticised. These early anthropologists and quasi-anthropologists were not fieldworkers. They did not work among living, so-called 'primitive' people, and so as more and more work came in from people who did indeed work directly among such people, the views of these armchair anthropologists became more or less discredited. Scholars such as Malinowski[1] began to actually go into the field and see how 'natives' *in fact* dealt with their intellectual problems, how *in fact* they actually thought on the ground and in context.

MILLER   Would you say that the view of the infantilism of the primitive mind as seen by people like Fraser and Tylor and perhaps to a lesser extent, Lévy-Bruhl was a reflection of political and social attitudes of colonial powers for whom it was convenient to think of such people as manipulable and manageable children?

GEERTZ   Well it may have been in some cases. But not, I think, in all. Frazer was about as pure a scholar as the world has ever seen. He hardly ever went out of his study. There's a story that once someone came to him in his rooms at St John's and said, 'There's a Fijian down in the street; would you like to go and see him?' and he said, 'My God, no!' He certainly was not politically motivated in any way that one can see. He did have a very strong anti-religious position. He was an agnostic, and along with Tylor, he was part of the great outburst of rationalist utilitarianism that accompanied the Industrial Revolution and the imperialism that accompanied it. But I don't think either one of them, Frazer or Tylor, consciously saw themselves as political, as consciously seeking to advocate the imperialist cause. But I think you are right in a more general way in the sense that their

---

[1]Bronislaw Malinowski (1884–1942) a Polish–American anthropologist whose studies of the Trobriand Islanders during World War II became a classic.

theories were part of the atmosphere of the time, part of the idea that somehow or other the whole history of mankind culminates in us, and therefore one has to discover the stages that led up to us, a view I think that would have seemed rather more plausible then than it does today.

MILLER Presumably it must have been fairly convenient to colonial administrators, to have scholars underwriting the view that the people that they were administering were children, and therefore had to be taken charge of. It allowed the colonial administrator to act *in loco parentis*, as it were.

GEERTZ I suppose so. They would probably have held those views without the help of scholars, but the scholars perhaps did have some role in fixing and justifying such views. Of course such notions are still around, if not so much any more in anthropology. Lots of discussions of what goes on in the world outside of the West still gets conducted in those terms, again for the reasons you mention. In addition, I think there is also a great fear – this goes back to the psychotic business – that there is something about the primitive and the child which is uncanny, like madness is. That of course is a rather Freudian way of putting it, but the 'primitive' like the 'unconscious' is rather frightening, and I think these scholars wanted to tame it, to domesticate it. They said: 'No, primitives are not beyond possible comprehension, totally irrational; they just represent normal stages on the way toward being what we are, and so therefore not to worry.'

MILLER So it was the first impact with *living* societies which began to undermine this view that there was such a thing as a primitive mind. And so what was it that Malinowski encountered which led him to think differently to this?

GEERTZ Well the first thing he found was that, in contrast to what people believed (they thought that 'primitives' couldn't make sense of the world), in practical affairs they were very effective. They really could build canoes so that they sailed and they knew a great deal about gardening and so on. They could hardly have survived if they had not. And even more important, he argued that 'magic' and 'rational thought' were not substitutes for one another. People built canoes as well as they could, made them as seaworthy as they could, and then they chanted over them as long as they could. So it makes very little sense to say, Malinowski claimed, that it all reduces to an intellective problem; there's an emotional dimension as well. Malinowski tried to develop a theory of his own, what he called a functionalist theory, about why then the extra part – extra from our point of view – was there. Why the chants? Why the magic?

There's a very famous passage in Malinowski which every anthropology student gets to hear all about in almost his first class, in which Malinowski contrasts fishing in a calm lagoon (he worked on a South Pacific island) and fishing in the open sea. When his people fished in the lagoon there was no magic involved at all because there was no anxiety, no concern for safety, the waters being calm and tranquil. But when they went out into the open sea with the high waves, there was lots of magic to sustain hope and confidence in a situation which was indeed very chancy. People drowned quite a lot in the open sea; if a storm came up you were more or less finished in one of those canoes, no matter how well it was built. So, he said, developing the functional theory of magic, the function of magic was to sustain confidence in the face of uncertainty – it was the doctrine, in a famous phrase of his, 'that hope cannot fail nor desire deceive'. If you want something badly enough, magic comes into play. The emotional, affective part of the matter becomes central and you begin to construct a set of ideas, an assortment of spells, or a system of religious practices, a cult or whatever, to sustain confidence in activities that are chancy.

Such a formulation does two things. First, it undermines the simply intellectualist kind of approach to the matter; and second, it brings out the social dimension, because this magic is often, especially with fleets of ships or with garden magic, a very complex social affair. So the individualist bias begins to dissolve, and indeed the psychologism with it, and you get a turn toward what is, I think, now the major way of thinking about these matters – namely, that it is illegitimate to attempt to read off from what people believe and do, how their individual minds work in any very simple way. Certainly most people would now hold, although there are always some people who dissent, that the essential cognitive processes of man, the kinds of thinking your brain makes possible, both peripherally and centrally, are essentially the same the world over.

If there are differences, they are very minor. What *is* different – and this goes back to Lévy-Bruhl, but without the sharp contrast he made – is the frame of thought within which people view the world, the conceptions of the world that they have. And insofar as there is any distinction between so-called 'primitives' and so-called 'civilised people' in these terms, it has been more recently ascribed – by an anthropologist named Robin Horton, an Africanist – to the fact the so-called primitive peoples live, or anyway lived, in a situation where there are or were no contrasting possibilities. Their interpretation of the world, while it has some internal complexities, is not tested in competition with other kinds of views. Their world is a closed world. It is not that it is irrational; it is indeed once again explanatory according to Horton (so that he and others who follow him are sometimes called 'neo-Tylorians'). The main reason that such a closed world view can sustain itself in the face of what we would regard as contrary evidence is that there is no other alternative available. That's one argument – or at least part of an argument, now popular in some anthropological circles, though I myself think there are some problems with it. There is another argument which is not contrary to it, but just another way of putting the matter, which is that literacy has made an enormous difference. This view is associated with Jack Goody, who is now the Professor of Anthropology at Cambridge. The notion is that after literacy it is possible to write things down and so to have critical checks on thought that are impossible when there is no writing. You can write things down, you can look at them and reflect upon them, so to speak, at your leisure; other people can look at them and reflect upon them, and you can share them with others much more widely, you can have a discussion of a sort that is not face to face, but is mediated by writing and indeed can reach historically over time so that you can even look back at others' thoughts as they have written them down and so on in a way which is very much harder, so far as it is possible at all, in the society without writing.

So the notion now is that if there is any distinction between 'primitive' thought and 'modern', it lies with the possibilities for self-criticism of thought made possible by contact with other ways of looking at things, either through writing or through widened contacts in general. But both of these matters are social; they are not (to my mind anyway, if not to Professor Goody's) psychological. Nor are they *biological*. There is nothing that has happened to the *brain*. There is nothing different between, say, an African group, and say a modern Western one, in neurological terms – or at least nothing significant at this level. What is significant is this multiplicity of world views that we all now live in and among. And of course it is now not only writing that brings this multiplicity and sustains it, but all sorts of other ways of inscribing thoughts – television, films, cassettes, whatever.

MILLER But nevertheless, one's tempted to ask about the *state* of mind of someone who performs magic over and above the technical manipulations that they use, for example, to make a canoe.

GEERTZ The first thing to say about that is that we really don't know much about it. Anthropology has done very little direct psychological work with so-called primitives. Most of what has been done has been, as I said before, the illegitimate reading from their beliefs to what's in their minds or supposedly so. That's the first part of an answer; that is, that there really isn't very much properly psychological work at all. There are a few studies. For example, those done in West Africa – in Liberia – by Michael Cole and some of his colleagues who have been trying to see how non-literate, mainly traditional Africans compare to educated ones, considered as a control group, how they learned mathematics, and the degree to which they are able to do so.

But there is very little of that kind of work around and even that tends to be again over on the intellective side rather than the affective. Anyway, that's the first part of an answer. The second part of the answer is that I think anthropologists now tend to be rather sceptical about state-of-mind ways of putting things anyway. In the sort of work that one associates with such scholars as Victor Turner, Mary Douglas, and, in a different way I suppose, myself, the view is that thought is, in great part anyway, a public activity. The way to look at thought is not to assume that there is a parallel thread of correlated affects or internal experiences that go with it in some regular way. It's not of course that people *don't* have internal experiences, of course they *do*; but that when you ask what is the state of mind of someone, say while he or she is performing a ritual, it's hard to believe that

such experiences are the same for all people involved, or that you really
ought to trust reports of inner states that you get when you ask questions
like that. The thinking, and indeed the feeling in an odd sort of way, is
really going on in public. They are really saying what they're saying, doing
what they're doing, meaning what they're meaning.

An example of this kind of approach, one which gets away from the
instrumental and the intellective, at least more or less all together, is an
analysis or argument that Susanne Langer[1] made some years ago in
connection with rain dancing among the Hopi Indians of the Southwest.
The usual Western view of this activity is that it's again a sort of Frazer's
false causation kind of reasoning; the Indians think they can make it rain
by dancing and they are wrong. And that's all there is to it. The question
then becomes once more, how could they be so wrong, and you get all sorts
of answers being produced. For example, there's the fallacy of the positive
instance; once in a while it in fact rains and that's enough because people
remember that and are impressed by it; the positive case impresses.

But the answers, this one or others like it, are fairly easily shown to be
quite implausible, and yet the ritual activity goes on, in this case it goes on
over and over again. The Frazer sort of explanation also doesn't really
work because as Evans-Pritchard[2] pointed out in one of his essays, if the
Indians, for example, throw water up in the air in an imitative magic sort of
way, in the dance, they don't really hold this view about the magical effect,
on imitative grounds, of water thrown into the air anytime they throw it up
in the air. They don't think it's going to rain anytime they throw water up
in the air; it's only when they do so in a ritual that it has that meaning or
significance. Just a simple imitative act, throwing water in the air is not the
point. The point is that it is done within a ritual and indeed at a certain
point in the ritual and surrounded by various other symbolic acts of
different sorts. What Susanne Langer suggested as the way to look at this
matter was to see the whole damn thing, the costumes and the rain, as all
parts of a single structure. That is to say the Indians are not trying to cause
the rain in the sense that we would cause rain by seeding clouds or
something; they are, she says, trying to think about the way in which the
various parts of the cosmos as they conceive it, explicitly or implicitly,
connect up with one another. And the cosmos includes them, includes
their dances, includes what they have to do in order to keep the cosmos
whole, to give it that kind of order – sustain, if you will, its order. If it rains,
the ritual of course is a great success. But it is a success rather more like a

[1] Susanne Langer (1895–   ). An American aesthetic philosopher famous for her first
philosophical work, *Philosophy in a New Key* (1942). Her symbolic theory of art is set out in
Feeling and Form and *Problems of Art* and her edited *Reflections on Art*. She is one of the
leading aesthetic philosophers of her time.

[2] Sir Edward Evan Evans-Pritchard (1902–1973). One of the most widely influential social
anthropologists of his day. His monograph, *Witchcraft, Oracles and Magic among the Azande*
(1937), demonstrated the inner coherence and self-validating character of an 'exotic' belief
system in its relation to the social system as a whole.

successful painting is a success, or a successful production of a play is a success. That is to say, as we say, it 'comes off'. When it doesn't rain, something went wrong. One often, perhaps even usually, doesn't know where it went wrong or what exactly went wrong. Sometimes one does; sometimes one doesn't. But in any case it's just a botched or moderately botched affair. The idea is to form the whole. When everything comes together, when you dance and you make all those long preparations that lead up to it, and then in the end it rains, what is reinforced is your conviction that you really understand what the cosmos is like and that indeed you understand your place and part in it.

This is the point that I've been trying to get to; the ritual activity is not conceived as instrumental in the first place. It is considered as expressive or representational or some other term of that sort, none of them quite what one would want. It's seen, by those involved, not necessarily explicitly of course, as an attempt to display to themselves and to reinforce in themselves the fact that the world is the way they think it is. In its way, instrumental activity of course does that as well, simply by indeed working – it shows that you have reliable empirical knowledge. But ritual activity is not, or anyway not necessarily, seen as instrumental in that way – that's not its intent. They, the Hopi or whoever, want rain; they dance for rain – or with rain is probably a better way to put it. But they aren't concerned with it as a bit of proto-science and to inquire into its causal efficacy is to put things the wrong way round and rather to miss the point. That is evident, I think, from the fact that they do both things together as I said before. Malinowski's 'natives' not only check out the fishing line but they also, at least in the open sea, chant. The chants have to be there because otherwise the meaning of the whole activity is not the same.

This is a rather different interpretation from Malinowski's. Malinowski was, as I said, a functionalist. All thought was instrumental for him. It was at the point where your empirical knowledge gives out that you use magical knowledge as a simple extension of it.

MILLER So far as he was concerned, magic *was* coercive in some way. So Malinowski was to some extent still expounding the original ideas of Frazer and Tylor.

GEERTZ Well in a way. He thought it maintained confidence; it did what it was supposed to do. As a functionalist, his main view of 'savages' or whatever – that's what he called them – was that they really were very commonsensical. This is of course quite the contrary to Lévi-Bruhl who thought that they were all caught up in all kinds of mystical confusions, or at least in mystical frames of their own that, logical as we are, we had difficulty understanding. Malinowski on the contrary thought his savages were really plain, sound, straightforward fellows. He claimed that magic was efficacious, or anyway practical, because without the magic and the belief in it you wouldn't put to sea in one of those boats, and you would never fish therefore outside the lagoon and therefore wouldn't get much in the way of fish. Magic works, so he claims, psychologically, to maintain confidence. That's why I and a lot of other people concern ourselves, *à la* Langer, much more with trying to understand what the people themselves think they are up to and try to explain *that*, try to get some sense of what is going on among *them*. We don't try to deduce their reasoning processes from psychological first principles; we try to get some understanding of what the meaning of whatever it is they're doing is for them, what they think they are up to, what, from their perspective, it's all about. If they do that, then I think that any really sharp distinction between primitive thought and modern thought rather dissolves because such a procedure is necessary to understand anyone. You have somehow to find out the frame of what they think they are about in order to understand what it is they are up to.

MILLER   In that case one would want to know what was so peculiar about '*civilised*' life, which led to the progressive withering away of such ornamental activities. If it is not just the growing-up of the mind what could it be said to be?

GEERTZ   Well, here I would say two things. First, I think it is easy to exaggerate how much it has withered away. It's not merely that there are superstitions and that people still do and believe all sorts of odd things. There are, more importantly, all kinds of symbolic frames around their activities to give them meaning.

A scientist puts on a white coat, there are all the trappings of politics and so forth and so on. Not everything we do is directly instrumental either, though the scientists will try to tell you a story about purity and antiseptic states and so on. We don't notice these frames, or at least not usually, because they're ours. But some future anthropologist or historian will look back on the sort of things that go on in British or American politics and wonder what the devil they were all about, why it was all this uninstrumental, expressive activity was going on. And he or she will try to understand it, in about the same way as I try to understand, for example, traditional Balinese politics in the nineteenth century as I look back on them not only in time but from a cultural distance.

Not all of the rituals of politics, whether they are royal marriages or openings of Parliament, are instrumental activities – activities functional to the governing of the country in a very narrow sense. They are a way of expressing what the participants – that is, us – think that the polity is all about, what we think politics *is*. Walter Bagehot[1], in *The British Constitution*, made a contrast between the efficient parts of government and the dignified parts of government. And the whole ceremony of public life, he tried to argue, was not just laid on top of things and basically irrational or silly. Rather it had something to do with sustaining belief in

[1]Walter Bagehot (1826–1877). An English economist and journalist. His *English Constitution* (1867) is still considered a classic work. He applied the theory of evolution to politics, as in *Physics and Politics* (1872).

authority; why people do the things they do without coercion much of the time, how authority is devolved and so on.

So the rituals that, for example, open Parliament here or that in my country surround elections, are all hardly to be understood as mere frills and ornamentation. Think of all the things that people do in American political campaigns. For example, they give the same speech over and over again. The reason for this has to do more with establishing a persona, establishing a sense of authority, and not, or anyway not very much, with formulating, or even promoting, policy. That kind of symbolic context still exists in all sorts of places in modern life. You can overestimate quite easily, I think, how rational we are, in the instrumental sense, anyway, of rationality. We don't really go around being quite so cold eyed as we think we do; we lack perspective on our own views. When one is working in Java or Morocco as I have, one finds the Javanese or Moroccans think *we* behave rather oddly, that we do rather peculiar things in the same way that we think at least some of the things that they do odd or at least difficult to comprehend. They don't see the purpose of what we're up to and why on earth we go through all the rigmarole we in fact go through.

The second aspect of the matter is the construction or development of social institutions which make it possible for society to be highly rational in certain contexts – science is the best example – without the people who are engaged in the activity being themselves necessarily particularly rational in general. I mean they can be, as persons, quite strange; but the procedures under which they operate are established and institutionalised. If you are going to be a doctor or a physicist, there are things you have to think and ways you have to think in, certain ways you have to act and behave as well, at least in the laboratory or on a ward. Again, there are lots of rituals connected with, for example, medicine, rituals which sociologists and anthropologists have in fact studied, analysing how doctors and nurses and patients in either regular hospitals or mental hospitals behave, stressing how much of what they do is designed to sustain a conception of what's going on in the place, independently of anything they may be doing to the body or the mind, in a therapeutic sense. So you have set-apart areas, roles even, where you can be rational in your thought and in your activity. But that is again partly because you or they are surrounded by a non-rational or arational or ritualistic or symbolic or expressive – the terms here involve all kinds of complicated controversies – context which sustains and makes such rationality possible.

MILLER Let's take the use of the word 'irrational'. Is it so unreasonable to say that such displays of 'irrational' activity, whether they're exemplified by a child or by an American politician at a convention, or by a tribesman, are instances of primitive thought. I can see that there are certain scruples which might be offended simply because we're bending over backwards in the attempt not to condescend any longer to primitive people. I notice how much you flinch at using the word primitive at all.

GEERTZ Yes, I do. It's not done in my circles any more. I think the analogy is – as I've said before – very dangerous. We're talking about 'primitives', – in shudder – quotes. But we're talking about 'primitive' *adults*. We're not talking about children, who have not yet become adults. We're not talking about adults whose minds have gone awry in some sort of way. We are talking about – for their society in any case – standard, normal, everyday adults. And the kind of rationality that we talked about before, that no one ever tries to grow corn just by chanting and so on, must have been there, as I also said earlier on, in the very beginning stages of truly human evolution. The hunters *did* know how to hunt. They may have chanted over their spear points but they also knew how to use them. So I don't want even to postulate two forms of thought. Dancing around in a circle before you went on a hunt, dancing like a deer so you could catch a deer, which we see even on the walls of the caves, and knowing how to make a good spear point, one which would actually bring down the deer – both of those ways of thinking have been there all along. They have both been there and both been developing since – well, there is no beginning – but since we began to have the interaction of culture and brain that I talked about.

I myself don't like actually the irrational-rational terminology, though I admit I don't quite know what words to use instead. But the important point is that instrumental activity of the hunting-gathering sort and symbolic expressive activity of the rain dancing sort have to have been there, have to have developed together. They have to have developed together over this period of time. That's not true for children, because other people see to it that they don't fall out of windows, or for psychotics, because somebody usually has to see to it that they don't jump out of windows. This is the part of Malinowski's point that I think is still valid; 'primitives' really are extraordinarily skilled. I have never myself worked with hunter-gatherers, but with people who are politically and technologically rather sophisticated, in Bali, Java, and Morocco. But in Bali, for example, they have a very developed irrigation system; they are among the best such traditional rice irrigators in the world. They know things about rice that they taught the Dutch when the Dutch came. Wet rice growing is a very complicated, highly technological business ecologically; a terrace is an aquarium. It has to be maintained and managed. It is quite demanding: the Balinese have water tunnels, aqueducts and dams. They are thus, if anything, *hyper*-rational about rice. But besides these, I think, quite advanced technical skills, they also have constructed an enormously elaborate ritual around rice growing. And it's hard to think there was any time when they had the one without the other, the technology without the rite. They may have been both less developed at one time, they may have been less good at the technical part and the ritual may have been simpler – who knows? But the notion that the ritual preceded the instrumental, that the symbolic part comes first or came first and then out of that people developed the rational part is the kind of mistake that the child-psychotic-primitive analogy can lead you into.

I don't think there is anything particularly primitive about artists or children or psychotics. In these terms peoples are all equally primitive and they are all equally modern. Where they differ, of course, is in degree of sophistication in any particular direction. You can develop matters in one line or the other, of course. The West certainly has specialised in science, at least since the seventeenth century, and before to some extent, in a rather striking way; developed it beyond, I think, anyplace else. There is no doubt about that. I think myself the Javanese have developed dance in an extraordinary way. But there is nothing more primitive or developed in that contrast as such. And there is nothing that I know of in the archaeological record to suggest that once we were all symbolic and then we got more and more rational as the symbolic sort of dropped away.

MILLER   Well in that case do you think that there is an inescapable degree of symbolic ritualistic activity which is as built into the human mind as the rationality which we now so much pride ourselves on? So that no matter how sophisticated we become, and no matter how many alternative opinions there are, techniques of literacy, electronic records and so forth, there would always be, no matter how 'civilised' we became, this element of the symbolic, the ritual, the protective, the 'superstitious'?

GEERTZ   Yes, that's exactly what I think. I think that, and I also think that the distinction between the instrumental and the ritual is not so sharp. This goes back to what I originally said about the brain – the human brain – being dependent upon culture; that it probably could not exist and that we could not function outside of culture. Apes can do things without a cultural context, or at least one of our sort, because a lot of things are wired in that are not wired in to us. We have to learn and develop, something that is true for so-called 'primitives' as much as for anyone else. They too need to have some sense that they know what's going on. They need to have a sense that the world is reasonable and even if they don't understand it, that it can be understood, and therefore they have, as we do, rituals to sustain that notion.

They, like us, have to answer questions, the reasons for premature death, for example, which just aren't answered by science, not because science is inadequate, but because it doesn't answer questions like *that* – it doesn't ask them, therefore it doesn't answer them. So life, for the acculturated animal, the culture-dependent animal we are, always involves at the centre of it, a search for at least *some* level of coherence of meaning, for the significance of what's going on. A sense that we know who we are, that we know what the world is *like*, and that we have some purchase on what's going on; that it isn't just one damn thing after another. That it isn't chaos. We have to think we have an understanding, however partial, of what's happening to us. And that 'have to' will never go away, because there's no way in which instrumental activity can altogether satisfy us. So I think that symbolic, ritual, 'primitive' thought, will always be with us. I can't imagine, for example – to resort to something we were talking about earlier – a wholly technocratic politics, because there would be then no foundation for authority. I don't think that technical efficacy alone could sustain the kinds of authority that we need in any complex society, perhaps any society at all, without some symbolic affirmation of prime ministers or presidents or queens or first secretaries or village chiefs or something. That sort of thing just has to be there, or at least so it seems to me. Panoply of some sort is inescapable. Even though as you say, those who actually indulge in it can hardly see it as irrational. And anyway I don't think it is irrational. I don't think ritual and so on is irrational any more than I think it's primitive. My argument is that it's all part of human rationality. Insofar as one can speak of 'rational' and 'irrational' thought – and I think we can – they occur in both instrumental and symbolic domains.

MILLER   Would you say that the recrudescence of mystical, occult practices that are going on in the West are the expression of a *flight* from rationality? Some attempt to reconceive the universe in terms other than the technological?

GEERTZ   Most certainly. It seems at least for many people that traditional modes of making sense of the world no longer seem to work. They seem to break down. For a long time after they begin to break down, people often hold to them mainly by force of will, because they have got to believe something. After a while that doesn't work any longer and people reach for ideas from all kinds of places. For most people that doesn't work either. The number of people in our civilisation who can really make, say, Buddhism work for them is, I think, rather small because it really doesn't go well with the rest of our lives, at least for most of us. For the rest, and as I say that's really the majority of us, the only hope is some sort of reconstruction, not of traditional views, but of an interpretation of the world growing out of what we now know about it, whether through science or otherwise. But certainly a flight from rationality is a great part of what is taking place now, especially among the thoroughly bewildered. People can stand not knowing or not understanding this or that; but they can't or at least not for very long stand the notion that the world is *absurd*, that you can't understand it at all, that there's no meaning to it at all.

As soon as that mood appears, some very odd – irrational, aberrant, whatever – phenomena occur because the normal course of symbolic formation has been frustrated. How the social imagination is going to work in the modern world to construct meanings that scientists and modern men and women can live with, without going off into strange cults or becoming hypertraditional – neither of which will work in my opinion anyway, in the modern world – is a deep question.

MILLER   But you wouldn't regard these new cults as regressions to primitive thought?

GEERTZ   No, I wouldn't. I think they're desperate, sometimes poignant attempts – especially by younger people – to try to use whatever's lying around in the world these days to get themselves oriented. They try to put their world together by themselves and that can't be done, or at least I don't see how it can be done. It's a social process, such meaning construction, not something to do by one's self or even with a few friends. But I don't think for the most part it's necessarily a regression. It's a matter of people who essentially don't know what to make of things, trying to make it up all by themselves, and therefore not doing a very good job of it. Some of this activity is regressive in a quite clinical sense. Jonestown is, or was, an example of what can happen as the whole thing snowballs and genuinely psychotic developments arise and take control of an entire group of people. But the attempt to try to make sense of the world, however ineptly or with whatever strange materials, is not in itself to my mind a psychotic or pre-psychotic sort of thing to do. Indeed everyone does it; it's just that it gets harder and harder for some people to do it; perhaps to some degree it gets harder and harder for all of us. And if they are psychologically disturbed themselves, then the whole thing can, as I say, snowball into a pathological process and you do get the Jonestown kind of outcome. But the effort doesn't seem to me to be regressive in and of itself, and indeed it's the absence of some way to make sense of things that leads to the collective madness.

12

dialogue with
Ernst Gombrich

PSYCHOLOGICAL ASPECTS OF THE VISUAL ARTS

INTRODUCTION

In a lecture which he gave at The Royal Society in 1974 Sir Ernst Gombrich recalls his Sunday walks in his native city of Vienna, where the Museum of Natural History and the Museum of Art History confront one another on opposite sides of the square. He remembers his eagerness to visit the Museum of Science, and points out that it was only later that he frequently took the turn to the right and 'got stuck, as it were' in the Museum of Art History. It turns out, however, that Sir Ernst Gombrich never 'got stuck' at all, and that although he went on to become one of Europe's most distinguished art historians he never lost his original interest in science. In a great book entitled *Art and Illusion* he triumphantly reconciled his two concerns by dealing with the psychology of visual representation. As soon as it was published in 1956, *Art and Illusion* was universally recognised as an intellectual landmark, and since then any serious discussion of pictorial representation has had to take Gombrich's argument as its starting point.

According to Sir Ernst Gombrich, the task of setting down a pictorial likeness on a flat surface bears a startling resemblance to the method used by scientists in arriving at a theoretical picture of the natural world. In representing the appearance of things the artist does not simply trace an outline of their visual contours, but prepares instead a hypothetical construction to be matched and then modified in the light of further experience. Through an alternating sequence of 'makings and matchings' the artist gradually eliminates the discrepancies between what is seen and what is drawn, until the image on the flat surface begins to resemble a view of the world as it might be seen through a transparent pane of glass. Gombrich's representation of picture-making coincides very closely with Professor Popper's conclusions about the construction of scientific theories. The 'makings and matchings' of the artist correspond to the 'conjectures and refutations' of the natural scientist. Both of these arguments coincide in their turn with Professor Gregory's views about the constructional character of visual perception. In all three we witness one of the most important aspects of the revolution that has recently taken place in the philosophy of mind. The traditional picture of the mind as a mirror of nature has given way to one in which active conjecture plays a leading role.

DISCUSSION

MILLER   In England where art and science are visualised as being at opposite poles it comes as rather a surprise to find an art historian considering the physiology and psychology of vision. So I'd like to start by asking you how and when you first moved from the consideration of the artefacts of art to a consideration of the way in which the artefacts of art illustrated something about the way in which we see and the way in which we represent the world around us.

GOMBRICH   Well, as you know, I studied the history of art in Vienna and the Viennese school of art history has always leaned towards a scientific, rational approach towards art. The great Alois Riegl[1], who wrote around the turn of the century, tried to explain the development of style in terms of various modes of perception; you may remember that Bernard Berenson[2] talks of 'tactile values' in painting. Riegl thought that in the age of the impressionists the whole history of art had moved from touch to purely optical sensations. I don't believe that he was right but you can see that this is an angle which prepares for my direction of interest.

Now I was lucky at the time when I studied to be asked by a friend, Ernst Kris, who was keeper at the Kunsthistorisches Museum and also a disciple of Freud, and editor of *Imago*, to join him in an investigation of the history of caricature; and caricature, of course, raises many psychological problems, including problems of perception. So I was introduced very early in my life to the general problems of images rather than of great works of art; after all, nobody would claim that every successful caricature is also a great work of art.

When I came from Austria to England in 1936, I joined the Warburg Institute which concerned itself no less with the symbolic meaning of humble images than with that of great works of art. When, later, I did war work in the BBC Monitoring Service, the problems of perception, at that time of auditory perception, impinged very directly on my work of listening to broadcasts, and on the relation between what one knows, what one expects, what one believes to hear and what one actually hears. All these things were our daily bread, as it were, and having started with interests of this kind, of course I pursued them. So when I returned to the Warburg Institute and to my previous work, it was natural that I asked myself these questions with ever greater urgency. What actually is going on in the development of a naturalistic or realistic style? This was the subject I chose for the Mellon Lectures in 1956, which turned into the book *Art and Illusion*.

MILLER   And in *Art and Illusion*, if I can try to summarise the thesis, you proposed the idea that we do not have an 'innocent eye' that produces the image, which we then merely copy on to paper when we make art.

GOMBRICH   Yes that was one of my main points. To compare the eye with the camera, which seems so obvious, is certainly misleading. We all know that painting or drawing has to be taught, that nobody who hasn't learnt it can produce a naturalistic image, a portrait or a topographical view, even though this is infinitely easier for us today than it once was, because we see images and photographs all around us. Before these aids or models came into being it

[1] Alois Riegl (1858–1905) was an eminent Austrian art historian whose writings on the history of ornament, on Late Roman Art and on the Dutch Group Portrait are of great theoretical interest.

[2] Bernard Berenson (1865–1959), the great American connoisseur who mainly lived in Florence first developed his psychological theory of aesthetics in his influential essay on *The Florentine Painters of the Renaissance*, 1896.

was certainly very difficult to create a naturalistic image. So the first question I had to ask was how this skill was acquired in a learning process extending over centuries.

MILLER   But you point out also that there is a sort of spectrum which extends from what one would call the conventional representation of the outside world to the naturalistic. Now perhaps we could try and illustrate what is meant by the distinction between the purely conventional and the so-called naturalistic. Let us take some well-known symbols. These (fig. 1) are conventional representations, in the sense that there is no resemblance between them and a woman and man. But nevertheless they can be read as standing for the two sexes.

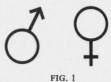

FIG. 1

GOMBRICH   These, if I may interrupt, are old astrological symbols for Mars and Venus which were very recently adapted for modern purposes but which had been adopted by biologists a little earlier.

MILLER   Yes, and yet there is absolutely no point of resemblance, no isomorphism, between these.

GOMBRICH   Well, I don't want to go into this in too much detail but there may be an element of isomorphism here after all. They might be less easily remembered if you switched them round.

MILLER   Well let's go, then, to the next stage. We have here something (fig. 2) which is a great deal nearer to the visible difference between men and women than the conventionalised astrological signs, although no one would pretend that they were actual illustrations of men and women.

FIG. 2

GOMBRICH   They show what in language are called distinctive features and it is these distinctive features which allow one to choose the right door in this particular situation.

MILLER   So in other words what's important about them is not so much the specific appearance of any one, but the fact that you know that one is an alternative to the other so that you don't make a disastrous mistake.

GOMBRICH   Precisely. Because there is, as you say, not a very great deal of photographic resemblance between these conventionalised signs which are conventionalised for easier reading from a distance. They are also easy to read because they are pictograms. I believe that this convention developed after the war and spread from airports, where there are many people who don't know the languages, to other such institutions. I remember having seen one in a genteel pub where the doors were marked by colour reproductions of paintings by Lawrence or Gainsborough: one representing a boy and another a pretty girl.

MILLER   With the Dürer *Adam and Eve* (plate 1) there is now a much closer resemblance.

GOMBRICH   This I would say is what is called an idealised representation of the male and female body based on the proportions of the antique; it allowed Dürer

PLATE 1

to construct the image in the right proportions which interested him so much when he came to Italy.

MILLER   And yet, although it's idealised, if this, for example, were to be included in a space capsule and launched out into outer space to convey some information of what the human race looked like, it might give some sort of information because there is a basis of resemblance.

GOMBRICH I wouldn't bet on this spacecraft image, because they might think that human beings have curious stripes and patches on their bodies and that this arm which is in fact foreshortened is just so short. You have to learn to 'read' such an image in order to get the right information. How should anybody guess that Eve very probably had long hair flowing down her back and this isolated bit wasn't a clipped lock?

MILLER   Yes but nevertheless within the limits of the convention of *engraved* representation, which has cross hatching and so forth, and within the limits of the idealisation and conventions and styles of that particular period, there would be more information conveyed about our appearance here than there would be by something which was purely convent-ionalised; where there was no attempt to represent our appearance.

GOMBRICH Given that you know what the conventions are, certainly it includes much more information.

MILLER   And, of course, we're apparently already proceeding towards much more resemblance with the photograph.

GOMBRICH The photograph not only *claims* to represent, it *does* in fact represent, one aspect of a person just as television images also represent people exactly from one particular point of view.

MILLER   Yes. But nevertheless I think the point that you make is that although one can construct a spectrum, which goes all the way from the purely conventional to what purports to be the realistic and the naturalistic, a point which you make so startlingly in *Art and Illusion*, is that even within what we take to be the idiom of realism, there are large elements of the conventional. And the artist cannot proceed in the absence of conventional schemata, to use a word you use frequently in *Art and Illusion*, when working towards representation. Now perhaps you could explain that exactly.

GOMBRICH Yes that is what I wanted to show. To build an image you have to start somewhere and the easiest starting point is a kind of minimal model of what you want to represent, be it a manikin or a house or a tree, which has to incorporate some of those distinctive features of which we have been talking. You can then go and correct or modify this minimal model – which I call a schema – till you approximate what you want to represent or what you see in front of you and this approximation I call matching. In this way making the model comes before matching it with reality. So you have these two formulas, 'schema and correction' and 'making comes before match-ing', which mean approximately the same.

MILLER   Now this, to some extent, goes against the commonsense view of what someone is doing when he or she is drawing an object. The commonsense view would be, I think, that it consists of a transcription of an image upon your own retina which you see as a privileged spectator sitting behind your eyes. And the outcome depends entirely on your manual skill rather than on some psychological skill.

GOMBRICH It seems to me that this naïve view of the 'innocent eye' is contradicted by the very fact that we have to learn to draw or paint – that you need to have a kind of language of schemata or representations in order to approximate what you can actually draw (on the canvas or on a piece of paper) to the appearance of what you have in front of you. On the other hand, I am always anxious to stress that this does not mean that there are no images which are less conventionalised than others and in particular I have never claimed that there are no such things as facsimiles or duplicates. When you speak of a three-dimensional object like a fruit it seems to me quite clear that you can make a replica of the fruit which looks very much like the real thing; in fact you may be tempted to bite into it. There is no room for relativism here because this possibility of deception exists for children and sophisticated people. We've all been foxed by three-dimensional wax images at Madame Tussaud's, so I am very anxious to stress, when discussing the development of naturalistic art by 'schema and correction', that I do not mean that the end-product cannot come pretty close to producing the identical perception we may have of the motif represented; only what we here mean by 'pretty close' differs according to the medium. Not only an artificial fruit but also a human head in the round, in other words a piece of sculpture, can be a closer imitation of nature than any two-dimensional image on canvas or paper. You cannot paint a 'facsimile' of the view from your window.

MILLER So you're saying, then, that most of the great problems in the history of the representation of the outside world consist of choosing to try and make our facsimiles out of materials other than those that the world is made of; and particularly by trying to show it on a flat surface.

I suppose the most vivid example of that is this sixteenth-century picture in the Castelvecchio in Verona (plate 2) where this child gleefully confronts posterity almost as if mischievously he knew the extent to which his self-portrait will resemble his counterparts in the twentieth century.

GOMBRICH Quite. It is also a manikin; it is a minimal model of a human being, two legs, two arms, eyes, nose, mouth, hair, but it isn't in the same sense a likeness as we presume the painter's portrait of the child must have been.

MILLER What we have in the same picture, of course, is the painter's portrayal of the little boy which is much more of a likeness than the little boy's portrayal of himself.

GOMBRICH Indeed, look how the gleam in the eye, the captivating smile, the texture of the hair, are rendered.

MILLER Now you say in *Art and Illusion* that we can learn a lot about the use of schemata by looking at the way in which a child draws. This has changed

PLATE 2

very little in 500 years, even 2000 years, and I'm sure that pictures by Egyptian children were exactly the same. The boy is using a schema which is always the same at a given stage in a child's development.

GOMBRICH   Yes I think that's roughly true. Though our children are also influenced nowadays by the picture books they see or the shows they watch they are pretty impermeable to these influences. They may be more dissatisfied with what they draw and say, 'Mummy how do I draw a tree?' but they do not therefore draw trees differently.

MILLER   Yes, but the point you make is that one should never run away with the idea that because a child *represents* its world like this, the child is in fact *seeing* its world like this. If the mother were to walk in looking like the child's picture of its mother, the child would be frightened.

GOMBRICH   I think it would be very frightened and rightly so. The main point here is the one you touched on before – that we live in a three–dimensional world, we move quite effortlessly around in the world, we have two eyes, we see the world in three dimensions. The problems of transposing this experience – this visual experience of our world – on to a flat piece of paper or canvas is much more formidable than earlier students of art may have realised; and that is perhaps the reason why they spoke so glibly about primitive art not being able to represent the world as we see it. You simply can't represent the world as you see it, because the world is three-dimensional and you see it as three-dimensional. What you have to perform is a reduction of a very complex character.

MILLER   And you're saying that in the child's attempt to represent the three-dimensional world in a two-dimensional fashion, it tends to proceed by some schema which at that stage is a long way from the sort of image that it might have produced if it had had a more sophisticated education. Now what would you say was the characteristic of the schema which is used by the child in representing its world? How does it differ from a more sophisticated representation like Constable's for example?

GOMBRICH   It is, to repeat, a kind of minimal model. If a child wants to make a motorcar out of those wooden blocks children are given as toys it may sometimes be happy with any block which can be pushed along, or it may try to add wheels, but it will never incorporate all the features of a motorcar. This minimal model serves it very well on the nursery floor in very many contexts, and serves it equally well in drawings. Look at a typical child's drawing; you see the trunks, leaves, and the fruit of the tree, the house with the smoke, the sun, the blue stripe of the sky which is a separate entity and not put behind the house because it is seen as something different.

MILLER   Do you think the child's model, the child's schema, is determined by a *linguistic* model of its world? There is a sense, as you point out in *Art and Illusion*, in which these pictures are not really pictures in the adult sense but are really enumerations or inventories of the things which the world contains. To what extent do you think this is determined by the fact that the child is beginning to learn a language which enumerates identifiable things in the world, and that in drawing, it is listing its vocabulary rather than showing its experience?

GOMBRICH   I would very much doubt that the parallel is quite so close. I've been toying with this idea but I do think that, first of all, the vocabulary of children differs much more than their drawings do. Children may very well know about, let us say, roof tiles, which they do not represent. It depends whether they have had any experience of this or other features, such as glass panes – 'open the window', 'close the window' – all these things which are not necessarily incorporated in the model. So I would be a little careful. I know that a comparison has been made between early speech and early drawing. But things are usually a little more complicated than such comparisons indicate.

MILLER   But what do you think is the next stage in child development – when it goes from a schema which is an enumeration of items towards a unified appearance of things as they look? How does the schema actually modify itself?

GOMBRICH   I don't think we can look at it in isolation as if the child were a sort of Robinson Crusoe. The child very soon looks across the drawing surface and peers at his neighbour's work at school. Sometimes a particular trick such as how to represent eyes or lips or ears sweeps through a classroom very quickly, sometimes not to the benefit of the beauty of these drawings. But children learn from each other. They, of course, also learn from their teachers unless the teachers are determined not to show them anything (which happens), and they learn from the pictures they see around them. So they are very soon aware of the fact that a tree, by and large, hasn't got such a huge trunk and that smoke doesn't look like that and they may ask: 'How do I represent smoke?' In other words they grow up in a world of images, unlike the craftsmen of 'primitive' tribes, with whom they have sometimes been compared. The social situation is totally different and the function of images is equally different in different cultures. After all, these children's drawings which we now admire or like are produced partly to pass away the time, though they are produced particularly to impress parents or teachers who will always say, 'my, isn't that lovely', and this determines the way the child goes on.

MILLER   One of the points that you're making is that to some extent our schemata – these models that we use as stepping stones towards representation – are thieved and borrowed from our friends and our colleagues and, of course, from tradition.

GOMBRICH   Yes they are.

MILLER   And you make the point very strongly in *Art and Illusion*, that there is hardly a great artist who has not proceeded from some model or precedent which he has borrowed from others.

GOMBRICH   Yes I am absolutely convinced of the fact that what we call style is something very similar in some respects (though not in other respects) to language. That art, like science, is cumulative in the sense that one generation learns from the other but modifies and corrects what the previous generation has done. This is not true of a very static civilisation like Ancient Egypt or Byzantium where there is no desire to surpass or improve on what has been done before but rather to create an image of the same power and the same expressiveness as the one you find in the Church or the temple.

MILLER   And this applies just as much to a great genius as it does to some amateur groping his way towards representation by using an art instruction book.

GOMBRICH   Most certainly. All geniuses also had teachers they studied, and they drew after other artists. We know that during the Renaissance it was a rule that the apprentice went to draw after works of art in churches. Michelangelo went out and drew after Masaccio's frescoes in the Carmine and, of course, though he might not have liked to admit it, he learnt a lot from his teacher

Ghirlandaio. There is no other way of becoming an artist. Constable said, 'a self-taught artist is one taught by a very ignorant person', which is all one need say about it.

MILLER   This often comes as a surprise to the public, many of whom think that the mark of a genius is the solitude of his enterprise, and that what distinguishes him as a genius is his ability to create these representations without guidance. Whereas the point you're making is that this never happens at all.

GOMBRICH   I don't think it *can* happen, though this doesn't exclude the fact that artists may be lonely; but artists, just as they had to learn to speak and to walk and to eat, had to learn to paint, to hold a brush, to stretch a canvas and, much more important, to plan a picture. I often say that a picture is not so much invented as discovered. The artist discovers fresh effects which he can put to use in his own work. If he had never seen, let us say, a picture which looks three-dimensional, in perspective, he couldn't have even been aware that this is a possibility. What he can do is to look at a painting which is three-dimensional but a little unconvincing in the way it hangs together spatially and say, 'I must really see whether I cannot improve on this', and this is what I mean by schema and correction.

MILLER   And making first and then matching.

GOMBRICH   Then matching. Stepping back from his canvas or fresco and looking at it as if he were the beholder and saying, 'there's still something wrong here, what can I do?' Sometimes this can be reasoned out; sometimes it is through trial and error that he arrives at a better solution. The importance of trial and error is illustrated in countless sketch books of artists where you see them experimenting with postures, positions, groupings, until they get it right. This is really the experimental part of all artistic enterprise.

MILLER   And some of those sketches or experiments may include models which are borrowed from another artist. You mention in *Art and Illusion* the touching relationship between Constable and Alexander Cozens, and point out that Constable, who is always thought of as the master of clouds, copied Cozens' etchings of clouds into his notebook.

GOMBRICH   Any great artist will always be interested in what his predecessors have done and will try to learn from their work. I think this has always been the case and is likely always to be so. Even cubism which looks like an entirely fresh beginning is known to have started from an observation of certain effects in Cézanne. Cézanne didn't want to be a cubist but he faceted his pictures in a way which intrigued Braque and Picasso, so they used this device as a starting point for a completely new style.

MILLER   Now in raising the distinction between making on the one hand and matching on the other, you mention the extent to which this process in art resembles a similar process in scientific discovery. And your friend Karl Popper, of course, has made much of this relationship between conjecture and discovery.

GOMBRICH   I think one must first say that this relationship exists, but only in styles which aim at the representation, or faultless representation, of, let us say, a human body or of a distance in a landscape or of a sunlit leaf. There is a passage in Leonardo in his *Treatise on Painting* in which he claims that he is the first artist ever to have painted the effect of sunlight showing through a transparent leaf. Here Leonardo speaks half as an artist and half as a scientist, and it is this ingredient of science – from the use of perspective and anatomy to the use of aerial perspective and certain visual effects including, if you like, 'Op Art' – that marks the development of the Western tradition of art as so similar to the development of science.

In many other civilisations the explanations of natural phenomena resemble myths and remain static. They are traditional and are told from generation to generation. The same is true of images which remain static. In Eastern Christendom you learn how to represent the Nativity on an icon. But in the Western tradition, you have this discontent, this feeling that it isn't yet right and if I do this it looks even worse. So we have to experiment and sort out the effects by watching them. I believe that just as the scientist tests his hypothesis, the artist, as I said before, tests his own picture by looking at it. It isn't that he looks at the model or out into the world and learns how to paint, it is that he looks at his paintings and learns to paint by improving them, by finding that they do not yet pass the test he has set himself.

MILLER   So he recognises some sort of mismatch.

GOMBRICH   Some sort of mismatch. And the greater the artist, the more sure is his capacity for self-criticism in all these respects and I believe that this can be shown to be the case in more complex phenomena like learning how to represent the sheen of silk. This is not something which you learn by looking at a piece of silk. You learn it by trying out how, through a bit of white pigment carefully applied, you suddenly get this surprising effect of a sheen which looks convincing. It doesn't really look like it at all, but it has the same effect. What the artist experiments with is *effects*.

MILLER   Would you say, then, that one of the difficulties in representing the world around us is that we are quite naturally and understandably enslaved to the idea that it's something furnished with objects rather than 'appearances'?

GOMBRICH   Yes that is certainly the case although I find that the longer I think about it, the more the word 'appearances' seems to elude my grasp. J.J. Gibson[1] has stressed it more than any other psychologist, that the world in which we live is a world of discrete objects which we apprehend as invariant, as he calls it; so that even to realise how little I see of a human head when I look at it from one side or exactly what an eye looks like when I see it in half profile, is something which needs trying out on paper or canvas and is by no means easy.

[1]J. J. Gibson (1904–   ) was Professor of Psychology at Cornell University. His main books on perception are *The Perception of the Visual World, The Senses Considered as Perceptual Systems* and *The Ecological Approach to Visual Perception*.

However, the question of 'appearances' raises some very difficult problems. What exactly is the appearance of the scenery or the landscape through the window? I can look at it in many ways according to how I focus or according to my expectations; there's always an element of interpretation there which maybe I slightly overstated in *Art and Illusion* – but I'd rather overstate it than not state it at all.

MILLER   I wonder if you could enlarge on the notion of the invariant and that favourite phrase of psychologists 'the regression to the real object'.

GOMBRICH   If you meet a friend in the street and he comes closer towards you, he doesn't appear to grow to double in size or when he goes away to shrink, because we always see the friend and not the projection of the friend on the flat surface. We discover this if we stretch out our hand and measure what we see against an upright pencil. If you are at the back of a room which has rows of chairs in it, they all look the same size because they *are* the same size and you are fully aware of their size. You don't think that those further forward will be too small for you and are only for dwarfs. While, of course, if we intend to draw the room realistically as seen from the back we must make the sidewalls converge and represent the front row of eight chairs as much shorter than the one close to us. These changes are normally hidden from us through the so-called perceptual constancies, the impression we have that the world is constant. This impression also applies to colour. We see the walls of a room in roughly uniform hues or colours; we abstract from the variations caused by shadows; we know these are shadows and we take this as red. The painter, of course, has to attend very carefully to the degree in which the colour is modified by the shadow or by the light, just as he has to attend to the fact that from a certain distance the scale of objects seems to diminish. I don't quite know what 'seems' is supposed to mean, but it diminishes in the projection, let us put it that way.

MILLER   So that, when you have the task of projecting something on to a flat surface, you must overcome your immediate experience of the world in which it seems to be furnished with constant objects, and concentrate instead on the image projected on the retina.

GOMBRICH   Quite. But the artist can never see his retina and therefore I believe he can only learn the trick of forgetting that the world is three-dimensional by studying other pictures and seeing what effect they make on him. For example, the surprising effect that when you photograph or paint a street with a row of receding lamp posts it will only look convincing if the fifth lamp post is reduced in height in relation to the first according to the rules of perspective. It is thus you learn to achieve the effect of three dimensions on a flat surface. As I sometimes say, to the annoyance of some of my philosopher friends, the method works, not because the world ever looks like a picture, but because a picture can be made to look like the world.

MILLER   One of the hardest problems of representation, apart from showing a world in three dimensions, has been the representation of the human face. What would you say were the peculiar problems of representing the human face, over and above the fact that it is a three-dimensional object which has to be projected on to a two-dimensional surface?

GOMBRICH   I think it is movement which is the great problem. And in particular the facial movement of expression which impresses us through its changes, through its melody. Somebody suddenly starts to smile or to frown and we are confronting a living being. To represent this constellation or configuration in a frozen form will often result in what impresses us as totally unlike. We are not aware of the various transitional phases which this mimetic or expressive movement has to go through. You as a producer are surely aware of the complexity in achieving a particular expression. There are more or less static expressions which are relatively easy to render but the characteristic of the person will always be the way they move, the melody of the expression; this can never be caught in snapshots except in lucky shots where you have the feeling 'I now can tell what he will look like in a second or two and what he looked like a second before'. Whether or not my guess is right is not so important; what matters is that this subjective conviction gives me the feeling of confronting a living human being.

MILLER   Would you say then that in representing the human face in a convincing and lively way, there are certain positions which will be chosen by an artist because they will lead the spectator to predict the way in which the model is likely to move in the next few minutes?

GOMBRICH   Oh most certainly. I mean just as the photographer asks a model to smile, so from very early on artists try to enliven a mask, as it were, or a head, by moving the corner of the mouth. You have the archaic smile of the Greeks

PLATE 3

(plate 3) and of early Gothic artists aiming at the same effect – of life animating the face. Later on more complex methods are used; an instantaneous turn of the head, the veiled smile of the Mona Lisa which is capable of so many interpretations that the image seems to change whenever you look at it. Leonardo played a very complex trick but something of this interpretability is, I think, part of the magic of some great portraits. For example, Rembrandt in particular, sometimes leaves the eyes in the shadow and, because of it, gives us the impression that here is a great intensity of gaze.

MILLER
So you're saying that the success of a representation depends to some extent on how much is *under*represented or left ambiguous.

GOMBRICH
Yes, it is the suggestiveness of the image, it suggests ways in which we can supplement it: in *Art and Illusion* I call it 'the beholder's share'. Of course there is a certain amount of 'learned' response in this which may not be born with us. We learn that certain images can be supplemented and therefore brought to life. There is a cultural element but it's difficult to assign exactly what role it plays.

MILLER
So there may be, in certain portraits, an artful blurring, an artful ambiguity which invites the beholder to increase his contribution.

GOMBRICH
This is exactly what Reynolds said about Gainsborough in a somewhat backhanded compliment. He says of Gainsborough's portraits that they impress because they allow the imagination to do the rest.

MILLER
So in other words, the vitality of the portrait may be largely due to the beholder's activity, although the actual choice of what is going to *be* the beholder's share is strategically chosen by the artist.

GOMBRICH
Exactly. It can't be done by everyone. You have to know precisely the one distinctive feature which you must not leave out. But, just as accurately, you must eliminate that which would be an obstacle, which would look frozen if it were there.

MILLER
Presumably the same principles apply to the representation of the body's movements.

GOMBRICH
The need for these movements occurs particularly in narrative art when you represent, for example, a battle, or a fight. There are easily legible configurations like the one where one man is striking a blow and the other fighter is trying to ward it off, which allow us to understand what is actually going on. If you look at Greek representations of battles (plate 4) you will see that these schemata are very much exploited; they can be made more moving and effective or more stereotyped according to the skill of the artist and to the requirements of his style. But there will always be the need to allow the beholder to read what is actually going on and therefore, on the whole, a clear silhouette is important in the representation of movement. If you think of any famous work, for example, Leonardo's *Last Supper*, or *The Creation of Adam* by Michelangelo, you will see how these famous gestures are silhouetted: you need to have clarity of all the movements.

PLATE 4

PLATE 5

MILLER This statue (plate 5) exemplifies the same principle. By showing a fixed posture which is easily legible as a movement.

GOMBRICH In this case, of course, it is an initial position rather than movement. He starts by extending his arm in order to throw the discus and therefore he could have stayed in this position, allowing the artist to study it for quite some time, before he started . . .

MILLER Yes . . . it's in equilibrium and therefore it's a pose that could be held. And the reason why it conveys a sense of movement is that the arm is at the limit of its excursion. And therefore expresses the possibility of acceleration in the *opposite* direction.

GOMBRICH Yes, it's like a taut spring, or a bow; you see that the arrow will leave immediately and will be hurled into the distance. In a similar way you find, through empathy in some of these representations of an actual moment that the muscles are tense.

MILLER That must be one of the reasons why the horse was so often shown in the rocking horse position, with both its front legs and hind legs extended in a position which its limbs never are in (plate 6). It was done in order to convey a legible image of its movement.

GOMBRICH Yes, that is very likely, though it did come as a surprise when artists were shown the 'instantaneous' photographs by Muybridge (plate 7) which showed that the horse moves its legs in different time rhythm. Ever since I discussed this example – and I was by no means the first who wrote about it; the first was the great French archaeologist, Salomon Reinach – I occasionally get a letter saying that I was wrong. Occasionally a race horse may move in this way but I think these are usually jumping rather than running, so I still hold fast to the fact that, by and large, the norm is the one which I illustrated in *The Story of Art*.

PLATE 6

PLATE 7

MILLER   But it took time for this to become a schema which was then accepted by artists.

GOMBRICH   It was much discussed in the nineteenth century; Degas and others were interested in the discovery of the camera, of what in fact we don't normally 'take in' (I wouldn't say 'see' which would be wrong) which we don't 'take in' because it's simply too fast.

MILLER   I've often wondered why the Degas images, borrowed from Muybridge's photographs, were as successful as they were in view of the fact they showed events which were invisible to all intents and purposes.

GOMBRICH   That's true but we are so conditioned by the pictures we see and once we are conditioned in this way, we don't mind any more. There's a very interesting recent development of this kind. When I was young, architectural photographers took great care always to photograph the building straight on and not to let it appear to be slanting by pointing the camera upwards or downwards. Now nobody minds. We have learnt to accept slanted shots as a way of representing a building when there is no other way of showing it; we are getting much more tolerant to certain photographic distortions which even a generation ago were considered intolerable. The same is true of the blurring due to movement in photographs. We see this in countless advertisements nowadays, and in books about cities where you see the blurred figures of people walking through them. No publisher would have published such a picture thirty years ago. So there always is a conditioning process in art. Just as we accept Picasso though we know that people on the whole do not quite look like his paintings, so we accept certain effects of the camera.

MILLER   So that an innovation in art may persuade people to *see* the world in a new way despite the fact that there is a mismatch between the new scheme and the world.

GOMBRICH   There isn't always a mismatch. We can see this convergence of a building when we look up and we can perhaps be aware of the blur when we see a rapid movement if we attend to it. Normally we are not attending to this, and the camera has conditioned us sometimes to attend to certain effects; like the movement of the horse to which we're not normally attending.

MILLER   But nevertheless Muybridge photographs show certain positions of the limbs which really are moving so fast that the eye couldn't possibly see them. And yet such improbable images are artistically successful; why *are* they successful, if they don't match up with the world?

GOMBRICH   Well I wouldn't say they don't match up with the world, they don't match up with what we can take in. I suppose we can say that we have been brain-washed up to a point by artists to accept certain things as possible.

MILLER   So is it fair to say that whereas in science there is a rigorous standard by which the model must approximate to reality, art is not necessarily in the business of creating a schema whose duty is to match reality.

GOMBRICH   Most certainly not, it very rarely is. Or only if an artist is committed to conveying the correct information. There still are, I think, medical artists who have to paint operations in the operating theatre. In their case, they are scientifically committed to make everything as clear and as correct as possible; in fact the picture must be better than the photograph because the operation is more visible as they represent it. But with this and similar exceptions where something must be represented accurately, for a police record, say, the social function of the visual image, on the whole, is not that of giving accurate information. It has many other functions – from maps to decorations, from didactic illustration to erotic titillation, from advertising to religious devotion.

Not all of them, by any means, demand attention to what we call natural appearances. I have postulated in *Art and Illusion* and elsewhere that this attention, which we quite wrongly take for granted, first came to the fore in ancient Greece in a religious context. There is a suggestive parallel, I believe, between the rise of naturalistic representation in art and the origins of the medium which you have made your own; I mean, of course, the theatre. It seems that it was in Greece that there arose the demand for the evocation of a mythical event as if it were actually happening before the spectator's eyes – what I have come to call the 'eyewitness principle'. It was this demand which, twice in history (in the ancient world and in the Renaissance) led to the process we have been talking about, the imitation of nature through 'schema and correction', through 'making and matching' by means of a systematic series of trial and error which allowed us finally to look across the flat picture surface into an imaginary world evoked by the artist.

13

dialogue with
B.A. Farrell

FREUDIAN PSYCHOLOGY AND ITS IMPLICATIONS

INTRODUCTION

In an essay on the concepts and mechanisms of perception Professor Richard Gregory pointed out with some dismay that the psychological studies which have made the greatest impact on the public imagination are the ones which have the most arguable claims to be considered as scientific, and that while the considerable achievements of experimental psychology have been largely unheeded the 'semi-mystical intuitions of the psychoanalysts have changed profoundly our conception of Man and Society'. Although there are many people who would understandably take exception to Professor Gregory's choice of the phrase semi-mystical, the fact remains that the scientific status of psychoanalysis is debatable to say the least, and that in spite of Freud's ambition to establish the subject within the province of natural science, psychoanalysis has had an influence which is quite out of proportion to its scientific credibility. In this respect, as in many others, Freud's enterprise resembles that of Karl Marx. Both men elaborated an intellectual system which claimed to make human affairs intelligible on the basis of materialistic laws. And while these claims have been largely unsubstantiated, the self-consciousness of twentieth-century man has been irreversibly changed by the insights of both Marx and Freud.

In Freud's case the discrepancy between social influence and scientific reliability has led some psychologists to despair at the gullibility of the general public, and there are many more who resent the money that can be made out of something which they regard as a seductive fraudulence.

It's difficult, however, to believe that the success of psychoanalysis can be explained in terms of public credulity, and the extent to which Freudian ideas have penetrated and replaced some of the more traditional views of human nature implies that they have a recognisable truthfulness which cannot, and perhaps ought not to, be weighed by the standards which are applied to laboratory science. A more generous interpretation is the one which identifies Freud as an imaginative moralist in the tradition of Saint Augustine, say, or Pascal. On the other hand it's difficult to acknowledge Freud's moral originality without taking into consideration the systematic mental picture upon which it is based. And although the scientific status of this picture is both ambiguous and controversial one is left with the impression that what makes it convincing is the fact that in some puzzling way it is true.

This is what makes the problem of psychoanalysis so interesting to philosophers, and in the effort to disentangle some of the intellectual issues which are raised by Freud, I invited Brian Farrell, a fellow of Corpus Christi College, Oxford, to discuss the theme against the background of his continuing work on the philosophy of the mind.

DISCUSSION

MILLER I suppose that when people consider the discipline of psychology the name of Freud is the one most commonly mentioned. People tend to identify psychology with the work of Freud and there could hardly be anyone who has been so frequently spoken of and at the same time so often misunderstood, misinterpreted and even misquoted. But I wonder if we could start by simply saying this: most people intuitively have a sense of being a single person, an integrated personality and might be surprised to learn that according to Freud we are in fact a structured establishment arranged with something which almost looks like an architecture. I wonder if you could try and describe what it was that Freud said about our mental structure and its organisation, and use that as a way in to discussing some of the other popular dogmas and misunderstandings of the great man.

FARRELL Well, I'll have a shot. I think it's important to understand that if we are going to regard Freud as a psychologist, rather than as a psychiatrist[1], then what he was concerned to do was to present us with a psychological model, or theory, of our mental functioning. Now psychological models and theories will be differentiated affairs. It's not, therefore, at all surprising that Freud's model contains parts. And it's not surprising that it is a very technical affair and difficult to understand, because psychological functioning *is* a very difficult thing to understand, and therefore we are almost certainly going to need a whole battery of technical notions to deal with it.

Perhaps the simplest way is to begin with it developmentally. The infant, when born, is supposed to have an undifferentiated mind. It is not yet differentiated into structures. It functions merely through the operations of the id. That is to say, it functions under the influence of its instincts alone, and it works to grab at any pleasures that are available to it under the influence of the pleasure principle. But it soon discovers that it cannot satisfy its pleasures immediately (for example, the mother sometimes is not there to give it the breast), and it has to learn to cope with reality – the reality of its own impulses and the reality of the environment. It does this by developing its ego functions. So first of all there is the id, and then we have the ego developing. But this becomes more complicated later on when, in going through certain stages of development, the child also develops its superego, which is, roughly speaking, its conscience. Now you might ask, what are the relations between these three parts? How do they interconnect? It is here that Freud used his instinct story. This is a very complicated affair. Let me just pick on the one thing that is

[1]A psychiatrist is a doctor whose speciality is the field of human disorders and their treatment. A psychologist, in one sense of the word, is a person concerned with understanding the conduct, behaviour, and so forth, of humans and animals – by the use and development of scientific methods. In another sense of the word, a psychologist is a person concerned with obtaining such understanding by the use of methods of enquiry that are not, or may not be, scientific in character. It is in this sense of the word that Freud's theory and clinical enquiry can be said to be psychological in nature. But when Freud is concerned with the treatment of patients, he is then acting as a psychiatrist.

important, namely the so-called sexual instinct, the energy of which he called 'libido'. This sexual instinct, according to him, went through certain, biologically fixed, stages of development.

First of all, it manifested itself in the oral stage, where the child was concerned with the satisfactions connected with the mouth. Then it went into the anal stage, where it was concerned with the control of the sphincters; then into the phallic stage, where the girl was concerned with clitoral sensations, and boy with his penis and connected sensations. After this the child graduated, so to speak, into the Oedipal period, and the end of infantile sexuality is achieved when he or she gets through the Oedipal stage at about the age of five or six. By that time according to Freud the personality is fixed or settled. After that there is the latency stage, and then the revival of sexuality with adolescence and adulthood.

MILLER And by the latency stage he means the period in which the overtly sexual feelings and motives are held in suspension.

FARRELL They are latent, yes. But of course this interaction between id, ego and superego is a very complicated business. It is complicated, in particular, by the fact that there are id impulses which, if they were allowed to come through to the consciousness of the child, would generate excitation that the child couldn't tolerate. This is something that the ego has to take account of, and it takes account of it by what is known as a mechanism of defence that is called 'repression'. This keeps the impulse out of consciousness and makes the child incapable of bringing it through to consciousness. But the mechanism of repression is a very complicated notion. If one sets about explaining it, one gets involved in great difficulties.

With the mechanism of repression at its disposal, the child can deal with the problems of the Oedipal period. When the child gets through the phallic period, the boy develops sexual interests in the mother and becomes jealous of the father; and the girl has a mirror-like history. The boy has to cope with his sexual interests in the mother, and he does this by repressing them, and by identifying himself with the father. Thereby he introjects the incest taboo, and his instinctual sexual interests in the mother then become aim-inhibited, become desexualised, and turn into affection towards the mother. He incorporates the attitudes of the father which become part of his superego. The girl's story is rather different.

MILLER I'd like to ask you one or two questions about the earlier stage of the development of the id, or the instinctual life. Many people are puzzled when they hear about this early sexual phase in the development of the self. Take so-called oral satisfaction, which is experienced when obtaining milk at the breast, or indeed the satisfaction of achieving control over the sphincters, which enables the child to become a continent creature. Why did Freud feel it necessary to think of these as exclusively sexual?

FARRELL This is a very important question; it's also a difficult one to answer shortly. But first I must point out that Freud did not think of these satisfactions as 'exclusively' sexual. When the child fed at the breast its satisfactions were partly nutritional, but, in addition, he believed the child sucked for pleasure – which was libidinal in character. Quite a lot of scientific work has been done on this to find out whether it does suck for pleasure, and the overall outcome seems to be that it does. Whether this pleasure has to be described as 'sexual' is, of course, a further question. My own view is that Freud made the most frightful mistake in describing it as sexual; his argument (in his *Three Essays on the Theory of Sexuality*) is extremely weak in my judgement. The sort of thing that misled him was this. When he dealt with an adult patient who had, say, a perversion, a compulsive masturbator for example, and he uncovered material which allegedly revealed a history of masturbation in the child (and I'll come to the validity of that inference later) – when he uncovered such material, he then went on to infer at once that, because the adult's interest was sexual, the child's interest when it played with its penis was also sexual in character. This is a whopping mistake. It is much more plausible, in the light of contemporary evidence, to say that what is going on in the early stages of the child's development is *preparatory* activity – activity which serves infantile functions and is preparatory to the later adult sexuality of the individual.

What has made this so plausible and cogent in recent years is the work of people such as Harlow. Harlow[1], as you know, took monkeys and subjected them experimentally to various forms of deprivation. For example, they took the young infant monkey and separated it from its fellows so that there were no peers around. Now when this happened it was discovered that those infants, when they became adults, were incapable of ordinary sexual activity. If it was a female, she was incapable of presenting herself satisfactorily for male copulation; if it was a male, he was not capable of mounting the female satisfactorily. This sort of evidence suggests a very important analogy. It suggests that something similar may be working with us – that when the child goes through the so-called oral stage, when the boy plays around with his penis and so on, he is preparing himself for later adult functioning. It is quite unnecessary to suppose that the child is driven here by a sexual instinct. I think Freud made a serious mistake here. Moreover, it led him into the further consequence of having to say that *all* pleasurable bodily feeling on the part of the infant was sexual in character. For, clearly, any sensual feeling, any part of the body, any activity of the infant, can be corrupted by the treatment given it into becoming a perversion later on. So the hypothesis of infantile sexuality is clearly an implausible one. It got Freud into the frightful muddle of having to extend the concept of sexuality in the way that he did, which has muddled and confused us ever since.

[1]Professor H. F. Harlow was Professor of Psychology at Wisconsin when, with M. K. Harlow in the 1960s, he developed methods of investigating conditions, in the lives of very young monkeys, which contributed to the growth, or otherwise, of the ability in the adult to mate and mother normally and efficiently.

MILLER   Well he seemed to draw rather odd analogies, did he not? I can remember one passage where he talks about the look of seraphic satisfaction on the face of the child who has had a satisfactory meal at the breast as being a similar expression to the expression of someone who has undergone a satisfactory sexual experience.

FARRELL   Yes, exactly, and this is, I think, illegitimate. One cannot argue on the basis of behavioural analogy alone, and conclude that the driving force behind the infant is the same as the driving force behind the adult. But what bothers me is that, because Freud made this howler, and analysts have been perpetuating it for some time after him (though some, or perhaps even many, of them no longer talk like that) – because of this, people have tended to overlook the importance, or the possible importance, of early infantile or early childhood experience *in general*. For it could be argued that it is in this field that one of the important 'discoveries' of Freud and company is to be found. What he has done is to point to what *may* be very important features of human functioning. The way in which the child copes with its oral interests, its anal interests, and so on, may be very important. Perhaps the best way of bringing this out is to think of just one or two examples.

Suppose we consider a boy who has a mother who is very self-conscious about her body and her breasts. The boy never sees her breasts, and the whole family atmosphere is one with a rather taut attitude, a restricted and closed attitude, so to speak, to the body, including his own. Then he undergoes some trauma. For example, he suddenly sees the mother's breasts or the breasts of the girl next door in a situation which upsets him. He has a traumatic experience or experiences . . .

MILLER   As in Freud's own case, when he suddenly saw his mother naked.

FARRELL   Well, suppose something of that sort happens and this experience is not worked through. It is not explained to him, and he is not reassured about it. He is left, therefore, with this unresolved trauma, and with a tight attitude, as a little fellow, towards his own body and towards the mother. He also incorporates a fairly severe superego from the father; and when he comes to adolescence and adulthood, he is, shall we say, a rather prissy man in respect of his own sexuality. He is very uneasy about his own genital sensations, his impulses to masturbate, and so on.

Now if that man were to arrive on the analyst's couch, the analyst would not be a bit surprised to find that the man had, on the one hand, a personal history of the sort just sketched – of trauma from the mother and the development of unrelaxed insecurity in respect of his own body – and that he was, on the other hand, campaigning in support of the Indecent Displays Bill (which, for example, would prevent cinemas advertising by publicly displaying naked breasts of females).

This is a hypothetical example. I could give a better one perhaps. A psychiatrist in this country, for example, the eminent psychiatrist Sir Martin Roth (and I refer to Sir Martin Roth because I am relying here on the standard text he wrote with Mayer-Gross and Slater)[1] – he might be inclined to say that Mrs Thatcher is a really prime example of an obsessional personality. When he says this, what he means is that Mrs Thatcher is a person who is rigid and inflexible, and who exhibits a lack of adaptability. As Roth and his fellow authors say, if you want to cover the obsessionals with one term, you could refer to them as showing an unusual degree of mental inertia. That is to say, they are slow to move, but when once set moving in a certain direction, they are very difficult to stop or to deflect. (I am almost quoting here from Mayer-Gross, Slater and Roth.)

At this point an analyst might go on to say: 'Yes, but I am interested in a particular type of obsessional personality, namely, the anal type. If it's true that you have an obsessional personality in front of you, it would not surprise me at all to find that this person is also an anal type. That is to say she or he is not merely obstinate, but is also very orderly and thrifty or parsimonious. If I were to get such a person on the analytic couch, I would expect to find a certain history coming up in the material – a history of difficulty in getting through the anal stage.'

MILLER   By the anal stage, do we mean that stage in which the child is undergoing the first difficulties in learning to control its bowels in order to be a sociable creature?

FARRELL   That's right, in essence.

MILLER   What is it that makes such experiences so painful and likely to lead to pathological thriftiness and rigidity, whereas others who presumably go through the same process survive it and are able to be generous and flexible?

FARRELL   Yes. This is not an easy question for the orthodox Freudian to answer. But if we liberalise Freud, and the Freudian picture, to allow for the influence of things other than the early bodily history of the individual, then I think the answer might be something like this. The early anal training and experience of the anal personality formed part of a family pattern in which rigidity was fairly prominent, in which the emotions were formally released or, so to speak, released on paper and dealt with, but without genuine inner depth, without any relaxed warmth underneath. So the person grew up rather clueless emotionally, in an environment which was generally rather tight and restricted.

MILLER   I see, you mean in which there was an emphasis upon etiquette, decorum and orderliness, of which bowel training would be only one part.

FARRELL   Exactly so. But you might say, and I think you would be quite right here to say: 'But what justification is there for producing these derogatory remarks about people?' – because they do sound derogatory – 'What on earth is the non-analytic evidence for this?' The first question to ask when we talk about the anal character in adults is this: 'Is there such a cluster of traits as obstinacy, orderliness, and parsimony?' Well, surprisingly enough

[1] W. Mayer-Gross, E. Slater and M. Roth. *Clinical Psychiatry*, 1954.

there is. For example, some work by a first-class British psychologist, Mrs Beloff,[1] has gone to show that there *is* such a cluster of traits. What has not yet been done, is to show that this cluster does in fact stem from that very early training – perhaps, because it is extremely difficult in our culture to organise any such experimental work. On the other hand, could I refer to a small experiment that has been done in this field? It was discovered that, if you give subjects faecal-like material to handle and manipulate, you can then use the difficulty they have in handling this material as indicative of their obstinacy about changing their beliefs in the face of contrary evidence. Now that is a finding which rather takes one aback. What on earth, apart from analytic theory and material, could have ever led anybody to think there was a connection here? Yet apparently there is this statistical connection. And one naturally is then inclined to say that there must be something behind this connection. So there are indicators that there may be something very important here; but there is no more than that. In general, one can simply say it has not been established that this early training does in fact produce the anal character, but we do have reason to believe there is such a cluster of traits.

MILLER But if there is such a cluster of traits, it would tend to corroborate certain historical generalisations which people have made – I mean, psychiatrists like Erik Erikson[2], who tend to identify the growth of capitalism with orderliness in the childhood training of the Protestant, for example. The idea of Protestantism and the rise of capitalism has been identified by Erikson as being traceable back to the punctilio of northern European bowel training.

Now this must sound to many people an extremely fanciful interpretation of history. Do you believe that it is as fanciful as all that?

FARRELL Well, let me say straight away that when you talk about cultures, you are talking sociology; and it is a very difficult business to make generalisations from the material and the case studies which the analysts have produced, and apply them to society in general. It's a hazardous business. It is hazardous enough when you deal with the individual, but if you start generalising about communities as a whole, you are asking for trouble. It's very difficult to explain institutions by reference to the way in which individuals in that society have been treated. Though an analyst may venture forth into such speculation, I would advise him not to do so.

MILLER But nevertheless, if there are institutional tendencies within a given society, about the age at which they impose control of the bowels upon their infants, one could imagine that it might result in permanent attitudes towards things like thrift, punctuality and so on.

FARRELL Oh yes, indeed it could. In fact, I think it was Geoffrey Gorer many years

---

[1]H. Beloff. 'The Structure and Origin of the Anal Character', *Genet. Psychology Monogr.* 55, 141.
[2]Erik Erikson (1902–   ), a German–U.S. psychoanalyst of the neo Freudian school.

ago, who gave this explanation of Japanese character and culture.[1] But how much there is in this, I really do not know, and I would strongly advise everybody to be very cautious indeed about it. It is, I think, speculation, if only because the original story here is still speculative – the original story being that the early anal training goes to produce a certain type of character. As soon as one gets into arguments about causation, one is in difficulties. And the psychoanalytic account of the anal personality, and likewise of the oral personality, is in part a causal story. Likewise, also, the Freudian theory of neurosis is largely a causal story, and causal claims are very difficult to sustain.

MILLER But likewise, aren't the developmental claims just as hard to establish. Is there any evidence to show, for example, that children do pass through successive stages which are oral and anal, and then into this supposedly phallic stage?

FARRELL Well, actually, there is. If we concentrate on the conduct of the child, the interests of the child, and if we look at them objectively, then we do in fact find such a progression. There is evidence to suppose that these stages *do* occur in the early period of infantile development. Matters are much more difficult when we come to the Oedipal story.

MILLER And this plays a central role in the Freudian drama of the family, doesn't it?

FARRELL Absolutely central, and it's a very complicated and difficult business. Let us deal, first of all, with the notion of repression. The boy is supposed to repress his wishes to have sexual intercourse with the mother, or, if we do not want to regard his situation quite so genitally, to get into bed with the mother. Well, it is not at all easy to find any evidence which shows that the boy *does* develop these attitudes to the mother, and jealous attitudes to the father. We might well think, as a matter of common sense, that the boy will be interested in going into the bedroom and having a look to see what his parents do; and this would be taken as evidence of the Oedipal story. But, oddly enough, perhaps, it is difficult to get any hard evidence to the effect that this happens.

If you say, 'it is understandable, because the boy has repressed his wish and interest', then we are using Freud's model. Now when Freud used the word 'repression', he was referring, essentially, to a complicated inner process. He was referring to energy being used to keep back certain wishes, and he was using it also to refer to energy being withdrawn from items associated with these wishes. In other words, a complicated internal process is going on, in which energy moves around. This means that the notion of repression is a theoretical notion – it is referring to an

[1]Geoffrey Gorer is a social anthropologist of British origin, who became noted during and after World War II for applying the methods and insights of social anthropology to large modern communities. Perhaps the best known example of his work is to be found in *The Americans, A Study in National Character*. He also wrote *Japanese Character Structure and Propaganda*.

unobservable. Therefore, we can only get at it by indirect means, we can only get at it by saying: 'Well, if this is going on, then we can infer that X, Y and Z which are observable, are going on too, or will do so.'

When this sort of indirect work is done on repression – and a lot of it has been attempted – it really fails to be conclusive and convincing. This is partly because other interpretations are available to explain what is going on. It means that the indirect proofs of the internal mechanisms and the internal operations of Freud's system have not been forthcoming. Therefore it is very difficult to maintain just like that, *simpliciter*, that the boy has repressed his castration fears, and so on. So what are we to make of the Oedipal story now?

MILLER   Why does Freud never talk about amputation fears?

FARRELL   I think it's because he was subject to the fallacy which we've spoken of before, namely that the child has a sexual impulse and he is really a little homunculus, whereas in fact he's not. But, of course, this is not to say that a child might not be corrupted and maltreated as an infant into having all sorts of bodily fears connected, in particular perhaps, with the penis, which affect him later on as an adult. Let us not forget that. But the Oedipal story is a generalisation about *all* boys, and also about *all* girls where penis envy comes in as an essential component. And, again, this has not been established.

MILLER   Presumably that's why Women's Liberation object to the doctrine. After all, it superimposes upon females a built-in biological inferiority, by insisting that they come into the world raging with envy about not having this part.

FARRELL   Yes. Insofar as objective work on female sexuality has been done, it goes against the Freudian story. For example, work has been done which shows that, to the extent in which adults are satisfied or dissatisfied with their bodies, women tend to be more satisfied with their bodies than men with theirs. Which is interesting. So one has to be very cautious about Freud's account.

MILLER   It certainly seems to be one of the more objectionable aspects of the Freudian theory.

FARRELL   Freud also argues that, when the girl comes to maturity, she moves from clitoral satisfactions to vaginal; and there is no evidence for this. Insofar as work has been done on female sexuality, Freud's account has, I think, been shown to be false, or to be without support.[1]

MILLER   But for many women in the post-Freudian era, Freudian doctrine seemed to provide a charter which guaranteed and underwrote their sexual inferiority and committed them to a state of permanent and insatiable envy.

[1] For this work and for a survey of scientific studies of Freud's theory and therapy, see S. Fisher and R.P. Greenberg, *The Scientific Credibility of Freud's Theories and Therapy*, Harvester Press, Basic Books, 1977, and P. Kline, *Fact and Fantasy in Freudian Theory*, Methuen, London 1972, 1981.

FARRELL   I think they can rest assured; I don't think it's been shown to be the case. The evidence goes rather the other way.

MILLER   I'd like to ask one more question about the Oedipus Complex. Is it necessary to dramatise the relationship between mother and son in terms of a Greek myth which is overtly sexual in order to explain the desire of a child to remain attached to what is the source of his security?

FARRELL   I do not think it's necessary at all. (You have brought out here how other, what one might call, behavioural explanations and learning theory accounts are more economical.) This is something which, I think, the non-genitally oriented analysts of the present-day would be ready to accept. What they would concentrate on is *not* what we've been concentrating on, namely infantile sexuality. What they would emphasise are the interpersonal relationships in the family. This is what they would regard as important; and what we've been concentrating on they would regard as rather *passé*.

MILLER   Well if we regard that as *passé*, if we set aside this slightly fanciful tale of the Oedipal situation within which the male child finds himself, what is left of the Freudian doctrine which we can still find valuable today, both for understanding the mind and also possibly for treating patients?

FARRELL   Yes, but one moment. Let me just go back to the infantile history. I do not think you can infer from what I said that you have to set it *all* aside. What I'm setting aside, or suggesting we set aside, is the early biological and sexual aspect of it.

MILLER   Yes, that's what I mean.

FARRELL   What is then left is something that may be very important indeed. What is left is – how shall I put this shortly? – the whole cluster of pointers which you can extract from Freud about the importance of the early period. One of the remarkable things about the material which analysts turn up – and I want to come to the validity of this material in a moment – one of the remarkable things about it is that it does uncover patterns of early development and history on the one hand, and patterns of later human difficulties on the other.

It is not easy to summarise these patterns because we are dealing with complicated clinical pictures, so to speak. (And this is one of the problems I have in explaining what analysts are up to.) The fact is that when one once gets inside their discourse, and hears them talking and operating, one realises that they are continually linking past and present. When a woman comes along and exhibits what is, to them, the typical picture of hysterical sexuality, they immediately begin to anticipate that they will find certain sorts of things in her past, and these do come up pretty regularly. Likewise, when confronted by a person with obsessional difficulties, they are likely to find certain sorts of things in the past, as I've indicated. Likewise, consider a girl who is, shall we say, an inadequate psychopath (to use the technical jargon), a girl who cannot take any frustration, who in spite of being intelligent, cannot get through her schoolwork because 'it's all so difficult', and who does not know *what* she wants to do with her life, who will take a taxi rather than walk fifty yards – that sort of thing. In short, she is a person who is quite hopeless and incompetent, and generally pathetic. An analyst will anticipate that a certain pattern of early experience in the family of this girl will probably be discovered.

Now all this is very important to a person working in psychopathology. It is particularly relevant when it comes to the Oedipal story because it will probably point to certain basic interests on the part of the child, both boy and girl. Anatomy may not be destiny in the way that Freud indicated, but it is obviously extremely important. A little girl is, no doubt, puzzled by her father's appendage if she sees it, and she naturally wants to explore it. 'I haven't got one – can't I feel you and yours?' But the father does not allow or encourage it. And presumably this will have consequences for the girl. Likewise, if she barges into Mummy's and Daddy's bedroom the parents may or may not explain what they're doing when they're naked on top of one another. This whole experience may be shocking to the child, may be upsetting and may have an influence later on.

So it may be that the child, up to and including the Oedipal period, is going through some very important learning. It is learning about its own body, it is learning about human differences, it is learning about the ways in which parents deal with their bodies and its own body. This early learning goes on in respect of men and women – the male and the female figure. And the fundamental dispositions of the child in respect of the mother image and the father image are learnt, or incorporated, by that time. That is to say, by the end of this period it may be the case that the child has acquired certain dispositions which are fundamental, in the sense that they go to determine, to some important degree, what sort of husband, or wife, the child will become as an adult, what sort of sexual partner, and what sort of parent. *If* this is so, then, clearly, when the adult person runs into difficulties as a husband or wife, sexual partner or parent, we must not be surprised to find that the sources of these difficulties are shown up – at least in part – in the analytic material. For this is likely to reveal the faulty and inadequate dispositions the person acquired as a child in trying to deal with the problems of the Oedipal period.

Now there is indeed a case for saying that, in all probability, something very important goes on during the Oedipal period. If one is at all perceptive as a father, one can recognise this, and recognise that as a parent one is faced with certain problems. For example, should one open one's bedroom door or not? Should one let one's child see one having sexual intercourse or not? Should one let one's child see one naked or not, and if so, under what circumstances? And so on. If one has been alerted by the whole Oedipal story, in psychoanalytic literature, then clearly one is sensitised to these difficulties, and realises the possible importance for the child of this particular period of its development. In this respect Freud was a pioneer in psychology and contemporary psychiatry. You may or may not agree about these possible causal connections, but at least he did point to, and emphasise, them; and this was historically a very important contribution.

MILLER   Let's consider the question of repression. Is repression, as an agency in the mind, as Freud conceives it, exclusively applied to feelings and experiences which are of a sexual character?

FARRELL   If we use the word 'repression' as it is used in Freud's model, then Freud took the view that it was only the sexual impulse that was subject to repression. Other (apparently) non-sexual impulses are repressed in virtue of their association with the sexual.

But of course the interesting thing here, I think, is how far all these claims about what's going on inside the mind can be supported by the material that the analysts produce. It *looks* as if they are doing a straightforward uncovering job. You have a patient on the couch, you uncover the facts, and then you reconstruct the past of the individual in the light of these facts. That was the original story. And of course it won't do. Analysts have realised this in recent years, and indeed Freud, at the end of his life, actually said that he thought it was not always the case that you got at the truth of what went on. What the analyst had to do was to convince the patient of the truth of a construction that the analyst was giving the patient about himself and about his past. *Conviction* of the truth was important, not whether the construction really was true or not. Now, when one looks at the material . . .

MILLER   And this is material yielded in the retelling of dreams.

FARRELL   Yes, and in the material produced in the analytic situation. When we look at this material we have to ask ourselves: how far does this material really allow one to infer to, say, the past of the patient? How far does this really allow one to infer confidently to what the individual here and now is repressing? One is faced with enormous difficulties.

First of all, one has to remember that the analyst comes to the patient with a certain point of view. He is seeing the material which the patient produces through his own theoretical spectacles; and he is liable, therefore, to select and to abstract and to emphasise features of the material in such a way that his own point of view comes to fit it.

MILLER   And so the patient's own material might itself come to fit the theory.

FARRELL   Indeed, that's the next point. Since you are dealing here with a procedure, namely analysis, which is designed to change people – designed to change their basic attitudes, designed to put them through a course of emotional relearning – you may succeed in changing the patient in the direction that you would really like him to go. So that a point soon comes when he tends to give you back material which fits in with your own particular story, as a result, at least in part, of your having given him that story in the first place.

MILLER   As with Christianity. The person who goes into the confessional yields material which is consistent with the Christian notion of sin. So if, for example, someone who was unfamiliar with Christian dogma were to arrive in the confessional and gave an account of how he tripped up and got his thumb caught in the door, the priest would not find that a satisfactory sort of confession.

FARRELL Yes, indeed. There is an important analogy here I think, and in more ways than one. One of the respects in which there is analogy, which you and I haven't mentioned yet, is that what tends to happen to the patient is that he is confused by the analytic situation; and at the same time the analyst indirectly gives him ways and means out of his confusion. The analyst does this by giving him a view of himself, which reduces his tension, the result of which is that the patient tends to come to accept this view of himself with conviction. Furthermore, because he's trapped through transference (the process in which he becomes emotionally involved with the analyst), he becomes a captive audience, so to speak; and he continues going through all his difficulties. So he comes out with a conviction about his own nature. Having been caught in this way, he then naturally falls into the sin that we all fall into, namely, of reading everybody in one's own image. 'What is true of me is true of everybody. And, since my difficulties were, for example, due to my anal difficulties early on, therefore everybody's difficulties of this sort will be due to anal difficulties earlier on; and Freud's story in general is true.'

MILLER But this problem is bound to get worse because now more people are aware of the dogmas of the Freudian church. When they arrive in the analyst's room they are prepared and rehearsed and they deliver material which is consistent, because it's a part of the popular myth, not just knowledge which belongs to a few initiates.

FARRELL Yes, this does tend to happen. On the other hand, I think what I've said applies to patients who are quite ignorant of what is involved, and of psychoanalytic doctrine in general. But, of course, if you are familiar with it, then naturally you will be disposed to produce the sort of material which you think the analyst wants.

MILLER Well certainly you get this when you go to America, and hear people who are not necessarily undergoing analysis. They swap anecdotes with one another about their own emotional lives, and they talk in psychoanalytic lingo. It's as if they've already rehearsed their part as psychoanalytic patients.

FARRELL Yes, indeed.

MILLER This must, to some extent, make one question the claim that psycho-analysis is a branch of psychological science. How would you rate that claim?

FARRELL It depends how you use the word 'psychology' here. If you use the word 'psychology' in the way in which it's used, generally speaking, in this country, then psychoanalysis is *not* psychology. For psychology is the sort of thing which is practised in British university laboratories of psychology. This is a standard, ordinary use of the word, in which it refers to objective experimental, hardheaded work. This work is concerned to get at conclusions which are reasonably well established. It is concerned with hard facts. It is concerned with reproducible phenomena.

Now in that sense, psychoanalysis is not psychology. But if you use psychology in a wider sense, which embraces any claims about mental functioning, then of course psychoanalysis *is* psychology; and the question *then* is: What is its character? How good a psychology is it? How well established is it?

14

dialogue with
Hanna Segal

KLEINIAN ANALYSIS

INTRODUCTION

In the introduction to the previous interview I pointed out that the work of Freud resembled that of Marx in claiming to make human affairs intelligible in terms of a systematic scientific generalisation. Apart from any detailed objections which might be raised against such claims, the fact that both psychoanalysis and Marxism have shown a tendency to be unremittingly schismatic lends weight to the argument that it would be a mistake to regard their underlying principles as scientific. This doesn't mean that genuine science is characterised by a lack of controversy, or that scientific discoveries are unarguably acceptable from the word go. The introduction of new theory is often accompanied by debate and dispute, but it is usually possible to recognise the criteria by which the dispute will be settled, and as time goes by some sort of consensus develops within the scientific community.

After nearly eighty years psychoanalysis has failed to arrive at anything which one could properly call consensus, and the vehemence with which the various schools disagree with one another has led some of the more uncharitable sceptics to conclude that the Freudian enterprise should be classified as a religious dogma and not as a scientific theory. In which case, the contribution made by Melanie Klein must surely be considered as one of its most interesting and influential heresies.

When Mrs Klein began her psychiatric work in 1919, Freud had already sketched in the basic outlines of his theory about the structure and development of the human mind. As a result of the pioneering work which he had done with hysterical patients Freud had already identified the unconscious processes of repression and symbolism, and by studying the symptoms and dreams of neurotic patients he was led to identify the energetic conflict that existed between instinct and social survival.

During the early 1920s Freud and his associates developed their picture of the child's psychosexual development, and it was within the context of these far-reaching revisions that Melanie Klein began to establish some of her distinctive theories, one of which was the emphasis given to the developmental importance of experiences which the child underwent during the first year of life, and in particular to the inaugural encounter between the baby and the breast. In a career which is too long and too distinguished to be summarised in a short introduction, Mrs Klein contributed original and startlingly controversial ideas about the foundation of envy and gratitude, and the meaning of depression. Regardless of their scientific status, Melanie Klein's ideas represent a persuasive way of visualising some of the more enigmatic aspects of human nature, and although it's difficult to identify the sort of evidence that would count for or against them, one is left with the inescapable impression that human existence is somewhat less unintelligible as a result.

Hanna Segal worked closely with Melanie Klein, and apart from the originality of her own psychoanalytic work, her professional association with Mrs Klein put her in a position to give an authoritative account of an aspect of psychoanalysis which has had a lasting influence upon both the ethical and cognitive ideas of twentieth-century psychology.

DISCUSSION

MILLER   Let's start with the broad statement that the adult human mind is an achievement rather than an endowment. What is the Kleinian and the post-Kleinian position with regard to the development of the human mind – and how would you evaluate this perspective of human development?

SEGAL   Perhaps I should first say something about what this word 'Kleinian' means, because there are many confusions and misconceptions about it.

I think it is important to remember that Kleinian analysis, certainly in the mind of Mrs Klein and her followers, is an extension of Freudian analysis – a development, not an opposition.

It derives more from the later Freud than from the early Freud.

Melanie Klein started working in the 1920s – an exciting time in the history of psychoanalysis. Freud had just published *Beyond the Pleasure Principle* and *The Ego and The Id*. These two books signalled important changes in Freud's thinking. His instinct theory acquired its final form. Basic psychic conflict arises out of the opposition of the two basic instincts – the life and death instinct – the sexual instincts being part of the life instinct, and aggression deriving from, and deflecting outwards, the death instinct. Melanie Klein, in her clinical work, was always concerned with the confrontation between love and aggression, and in her theoretical formulations she used the concept of the life and death instincts. In the same decade Freud gave what we call his structural model of the mind, describing the structure of the mind in terms of the ego, super-ego and the id. Examining this structure, particularly the nature of the super-ego in children, led Mrs Klein to her emphasis on the internal world and internal objects.

In the early 1920s Melanie Klein devised the technique for psycho-analysing children. Since children cannot be instructed in free association and the main expression of their phantasy life is through free play, she provided her little patients with simple toys and play material and used the children's free play, as well as their verbal communications, to gain access to their unconscious phantasies.

When Melanie Klein started analysing children (two and three-quarter years old being the youngest) she realised that these children had already a long psychic history and a complex internal world. For instance, the Oedipus Complex was supposed to start at the age of three or four, but she found evidence of very violent Oedipal conflicts at a very much younger age. She also discovered that children had phantasies of very primitive and violent internal figures very early on, and that their super-ego was more primitive than the super-ego described by Freud.

One could say that Freud acquainted us with the child in the adult, and Klein with the infant in the child and the adult.

Freud certainly did have theories about infancy, some of them extremely illuminating, but they were theories; he didn't really work with the infant on the couch. Just recently I was rereading some of Freud's work on female sexuality, where he speaks of penis envy and how he used the concept in his session, and then there is a little footnote to the effect that he noticed that whenever there is a lot of material about penis envy, soon after the patients start complaining of their mothers not having given them enough milk, and he adds that he does not know what to make of this observation. So he obviously was perceptive when observing the infant on the couch, but he didn't put his discoveries to practical use.

MILLER So Freud's idea about the infant was inferred retrospectively from the material which came up from adults during the analysis, rather than from direct acquaintance with the child.

SEGAL Yes, but it's not quite like that, because although we don't analyse infants on the couch, we do make inferences about infants. Obviously when analysing a small child, it's easier to observe the infant within the child than directly in the adult.

Of course when you speak of the mind as an achievement, those first two years of life – what I call the infant within the child, within the adult – are of fundamental importance because it is in those years that we develop thinking, symbolisation, capacity to play, talking; that is, we really develop the basis of the mental apparatus. And according to Melanie Klein, it is in the first years that certain basic patterns of object relationships, thinking, symbolisation, speech, etc. are laid.

MILLER What do you mean exactly by an object relationship?

SEGAL Freud thought of an object as the object of instincts; every instinct has its object. The breast is the object of the oral drives, i.e. hunger. Our genitals are the objects of the sexual instincts, etc. It is a little different with the death instinct, of course, which has no object but oneself. Melanie Klein never formulated the concept of the object quite like that; for her the object became much more an object of the infant itself; rather than an object of the infant's instinct. Which doesn't mean that it's not an object of instinctual strivings as well, but probably a great deal more enters into it. And according to Klein, object relationships are formed from the start.

To come to your more general question – the growth of the mind. One could put it this way: when the infant is first born, he is assailed by a medley of perceptions – of external and internal origin – and the infant reacts to this abrupt change with ambivalence. One can think of the life and death instincts as very theoretical concepts but to me they have a clinical reality. Faced with the impact of this medley of perceptions, the infant reacts in two ways; he wants to grab at life, to breathe, to feed, to find an object of satisfaction and he wants the opposite – to annihilate this awful change which happened to him.

To me the death instinct is not a biological drive to return to the inorganic (as Freud described it) but it is a psychological wish to annihilate this sudden change brought about by birth. So the infant is born into a sort of chaos of contradictory perceptions – pleasant and unpleasant – and of contradictory desires; very soon he starts to sort them out and the sorting out is called 'splitting'. This is a term Freud applies to later phases of development, but which Melanie Klein applied to the earlier phases. The infant is trying to make sense of this medley, and the way he makes sense of it is by attributing everything that is desirable to something which we call the breast. But used this way the concept of the breast is a very psychosomatic[1] idea. It's not just the physical breast but an experience coming from an object that satisfies hunger, takes away the cold, makes one feel totally happy, maybe brings back even some feeling of being back in the womb. And equally, the infant attributes his bad experiences to a bad object/breast. At this point, there is no perception of absence, for instance, of a good object. One is assailed by bad things, or one experiences something very ideal.

MILLER   So the good things are all that is promising and flourishing and nourishing.
SEGAL   The experience is conceptualised as the breast. When the analyst speaks of the early infant in relation to the breast, he doesn't mean that the infant from the start actually has an anatomical perception of the breast. He has a perception of an alive object, satisfying physical and emotional needs.

To return to my theme. From the beginning there are active processes in the mind, which we call splitting, introjection and projection. The infant desires to incorporate into himself the good thing and to make it part of itself, and to push out everything that is bad. Freud in his essay on Negation said that the first psychological move of the infant is, 'This I'll take in – that I'll spit out'. And those ways of perceiving or misperceiving in black and white often persist in the adult personality.

Examples are not hard to find, because you can think of normal adults who consider one nation bad, the other nation good; one race bad, the other race good, etc.

I'll give two clinical vignettes – one concerning an adult and one concerning a child, and I will come back to them later from a slightly different angle. The first is about a patient who was very apt to function in a paranoid way, as we would call it, seeing things in black and white. She heard that there was a party given by a Swiss analyst Dr S, who had a beautiful castle in beautiful mountains, and she heard that there was marvellous food at this party. She dreamt that she was about to enter a balcony, but she didn't know which because there were two balconies. One was in full light, in sunshine, and had lovely food on it; the other one was dark and filled her with a sense of apprehension. Her association was that somebody had joked that Dr S's castle had a balcony over a precipice from

[1]'Somatic' means bodily and 'psycho' means psychological. So the breast in this context is not just the physical breast but also a mental object.

which he used to throw his patients down when he was fed up with them. She was, in this dream, communicating her anxiety about coming to her session – Dr S representing me. Will she go to the blissful party – the breast – or to the death-bringing one.

My second example concerns the material of a little three-year-old girl. After a vacation she gave a lovely warm smile to the analyst, but then became petrified because she saw on the wall a black lady – she called her 'wall lady' – who was going to devour her and she wanted to run out of the room. When the analyst interpreted why there was this black lady on the wall (I'll report this interpretation later), she, the child, went to her drawer, took out a doll, took a beaker, got some water, gave the water to the doll and said: 'That's milk for the baby, now she can feed.' She was reproducing a very early process in which things are black and white, but it was particularly at the moment of frustration – the vacation – that the black lady appeared on the wall.

It would be nice if it were so easy but it isn't because it is not simply only that there is this relation to the ideal and the persecutory object. We are all familiar with the fact that for a very young baby bliss or disaster are a second away from each other. But the experience is also governed by projection – what Mrs Klein later called projective identification[1], the third of the active processes mentioned earlier. The bad breast is not only the bad experience which is inflicted by the environment, it is also a projected part of the infant himself. The infant who wants to get rid of all sorts of bad internal feelings, deals with them by projecting them outside. Therefore this bad object also acquires the characteristic of one's own bad impulses, or parts of the self which one wants to get rid of.

And here I'll come back to my examples. Another dream my adult patient had was as follows. She dreamed that she was lying on the couch, feeling a complete baby; she was greedily eating her way into me. She was feeling it quite physically, feeling it as a blissful situation; and then something like two enormous spiders came and started pulling her away. It was obvious that she associated this with the end of the session. She also had a spider phobia. There was also an association with hands; the dream spiders looked like hands. Her experience of her mother's hands taking her away from the breast was that the hands had the characteristics of her own greed. She was eating her way greedily into me, and these hands came and were greedily devouring her.

MILLER If I can recapitulate for a moment. There are two sources of bad feelings. There are bad feelings which arise from unpromising and unpleasant experiences which occur in the outside world, and those are, as it were, emblematically represented as a bad breast. And then there are feelings which are uncontrollable desires or impulses, which arise from within and seem to threaten the personality, because they seem to burst out from

[1] A process by which a person imagines himself to be inside some object external to himself.

inside, and therefore have to be projected into the outside world. Have I got it right?

SEGAL But the two are not separate. You saw what happened to my patient. Her dream showed frustration, a bad experience, which was like the end of the analytic session – like the end of a feed. But it is experienced by her in terms of her projection – greedy hands attacking her. You see, hunger gnaws you. In other words, hunger is not felt at that primitive level as the absence of a good thing or as frustration, it is felt as something gnawing you. In other words, you attribute to the bad experience the characteristics of that part of yourself which had been projected. Another patient may experience the end of the session quite differently. For instance, he may be aware of his own frustration and anger.

MILLER But the frustrations of which you speak must partly arise from strong impulses from within.

SEGAL Yes, the infant deals with his bad impulses originally by trying to project them into the object. But this in turn gives rise to anxiety. Because the threat is that if one projects all these bad feelings outside, then everything outside becomes bad. And, indeed, with infants when mother returns after an absence they sometimes turn away from her and will not feed. This was experienced by the little girl I described who wanted to run out of the analyst's room, which, in her mind, turned bad during the holiday. She was fleeing the 'wall lady'.

The history of the patch on the wall was that she had splashed water on the wall before going on holiday and indeed there was some discoloration. She also had diarrhoea the last day of the term, so the bad lady on the wall is the place where she phantasised she had put her own urine and faeces, and therefore when she came back she couldn't feed – because she perceived it that way. As a small child she had feeding difficulties, repeatedly turning away from her food. The interpretation, first of the split between the ideal analyst and the wall lady and then of the projection, enabled her to integrate the good and bad aspects of her object, lessen the persecution by the wall lady, and enabled her to relate to the analyst again as a feeding mother. This was expressed in her play with the doll when she said: 'Now she can feed'.

MILLER Well now, once the infant has segregated the world into these two alternatives – and it's in a sense rather a Manichean view of the world with everything either good or bad – how does he actually handle his further development?

SEGAL To answer your question I shall here introduce a technical term; these are terms bandied about but not always understood. That phase of the development – when the infant copes with the chaos by producing the ideal object related also to the loving self and the bad object, which is then hated – Mrs Klein called the paranoid-schizoid position. She did not mean that all infants are mad, but that this is a phase of development which becomes probably the fixation point of paranoid-schizoid pathology.

MILLER   So by fixation point, you mean that although this stage of development is not itself pathological, it *would* be pathological if that was the stage to which the adult reverted.

SEGAL   Roughly. I don't want to go into details of psychopathology, but one never simply regresses to a previous phase of development. Also, the fixation points are points at which a pathological nexus exists already. One could think of it that way: if things go wrong, islets of illness are formed which disturb later development, and in case of the breakdown of later defences, may be fully reactivated in a psychotic illness.

But to come back to development. If the split I describe persisted, we would remain incapable of developing a more realistic perception of the world. If the development proceeds smoothly, gradually an integration occurs. As the infant internalises the good object and partly identifies with it, the infant ego becomes stronger. The growth and strengthening of the ego is due partly to physiological growth but partly also to the internalisation of good experiences which allow psychological growth.

As the infant becomes stronger he is less drawn to projecting badness outside. As he feels stronger he feels less threatened and can tolerate internal stress. A benevolent circle is established; the stronger the ego of the infant, the less he feels threatened and the less he projects. And as he projects less, so his objects become less threatening.

MILLER   I see. So that by incorporating an image or an emblem of what is promising and nourishing in the outside world into his or her mind, the infant is better placed to accommodate the bad feelings that he might have.

SEGAL   Yes, and therefore he's less given to attribute badness all the time to an external object; therefore his picture of a terrifying object becomes much less horrible, and in that way the two get closer together. And he gets closer to a reality perception of what his object is really like.

A number of factors become integrated, partly through the physiological development of the infant, but partly through this emotional development which I described (and if that doesn't happen even the physiological growth can get retarded). Gradually the infant becomes aware of something that Mrs Klein calls 'mother as the whole object'. He becomes less egocentrically related to *bits* of mother that give satisfaction or persecution. He becomes more able to perceive his mother as a person who comes and goes, who is the source of gratification but also the source of frustration and pain. That she's not two or more objects but she's one, and she's not an object solely related to the infant but a person who comes and goes; the concept of absence comes in, the concept of mother as a person who has life of her own. And simultaneously with that integration, the infant, through withdrawing his projections, becomes more aware that it is he himself who loves and who hates. And who loves and who hates the same person. And this brings in a different register of feelings from the ideal and persecutory ones because the awareness of feelings of aggression towards a loved person, the beginning of ambivalence, brings in such feelings as guilt, the fear of loss of the object, and longing for the object. We call that type of relation to the object, that constellation of feelings and anxieties, the depressive position.

MILLER A clinical psychiatric term.

SEGAL A psychiatric reference, except less than the paranoid-schizoid position, because being capable of feeling depressed when your loved object goes away is recognised as a normal feeling. It is abnormal *not* to be able to feel sadness, or longing, or not to be capable of having feelings of guilt.

MILLER So this depressive phase, once again like the paranoid-schizoid phase, is only so-called because if the adult were, as the result of some illness, to revert to that infantile stage, it would be considered an illness.

SEGAL Yes. But it's also a matter of degree, because we must be capable of depressive feelings, which is not the same thing as having a depressive illness. Mourning, for instance, reawakens feelings pertaining to the original depressive position, the loss of one's first good objects, without its being pathological.

When in the depressive position destructive feelings predominate and the infant feels that he has irreparably annihilated goodness, and he is left in a state of despair; then a kernel of pathological depression is formed, which can be a fixation point for later pathological depression and/or gives rise to such defensive structures as determine later neurosis.

But in a normal infant, the depressive feelings, his anxieties of having lost the breast or lost the mother also give rise to reparative feelings, to feelings that what has been destroyed by hate can be restored by love, and that the state of having a good internal object can return again, much less idealised than previously because it is an object that had frustrated one; it is an object that had been attacked; it is an object that needed a restoration and would therefore acquire different characteristics.

Internal figures formed in the paranoid-schizoid, and in the depressive, position enter into the composition of the later super-ego. The earlier experiences give rise to an extremely persecutory super-ego, and an ideal aspect of the super-ego, which Freud also spoke about, which also becomes persecutory through demanding such ideal perfection. Once the infant reaches the depressive position, and more integration, the super-ego becomes more realistic. It only makes you aware if you attack something that you value.

And it's not punitive, but it's pushing towards reparation, restoration, and towards regaining a good state of affairs.

MILLER So then if I read you aright here, if all goes well in the process of development, the infant, having passed through this stage of splitting, and of seeing the world in terms of good and bad, promising and the reverse, proceeds to a stage in which it is capable of identifying the mother as a whole person who can be there or not there, but whose absences are not seen as annihilating threats; and am I right also in saying that in reaching this stage, the infant is learning to recognise and identify with the forces of conscience, which is simply another name for the super-ego presumably? And that these are to some extent identified with the mother who is now seen as a whole object?

SEGAL   Yes. And the father. I left the father out of it, but in this phase I think it's also very important that the infant recognises independent people who lead lives of their own; the father, and the parents as a couple, acquire an ever increasing significance.

That is where Mrs Klein disagreed with Freud about the timing. For Freud, I think, the father really achieves significance when the child's three to four years old: in Mrs Klein's view, what she names the depressive position already begins to include the father as a separate person, and the beginning of the Oedipus Complex. Nowadays we are inclined to believe that the father's presence is, in fact, felt by the infant from the beginning.

MILLER   Now in arriving at these stages, if one sees these as milestones of emotional progress and development, what is it that determines the outcome? Are these stages delayed or frustrated by events in the outside world or by the vicissitudes of the internal life, over which, after all, we have no control?

SEGAL   I think that this is one of those areas about which there are endless discussions which to me seem fruitless. For instance, if one were to think that non-Kleinian analysts such as Winnicott, let's say, or Bowlby, or Balint, really think that the infant is a *tabula rasa*[1], that all infants are identical and only the external events impinging on their consciences change them, it would be attributing to them a ridiculous view.

Some people attribute to Mrs Klein a totally ridiculous view which is that everything is internal and the external world doesn't matter: that an infant who would be abandoned by parents and brought up by the orphanage is just the same as an infant who is lovingly reared.

Either extreme is ridiculous. But it is true that some people tend more one way, some another. I would say that the outcome is always an interplay of internal and external factors; that for a given baby that mother wasn't good enough, but she might have been for an infant who had a better constitution, and the other way round; that there are infants who maybe are born with such a weakness of the ego and such an inability to cope with their hostilities, that it would take an exceptional mother indeed to deal with them.

But certainly there are people who tend to attribute more to the external and people who attribute more to the internal. Mrs Klein, and I myself, attribute a great deal of importance to the internal factor – to how a given infant deals with the situation.

MILLER   I'm sure that many people must be very concerned about bringing up their children. If the emphasis lies upon the accidents and the unexpected events of the *outside* world, they're going to feel that they can, as parents, have much greater control over the environments within which their

[1] *Tabula rasa* – a blank tablet, which is analogous to the idea that the infant's mind is empty at birth and all psychological functions develop from experience alone.

Melanie Klein

children are reared, because they can, in that case, powerfully determine the mental health of their children. But if the outcome is genuinely determined by *internal* idiosyncrasies of the individual, then the parent is powerless to influence the outcome.

SEGAL Parents should take responsibility for their children; I have to say that there's absolutely no doubt about it. For example, obviously the infant who gains the good breast very frequently and happily, will have a greater chance of building up the strength of the ideal component as opposed to the persecutory component, at the paranoid-schizoid position.

MILLER So, whether the breast, emblematically or realistically, is seen to be good or bad, may be partly determined by something which the mother either does or fails to do. On the other hand, if, for example, due to some personal idiosyncrasy of the child, it attacks the breast with a ferocity which the mother can't satisfy, then it also becomes a bad breast.

SEGAL Yes. Well I'm saying that the breast can become bad for external or internal factors. Nevertheless the responsibility of the parent is to ensure the external environment is the best they can manage. But I'm glad you raised this point because there is a tendency sometimes to induce a sense of guilt in parents which doesn't help at all – to make mothers feel that the child is a *tabula rasa* and every time they do this wrong or that wrong, it's going to have nefarious consequences. This doesn't help the situation.

MILLER But then arises a purely practical issue. If a mother, for reasons which have nothing to do with her, has a child that happens to be ferocious in the way it attacks the breast, and seems to be an unco-ordinated child; although the mother herself has generous and graceful feelings about her own body, nevertheless she will become frustrated as a mother. What then happens in that relationship – how can she actually accommodate that?

SEGAL With difficulty. The only thing one can say is that some mothers do have very difficult infants. The projective identification, the projection I spoke about, is not only in the infant's phantasy. Infants have a way of inducing uncomfortable states of mind in parents, and it is very important how parents can deal with those feelings of discomfort that the infant produces.

This is a very important area of work which Wilfred Bion[1] worked on. He speaks of 'the breast capable of containing the infant's projective identifications'. That is, a mother who responds to the infant's distress with an appropriate anxiety, leading to an appropriate response. Some parents react to the infant's projection of distress by denial, they refuse to be moved, or by collapsing themselves, or by becoming hostile. Parents who can tolerate the hostility and anxiety of a child and can give him relief, help him to reintegrate the projected parts of himself. But of course with some infants it is very difficult, because they can induce states of real panic, distress or hostility.

MILLER Well, my first feeling about what you have said is the amazing fragility of the human personality in the face of the risks which arise from the outside

[1]Wilfred Bion, an eminent English psychiatrist who was analysed by Melanie Klein.

world on the one hand, and the terrible unpredictable risks which arise from the idiosyncrasies of the individual on the other. It is surprising that *anyone* achieves any state of mental equilibrium when you think of the appalling risks and the small chance of there being some balance struck in this reciprocal relationship.

SEGAL   Well there are two things to say. One is that infants are tough. It's amazing how much an infant can sometimes build from a very poor environment. The child's life instinct is very strong – the desire for life, the capacity to have pleasure, gratification, the gratitude for, and incorporating of, the good experience. The life instinct is a powerful force. And from the external point of view it's again not quite so fragile. Parents can make many mistakes but if they have basically the right attitude the infant and the child will perceive it.

You spoke at the beginning about the mind being an achievement. It is by overcoming these anxieties and stresses that we develop a mind capable of dealing with the internal and the external world, and that is what makes the human mind so complex and so fascinating.

Then the occasional frustrations which all infants have to go through – even, occasionally, separations, which can be more traumatic – can be worked through. Particularly when the infant already reaches the depressive position and is capable of restoring himself from his own inner resources.

MILLER   So it's a much more elastic-sided relationship than a straightforward naïve account would give one to believe.

SEGAL   Yes.

MILLER   I see. But in all this one can see that there are mechanisms of protection and defence which the personality has to use in order to arrive at an adult healthy state of mind. And, in this, reparation is a very important defence mechanism.

SEGAL   I'm not sure I would call reparation defensive. In a way one could say it is defensive because it restores the object and does away with the pain. In a way it is not defensive, because defensive – the way Freud used it – means using defences so as not to be in touch with psychic pain. Doing something which is restorative means being in touch with the psychic pain, and doing something about it.

MILLER   As in the process of mourning, presumably.

SEGAL   Yes. Whereas the manic defences, for example, deny the psychic pain.

MILLER   This is the process which Freud described as the *work* of mourning.

SEGAL   Yes, it is the work of mourning. I would not call it defensive.

MILLER   So in all of this, one begins to see that phantasy plays a very large part in the development of the mind. Now, I wonder if you could outline the role of a phantasy and phantasy-building in the development of the mind.

SEGAL   I'll use a formulation that Susan Isaacs[1] gave to phantasy as a mental

[1] Susan Isaacs (1885–1948). Author of standard works on various aspects of the welfare and education of young children.

264 · STATES OF MIND

representative of instincts. Freud spoke of early hallucinatory wish fulfilment. To say that the infant lives in a world of omnipotence is the same as to say that he lives in a world of phantasy; that his wishes for a satisfying object are experienced as fulfilled by the phantasy. And that goes not only for his libidinal wishes, but also for destructive wishes which are stirred by frustration or by envy. But this omnipotence from the very beginning is in conflict with a budding reality sense.

Freud, in the *Two Principles of Mental Functioning*, where he writes of an organism living on the pleasure–pain principle, adds in a footnote, 'if such an organism ever existed'. That is, we assume that from the beginning there are reality perceptions. But those reality perceptions may be overridden by phantasy and *do* get overridden by phantasy.

There is a constant interplay between phantasy, which may override and distort reality, and reality, which comes in and modifies the phantasy.

MILLER   Yes, and were reality not to do so, the infant mind would remain in a state of isolated omnipotence from which it could never recover normal relationships with the outside world.

So these phantasies which the child experiences are the phantasies of a satisfaction which the world won't or can't provide, or phantasies of destruction which the child visualises the world actually being destroyed by.

SEGAL   Being destroyed and destroying him. That would be the very early ones.

When the infant does get actual satisfaction, there is a merging and a correction within the infant mind, because there is always some discrepancy between this ideal breast and the breast that actually comes to feed.

So even in the best feeding and loving situation there is some correction from reality which makes it a bit more real again, a bit less excessive. And when we think of mental health, I think it's the infant's capacity to tolerate those discrepancies which are tremendously important for his mental development. From the external point of view, the discrepancies may be too devastating. There may be discrepancies that cannot be overcome; but in a good environment it is crucial that the infant has the capacity to tolerate discrepancies and keep, as it were, adjusting. And a very fundamental change happens in the functioning of phantasy with the depressive position. Not only the content of the phantasy changes from the ideal, the persecutory and the fragmented, to the more integrated but it also changes more towards the phantasy of what one has done to the object oneself. Also a greater differentiation is established between the inner and outer world and the content of the phantasy gets more stabilised.

For me the depressive position is very much the battle ground of what Freud described as the reality principle overcoming the pleasure–pain principle. In withdrawing projective identifications, in allowing mother to become a real external person, the infant begins to differentiate phantasy and psychic realities from the real external object, and that is the point at which the infant could verbalise to himself, if he was able: ' "This is what I imagine", but that is "what is" '. Which means that the phantasy life goes on, but it's not identified with what is. And that is also the moment when repression takes over from splitting. In other words, when at the beginning there was the bad and the good in the object and in the self, as concrete things fighting one another, now there is an awareness of one's self with good and bad impulses related to an object which stirs both.

I don't mean, of course, that all that happens in six months. In fact I had to fight that battle out with a man of seventy-four before I completed his analysis. But those are two modes of functioning, and as the depressive mode of functioning takes over, part of it is a differentiation of phantasy from reality. And that, of course, has a fundamental relevance to thinking, to symbolisation, and to the whole area of mental functioning. Projective identification gives rise to – what I call symbolic equations; symbolic equations which, I think, lie at the root of what psychiatrists call the concrete thinking of the psychotic.

MILLER And what are these exactly?

SEGAL What to the normal person would be the *symbol* of something, to the person who thinks concretely *is* the thing. The example I give in one of my papers is of two patients. One was a schizophrenic who was a great violinist when a youngster. When I asked him: 'Why don't you play your violin?' he said, 'I won't masturbate in public'. So for him playing the violin was an act of masturbation, and his violin was the penis.

I had, simultaneously, another patient, who played the violin, and for him, too, playing the violin represented a masturbation phantasy, and the violin had various symbolic meanings, one of them being the penis. But for him playing the violin *symbolised* a masturbation phantasy. It was not an *equivalent* of masturbation.

That kind of more mature symbolisation is like a completion of the process of mourning; the object is given up and symbolised in other ways. But my schizophrenic never gave up certain things, and concretely wanted to find the penis in the violin.

MILLER And couldn't actually distinguish between the two. I see. So there is what one would call a pathological process of symbolisation in which the patient actually *equates* some part of the body, say the penis, with something such as a violin, but sees them as identical.

SEGAL As identical. Exactly. And is not able to differentiate his phantasy from reality.

MILLER I see. Am I right in saying that what happens to the phantasy life as the child encounters the vicissitudes of the real world is that reality becomes accommodated in some way, and the element of phantasy therefore shrinks, or withdraws its frontiers as the person learns to recognise what is self and what is non self?

SEGAL But I don't think phantasy life shrinks. No, the process is different. You know, the traditional idea of the scientist is that the scientist is rational; he puts his phantasy life away; he observes reality and draws conclusions. Now we know that this is a naïve view. The scientist comes with hypotheses in his mind, conscious or preconscious, or even unconscious, which he tests. To me the reality principle doesn't mean we put our phantasies away and become rational human beings. It's more complicated than that. I think our phantasy life goes on but it is repressed; it is symbolised, and it is constantly tested. Our phantasies are like hypotheses of what the world is like, which is constantly being retested. If you repress the phantasy too much, our lives become very very narrow, and our rationality isn't really rational because it leaves too much out of account. I would say that it is the richness of our phantasy life which gives richness to our thinking and rationality; and it is our capacity for reality testing and distinguishing the psychic from the external which gives it its rationality – that is, its precision and correctness. But I would certainly not advocate a shrinkage of phantasy, but let's say the lessening of its concreteness.

Maybe I should here say something about the repressive barrier. Freud spoke of conditions in which it is either too rigid or too loose. The kind of repression which Freud calls too rigid and which gives rise to pathology is like a splitting; it's cutting off of phantasies which remain concrete and unworked through. When repression works well our unconscious phantasy is in constant contact with reality, through various symbolic expressions. Repression becomes a contact barrier.

MILLER So symbolism plays a fundamental part in our negotiations with reality. It really represents a sort of courier service which passes between the carriers of the internal phantasy life of the mind, and all that goes on out there.

SEGAL Symbol formation is strongly linked to our interest in our mother's body. One of Mrs Klein's most important papers is 'Symbol Formation and Its Importance for the Development of the Ego'. The infant has an enormous wish to explore and know the mother's body. It is what could be called the epistemophilic instinct. It can be linked with love or it can be linked with destructiveness, but I think it's also an impulse on its own.

Phantasising that he is entering and exploring his mother's body, about which the child feels ambivalent, gives rise, of course, to enormous anxiety. Therefore the child displaces his interests and symbolises them in the world, and this gives rise to an interest in the world. I think that things which are not endowed with symbolic meaning at some level probably don't interest us.

It is because the external world is endowed with symbolic meaning, that it arouses such enormous interest. Of course, it might interest us for the purposes of survival. We would still need food and shelter, but our epistemophilic interest, the creative interest in external reality, is because we endow it with symbolic meaning which refer to all the things that the infant wanted to find out and touch in relation to its primary objects.

MILLER So are you saying that, apart from those purely expedient relationships which we have with the outside world where the cognitive capacities obviously have survival value, the *apparently* intellectual interests which we display as human beings – scientific curiosity, for example, or our interests in art – are fundamentally modelled on the symbolic relationships which we first learn in our attitude to our mother's body.

SEGAL   To our mother's body and ourselves, because there is also the search for oneself and one's own psychological and psychic realities.

MILLER   But nevertheless, our curiosity in what we think of as our intellectual pursuits is ultimately modelled on a world of libidinal feelings towards objects which are in the outside world. I think that a lot of scientists would find it very hard to accept that the impulse of curiosity, which seems to them to spring simply from a direct and concrete interest in the way the world is, would have to come from something as primitive and as personal as that. Could it not be postulated as an alternative that science could just as well spring from an over-development of the cognitive capacities which we need to survive in a difficult world, as much as our relationship to our mother?

SEGAL   Well, at the beginning of our life our survival is dependent on our parents and that is carried over to the world together with other impulses. But the scientists I worked with were animated much more by what you call curiosity than by the pragmatic need to survive.

MILLER   But in all of this, the role of symbolism is an indispensable process for actually undertaking relationships with the outside world. And you're saying, that in the absence of the capacity to form symbols, the mind actually becomes stunted.

SEGAL   Well you can see that starting in the autistic child. It was work with an autistic child that brought the problem of symbol formation forcibly to Mrs Klein's attention and became the basis of her paper 'Symbol Formation and Its Importance for the Development of the Ego'.

The autistic child doesn't play, doesn't talk, can't relate to the external world, doesn't have a cognitive interest in the world. The little boy, in her paper, was interested in two things which enabled his analysis to start (he was a non-speaking child): door handles and trains – a tiny bit of something that survived and still symbolised an interest in the world.

The train was related to parental intercourse I think, and the door handle with entering his mother's body. And it was through following that tiny thread that in the analysis she could discover his interest in his mother's body, which in his case was blocked because it was too sadistic and too projective, parts of his body were too concretely identified with his mother's body. As soon as his phantasies and anxieties about his mother's body started to be liberated, he showed anxiety and started displacing and becoming interested in the world around him – a cognitive interest. He became capable of symbolisation and his speech developed rapidly.

MILLER   So the first step towards his treatment was achieved by identifying those residual symbolic capacities which the child had retained.

SEGAL   He had no interest in anything else; his mother or nanny could leave him and he wouldn't notice it. If he had not had this interest in door handles and trains, it would have been difficult to get access to his internal world.

MILLER But these symbols themselves had arisen in his mind only because they were, albeit very small and stunted, representations of primal relationships with his mother. So that in every case here, we're going back to a picture of the mind which visualises the relationship of a child to its mother as being the prototype of the general relationship to the outside world.

SEGAL I would extend it a little bit, first to the part object which is a maternal breast: when it becomes mother, it really becomes mother and father. This happens very early on – the idea of two objects coming together, two complementary objects.

MILLER If we can begin to summarise, I think the first question that occurs to me is, how does the analyst distinguish between what would be a valid interpretation of a particular lot of material, and an invalid one? Presumably it's not quite like the process of verification that goes on in natural science.

SEGAL If we started treating our patients' associations as something that has to be weighed or measured in that kind of way we would be thinking too concretely. What you are asking is the most important question relating not only to Kleinian analysis, but to psychoanalysis in general. I think psychoanalysis *tends* towards being a science rather than completely being a science, because so much still depends on our intuitive faculties. The criteria that we have to develop for validation must be different in many ways from the criteria of validation in physical science. We're dealing with psychic reality and psychic life.

There is also a complication that a psychoanalytic interpretation given to the patient is an action. It is not like, say, an interpretation of a text or a hypothesis about an unconscious meaning. It is also a communication that is meant to affect the patient and produce a change so that the question of correctness – 'Was it a good interpretation?' – is not only the question: 'Was it a valid translation of what the patient said or did?' It raises also such questions as, 'was that the important aspect of the patient's communication' or 'was it the right time to communicate to him a particular understanding'. And the validation comes from the patient's response.

I would take, for myself, as a validation of an interpretation something that I would feel is a move towards integration in the patient's inner world. If I think that something that was erroneously felt by him to be a piece of the outside world is now becoming experienced by him as his own feeling or phantasy, that would be one point. The other point which maybe links with it is if I felt that the interpretation put the patient more in touch with his reality sense.

But here I have to say what I mean by reality sense. The reality sense doesn't mean you suddenly become 'realistic' and give up your emotional life. What I mean by the reality sense is being aware of one's own inner reality which is one's wishes, one's phantasies, one's misconceptions; and being capable of testing them with the external reality. I think that the reality sense is the capacity to relate one's phantasy to the real world and see which is which.

MILLER So it's the patient's testimonial that becomes the criterion of validity. Since the patient is identified as the author of his or her own dreams and phantasies, then the validity of the analyst's interpretation must be something with which the patient himself personally identifies, and *that* must be the validating principle.

SEGAL Yes, I think that the validation of the interpretation can only be from the patient's response.

MILLER And is the patient a reliable witness of his response?

SEGAL By response I don't mean the patient saying 'yes' or 'no', or agreeing or disagreeing but the response in terms of what I see happens to his reality sense, in the sense in which I mean it.

MILLER Not just his becoming more socially efficient?

SEGAL No. And one can see it in the long-term. But, in the short-term, what I watch for is mostly moves towards integration, and that also means usually a change in the relationship to me as the interpreter.

Take the small child I spoke about, who first smiled at the analyst, a good analyst, then became frightened of the 'wall lady' and wanted to run away. When the analyst interpreted the split and identified the wall lady as being the analyst onto whom she'd peed, the child responded by giving the doll the milk and saying: 'Now she can feed'. To me that response was a validation of the interpretation. The persecution lessened, the ideal and the persecutory became a more real feeding object and that now the child could feed: a moment of integration.

dialogue with
Thomas Szasz

OBJECTIONS
TO PSYCHIATRY

INTRODUCTION

The remarkable advances in neurological knowledge that took place during the twentieth century encouraged the hope that insanity would yield to the same sort of analysis, and that with progress in biochemistry and pharmacology conditions such as schizophrenia and acute depression would become medically manageable. These ambitions have not been realised on the scale that some of the more optimistic clinicians would have hoped.

There is as yet no consistent theory to explain psychotic illness on the basis of biochemical neurology, and although pharmacological research has produced drugs which exert a powerful influence on the behaviour and mood of mentally disturbed patients, the suspicion remains that such treatment suppresses the symptoms and leaves the underlying disorder untouched. In any case, the alleviation of symptoms is often purchased at the expense of distressing side effects.

In recent years there has been a growing opposition to such an approach, and the opponents frequently raise the objection that patients who are treated in this way are being poisoned into submission in the effort to suppress behaviour which the community finds embarrassing and unmanageable. Such critics point out that the medical approach to insanity embodies a fundamental misconception about the nature of so-called mental illness.

The leading critic of this medical approach to madness has been Thomas Szasz, an American psychiatrist of Hungarian origin. For the past twenty-five years or more, Szasz has argued that madness has been misrepresented as a disease, and that the myth of mental illness has given the psychiatric profession a dangerously unlimited licence to imprison and manipulate mad people in the name of philanthropy or therapy, as well as a strategic misuse of language in the service of justifying a variety of repressive policies. In a long list of books published over the last twenty-five years he has argued that the failure to recognise this error has led to the loss of a precious human birthright.

DISCUSSION

MILLER When someone coins a vivid slogan, they often become associated with it for the rest of their lives. Your name is associated with the idea that mental illness is a myth. I wonder if you'd like to start by saying what you mean by the 'myth of mental illness'.

SZASZ By the 'myth of mental illness' I mean the same sort of thing as Gilbert Ryle[1] means by a 'category error'. The liver can be sick; the heart can be sick; the brain can be sick – using sick in the modern scientific sense, meaning that there is something biologically amiss with a part of the body. Since the mind is not a part of the body, is not an organ – since the mind is

[1] See note on page 60.

an abstract noun that lacks a concrete referent – it cannot be sick. It's as simple as that.

Of course, the term 'mental illness' means something. But what it means is very different from what it's supposed to mean. For decades, the American people have been bombarded with the message that 'mental illness is like any other illness'. That was the official, supposedly scientific position. It still is. Well, the one thing that's obvious about mental illness is that it is not like any other illness. In my view, it's not an illness at all.

MILLER   So you're saying then, in Ryle's sense, that we've mistaken the categories of illness by applying it to the mind. You feel that this is logically wrong as well as factually wrong.

SZASZ   That is correct. But to say that the idea of mental illness is a mistake is true only in a very benign philosophical sense. Because, in a sense, it's not really a mistake: nearly everyone knows that mental illness is not like cancer or heart disease.

So, if we are going to call this sort of talk a mistake – as Ryle, of course, has often done – then I would want to amplify that. I would want to talk about tactical mistakes. The whole history of psychiatry shows that the way mental illness is talked about is not simply a mistake, but is rather a particular way of using language to gain certain practical ends. So instead of talking about mental illness, we should talk about what doctors, surgeons and psychiatrists *do*.

To use some philosophical concepts again, we now know, or understand, that, empirically, a word means the habits it involves or engenders. We must stick to that, especially when it comes to psychiatric words. There is not much point in looking up such words, any kinds of words, in dictionaries. Of course, it's all right to do so when you begin to learn a foreign language. But if you want to know what a word really means, you have got to know how people actually use it. Because that's what it means.

MILLER   So, how and when, then, was the notion of sickness first applied or *mis*applied to the mind?

SZASZ   That's easy to answer and it ties right in with my argument. The idea of illness as applied to the mind is roughly coeval with the idea of illness, in the modern sense, as applied to the body. The contemporary, scientific idea of illness is not that old, either. Without going into too many details, remember that up to the end of the eighteenth century – say, until 1800 – doctors and scientists believed that a person was ill when he suffered from various disturbances of what were called the 'humours'. That was the humoural theory of disease. So it really wasn't until after the Enlightenment – actually not until about 1850, when medical microscopy developed – that a wholly different concept of disease arose: that is, the concept of disease as tissue damage, as bodily illness. It was during this same period, during the period when the medical concept of illness changed from the humoural to the cellular, that the idea of insanity changed from madness to mental illness.

The idea of madness is, of course, very old. It goes back to antiquity. But it didn't mean then, in the New Testament for example, what it means now. So the modern idea of mental illness developed parallel with the modern idea of bodily illness. But we must connect all this with an operational approach to mental illness, to psychiatry. So I think we should raise here the question of what psychiatrists traditionally and typically do and have done in the past. They have operated mental institutions, called madhouses or mental hospitals and confined people in buildings so labelled. Ostensibly the inmates were confined for the treatment of their mental illnesses. But that wasn't the real reason.

MILLER But prior to the identification of the mad with the sick, the custody of the mad was not necessarily legitimised in terms of illness or sickness. It was to do with the protection of the individual, or the protection of society, from the mad person. But you're saying that, with the advent of pathological notions of tissues and organs in physical disease, this extended to include madness, and that the mad person was now put in custody, as a *sick* person, rather than as an aberrant one.

SZASZ That's right. But now we have to fill in some blank spaces. As you know, as historians have shown, the idea of madness had been abroad in Western culture for a very long time. However, in the Middle Ages and before, madness didn't mean what it means now. Moreover, we can't really speak of the custody of madness before the modern era, because, for all practical purposes, there was no such thing. There were no madhouses or mental hospitals, to speak of, before the middle of the seventeenth century. In England there was Bedlam, of course. But that institution served a variety of purposes; housing the insane was just one of them. If we go back in history, say to classical Rome at its height, we find that it was a city of about two million people – and it had no institutions for housing mad people. The same holds for ancient Greece.

The point is that the increase in mental patients occurred in tandem, as it were, with the development of mental hospitals. The buildings, the patients, and the psychiatrists grew together, one after the other.

MILLER So you're saying then that the patient is a creation of the profession of psychiatry.

SZASZ I hope that's not too shocking. It's a simple idea, really, similar to the idea that the heretic is a creation of the theologian. Obviously, if there is no dogmatic, militant religion, there is no heresy and there are no heretics.

MILLER And you're also insisting that the development of the psychiatrist in his turn is the consequence of the misapplication of pathological ideas to the mind. Now why do you think, in the middle of the eighteenth century, it became necessary or attractive to categorise madness as the expression of sickness, rather than as some other denomination?

SZASZ Well, that ties in both with the development of the idea of illness and with the development, in Western culture, of urbanisation and the resulting problems of pauperism, vagrancy, and so forth. We are talking now, in a way, about the earliest form of the problem of unemployment. I am oversimplifying now, but this is the central problem of psychiatry: people in society who somehow can't make it; who don't make it; who are, or who have become, outsiders. This image is captured very nicely in the old-fashioned English term 'alienation'. In the eighteenth century the victims, the clients, the patients – it's hard to know what to call them – were alienated. The doctors who became their managers were called alienists. That's what mad-doctoring was all about. That's what psychiatry is still all about.

But there is something sticky about all this. We are talking about the eighteenth century, not the Middle Ages or Biblical times. We are talking about the West. There was already a sense of human rights abroad in the land. There was already a sense that you can't just sweep people off the streets and lock them up – unless they are criminals. But society – the dominant class of society – was now confronted with a lot of people who didn't fit in, who had no place in society, who lost their place in society – but who were not criminals. What justified locking them up? Illness.

In my opinion, illness – and especially mental illness – is one of the core concepts in the justificatory rhetoric of the modern world. It replaces God, in a way. From times immemorial until AD 1800, God was the centrepiece of justificatory rhetoric; since AD 1800, it's mental illness. In the name of God, people waged wars, killed and enslaved others. Religion justified all. Now medicine does.

Now people are locked up in the name of mental illness. When the Russians do that, the journalists in America and England say, 'that's awful, they are locking up dissidents'. That's not the way the Russians see it, of course. They say they are locking up schizophrenics. The sad part of it is that long before *they* did it, *we*, in the West, did it. Of course, we were not 'locking' up innocent persons, we were 'hospitalising' mental patients. And that's what we do today.

MILLER   So you're saying that the justification for putting away the awkward, the unpleasant or the disgusting or . . .

SZASZ   The helpless.

MILLER   . . . or the helpless . . .

SZASZ   . . . and the hopeless and the lonely . . .

MILLER   . . . was in fact pathological, and that unless someone could be described as sick, they had to be identified as mentally ill before people felt justified in putting them away.

SZASZ   Right. We see this idea developing already in Shakespeare's plays, at the very dawn – even before the dawn – of psychiatry. Hamlet's mother and uncle, for example, tried to get rid of him by classifying him as mad, but it wasn't so easy. No one locked up Lear, either, though he had what psychiatrists would now call a mental illness.

MILLER   You go on to insist that this is a disguised form of social control and that it's the exercise of a tyranny. Medicine has tyrannised the individual.

SZASZ   Well, yes, but let's go a little slower. You see, it's more complicated than that. Of course, psychiatric controls are a form of tyranny; but they are a form of protection, too. I am not softening my position, but I have always emphasised that psychiatric tyranny, like so many tyrannies, is a type of paternalism. So psychiatric controls satisfy two kinds of needs. On the one hand, psychiatrists help families, help society, by removing certain unpleasant or unmanageable people from their midst. On the other hand, psychiatrists also help individuals by providing housing and care – really, room-and-board – for people who can't or won't take care of themselves. In Calcutta, people live on the streets. You can't do that in London or New York, though in New York it's going a bit that way now. So in London and New York, the outcasts and the homeless people end up in mental hospitals. Many of these people may be ambivalent about this arrangement: they may not want to be there but have no better alternative. That is why, if psychiatric hospitals are half-way pleasant, the psychiatrists have trouble getting people discharged. These so-called hospitals are really homes for the homeless. They are orphanages for abandoned, solitary adults. It's a very sad affair, really. And what makes it sadder still, and economically ruinous and conceptually unmanageable in our society, is that this whole business is medicalised. The inmates are supposed to have mental illnesses, are supposed to get treatments for these illnesses, and so on. Everyone is looking for an illness where there isn't one. Just miserable, tragic lives.

MILLER   But is it merely because it's economically unviable that you regard the medicalisation of madness as objectionable, or do you think that there's some more fundamental ethical reason for removing the medical from the domain of the insane?

SZASZ   Both. I object to the medicalisation undergirding – or, better, inspiriting – psychiatry for both economic and ethical reasons. And for conceptual reasons, too, of course. But I think that's too abstract. Let's get back to what the psychiatrist does. The psychiatrist is a doctor, a physician. He is trained and licensed as a doctor. He claims to be a doctor. But what does he do?

    Well, what do other specialists do? The surgeon operates. The internist makes diagnoses and prescribes medicines. The psychiatrist, for his part, does two things. He takes innocent persons and deprives them of liberty; that's called civil commitment. And he takes guilty persons and claims that they are innocent; that's called the insanity defence. Ostensibly, both of these things are done in the name of mental illness, in the name of diagnosing and treating mental illness. That's the ideology. That's the justification. But the fact remains that they incriminate the innocent and excuse the guilty. Therein, precisely, lies much of their power.

MILLER   Perhaps I can take the legal case first of all, and offer an objection. Wouldn't it be true to say that until the abolition of capital punishment at least, the psychiatrist was not, in fact, proving the *innocence* of the murderer or whatever, but he was in fact exercising a humane function in offering some sort of mitigation. It was a life-saving manoeuvre, because at least it saved these wretches from the gallows; in that sense the psychiatrist was exercising a humane function and not simply inflicting a medical category on someone who ought to have been punished. He was softening the violence of a vindictive law.

SZASZ Of course, you are right. You know your medical history. That is what happened and *that*, by the way, is one of the reasons why psychiatrists have acquired, from early on, the mantle of being humanists. This sort of softening of the laws – really, evasion of the laws – has continued to the present day. For example, before abortion on demand became legal in America about ten years ago a pregnant woman who wanted an abortion had a choice between an illegal abortion and a legal abortion. This meant first going to a psychiatrist and, in effect, paying him to declare that she needs a 'therapeutic' abortion. I wrote about that, many years ago, and called it 'bootlegging humanism'.

So far so good. But social life is a complex dialectical process. Ideas have consequences. Let's go back and look at what the psychiatrists did in the nineteenth century when they used the insanity defence to save men from the gallows. If they objected to capital punishment, why didn't they – why didn't the British Psychiatric Association or the American Psychiatric Association – lobby against capital punishment? Why did they instead lie about mental diseases? Such lobbying would have been genuinely altruistic. But it would not have given them the mystique and the power, as professionals, that they craved. That they still crave.

Actually, what the nineteenth-century psychiatrists who called murderers insane did, had nothing to do with medicine or science. Rather, it was similar to what the legendary Raoul Wallenberg – the Swedish diplomat in Budapest in 1944 – did; and what a few other diplomatic representatives did. The Jews were threatened with deportation and murder in the gas chambers. So what did these diplomats do to save their lives? They said to the German authorities: 'Look, you can't kill these people. You can kill only Hungarian Jews. But these are not Hungarian Jews, these are Swedes . . .' What a horrible joke! Of course, unless one sympathised with the Nazi goal that *all* Jews should be killed, anything that saved some Jews from such a fate was permissible, was right. But let's trace this actual example and see what happened after the Nazis were defeated. After the war was over, no one claimed that these Hungarian Jews – who were never even near Sweden, who didn't speak Swedish – were Swedes. That claim was just a tactic which had served its purpose.

But that's not the way it has worked in psychiatry. In the nineteenth century, struggling against capital punishment, the psychiatrists often claimed that offenders subject to that penalty were mentally ill. But capital punishment is no longer a serious problem. In most western countries it is, for all practical purposes, a thing of the past. But the psychiatrists still insist that murderers – and, of course, all kinds of other persons who break the law too – are mentally ill. Moreover, many psychiatrists do not merely want to save people from execution, they want to 'save' them from all penal sanctions.

Take the case of the Yorkshire Ripper. Several psychiatrists testified that he was not responsible for the killings because he was sick. It seems likely that they genuinely believed that the Yorkshire Ripper killed women because he had a disease, just as some people have sugar in their urine because they have diabetes. This is what I mean when I say that ideas have consequences. The idea of mental illness has consequences. It may have started out as a metaphor and as a strategy, but now it has become real. The metaphor is now taken literally. This is one of the reasons why I believe that psychiatry is much like a religion.

MILLER Well, let us concede that certain forms of insanity may not be so readily identifiable with a physical pathology such as, say, jaundice which can be identified with a disorder of the liver, and which you can discover at autopsy, and say that psychiatrists have found it very hard to associate certain aberrations of behaviour with corresponding disorders of the brain.

But wouldn't it be reasonable to say that certain forms of conduct are so consistently unrepresentative of the main mass of human behaviour – like ripping ladies, and going out and doing it again and again in a compulsive way – and are so similar to disease, in the sense that they exhibit a certain sort of coherent consistency, that it's only hair-splitting to say that it's not a disease because you can't find some sort of organic lesion associated with it. The fact that someone is compelled to go on acting-out some antisocial violence is in itself enough to justify calling it a disorder, and indeed an illness?

SZASZ That is a very forceful way of framing the argument – the argument against *my* view, that is. Obviously, if my argument were the only one, it would have prevailed already and no one would think anything else. Your counter-argument goes to the heart of why that hasn't happened and is not about to happen.

Everything you said is plausible. But, let me try to sort out what, I think, is wrong with it, what is problematic – to put it mildly – about it. First of all, implicit in your argument is a subtle switching of the ground rules about what constitutes disease. Biological scientists and non-psychiatric physicians continue to stick to the idea that a disease is a demonstrable lesion, not a package of behaviours. That was the definition I used too. You are, in effect, suggesting another definition.

That's not all. You have also introduced the concept of behaviours that exhibit a 'coherent consistency'. Now, that will prove to be troublesome because there are all kinds of assemblages or configurations of behaviours that exhibit such coherence and consistency which we do not call diseases. For example, religious behaviour. If a person doesn't share the religious beliefs that inspire the behaviours he observes, then such behaviours may very well seem strange or peculiar to him. He may even call the religion a 'cult'. As you know, it is quite popular now in the United States for psychiatrists to call certain minority religions cults and to diagnose their adherents as suffering from mental illnesses. Of course, before it became a dominant religion, Christianity itself was a minority religion – a cult, if you like. My point is that you have provided no guidance about how we should distinguish between those assemblages of behaviour that are diseases, or that may be diseases, and those that are not, those that we need not suspect of being diseases.

Finally, you introduced the idea of law-breaking, of violence, as a disease. That I don't like at all. I hope we can expand on that. Let me now add only that I think it's a serious mistake to intermingle crime and disease. Crime is crime and disease is disease. One quick way to see the trouble we create for ourselves if we mix these categories is by coming back, once more, to the question of the duty of the doctor. Is it the duty of the doctor to help people recover from diseases? Or is it his duty to enforce the law and punish people? Obviously, if someone goes around killing women, like the Yorkshire Ripper did, once he is caught, any civilised society will do something to him. Even if what's done to him is called 'hospitalisation' or 'treatment', the subject will experience it as punishment.

MILLER   Simply in the sense that their liberty is curtailed . . .

SZASZ   Isn't that enough? Of course, they may suffer other indignities or punishments, in addition to their liberty being curtailed. They may be forced to ingest chemicals they don't want. They may be subjected to various interventions called 'psychiatric treatments'. But talking about those things will get us off our target. Let's stick to liberty, to the deprivation of liberty. Is it the proper function of a doctor to deprive a person of liberty?

MILLER   No, but it may be a doctor's function, in cases where there are unpleasantly violent penalties to be inflicted for such crimes, to exert an advocacy on behalf of the subject, simply to make sure that he does not suffer such violent penalties.

SZASZ   I don't believe that. I don't like that. After all, a doctor, like anyone else in modern society, is primarily an individual moral agent, a citizen. Only secondarily is he a doctor. Now, in his role as a person, as a citizen, it is his job to exert the sort of advocacy you speak of, to do the morally right thing, whatever that may be for him: protesting against irrational or vicious laws, sacrificing his life . . . leaving the country . . . If you are a conscientious doctor in Nazi Germany, then, I would say, the thing to do is to leave, to go to America, rather than to practise in that system.

MILLER   But if it's the function of the *legal* defence to point out causes of reduced responsibility, which may be simply a question of ignorance or carelessness, it may require someone who is *medically* expert to point out more occult sources of diminished responsibility, something which the doctor calls illness. Surely that's a perfectly reasonable and legitimate thing to do?

SZASZ   I have no objection to that. It cuts across medicine and psychiatry. Medical doctors may be involved in giving that sort of testimony too – a patient may have diabetes or epilepsy, for example. But this is really not the way things happen in psychiatry. In psychiatry, doctors typically testify about reduced responsibility; about how this or that defendant was not responsible for what he did because of his mental illness. That's the typical scenario. Why don't they ever testify about increased responsibility? There is an excellent example to illustrate this point, which is interesting both legally and historically, namely: drunkenness. In America, psychiatrists take it for granted that a so-called alcoholic who breaks the law should be dealt with more leniently than a normal, healthy person. But why should that be so? Why shouldn't drunkenness be an aggravating circumstance, as it was in Roman law?

MILLER   Well indeed it is.

SZASZ   Well, perhaps it still is, in some jurisdictions. But let's not get away from the typical psychiatric-legal situation. As you know, psychiatrists who testify in criminal trials to exculpate the defendant are looked upon as great humanitarians. Now, so far as drinking goes, we know perfectly well that alcohol relaxes a person's inhibitions. So you might expect that psychiatrists would systematically testify that persons who commit crimes while drunk are not only fully responsible for their acts but deserve to be judged especially severely. But that's not the way the game is played. You know how many vehicular accidents in America are due to drunken driving; some very famous Americans have been involved in such accidents. And what has happened to them? Not much. Because drunkenness is regarded as an exculpating condition, not as an inculpating condition.

MILLER   But it also may be an *in*culpating one. It's an aggravating circumstance to be in command of a vehicle when drunk, because in fact you know that to take in drink does in fact diminish your responsibility.

SZASZ   When was the last time that a British psychiatrist testified to that effect in court?

MILLER   It doesn't need psychiatric expertise to demonstrate that. But there may be sources of diminished responsibility which arise from something other than the intake of substances. There may well be susceptibility to substances which are simply being secreted inside your head, unknown to you. So that you may be an 'alcoholic' of your own making. In other words clinically insane.

SZASZ   Now you have constructed a purely hypothetical situation. In fact, no such internally secreted substances have been isolated. But let's *assume* that such substances existed; that they would predispose a person towards breaking the law, towards committing violent acts. There would still remain the question of how we should deal with him, of what we should do with him or to him. That's a legal question, a policy question, not a scientific question – though the answer may be informed by what we know, scientifically. So that question would still remain. The question would be: should such a person, as you have hypothesised, have more freedom to break the law, should he be penalised less for breaking the law, than you or I? Where does identifying him as different from you and me leave us? What intervention towards him, or against him, are you envisioning?

MILLER Well, then intervention might in fact be required. Having been identified as a person who was a victim of such-and-such disorder of his neurones, it would be both reasonable and humane to deprive him of the liberty of driving a car, as with an epileptic. Or it may well be that the curtailing of liberty had to be even more stringent, and that in the case of someone who was the victim of substances which made him violent, in or out of cars, he might actually have to be kept not merely off the road, but off society's back and put in custody.

Now I'm simply playing devil's advocate here. I'm not saying this is *necessarily* so. But it seems to be a defensible argument.

SZASZ Sure, it's a defensible argument. I'll even join you in it. If you are willing to be the devil's advocate, I am willing to be the devil. But the devil, as I see his role here, is on the side of the angels. I very much agree with the practice of not letting epileptics who have seizures drive cars, or of not letting them pilot 747s across the ocean, even if their seizures are controlled with dilantin. My criticisms of certain psychiatric practices do not commit me to opposing these perfectly sound policies based on what we know about certain medical conditions. But, you see, we have again slipped away from mental illnesses to medical illnesses. Medical illnesses are demonstrable conditions. A person may be thought to have epilepsy, he may be mistakenly accused of having epilepsy, his name might have got mixed with someone else's, let's say, and such a person could go to court and say: 'Look, I am accused of having epilepsy, but here is the evidence – my medical history, the neurological examinations, the electroencephalo- grams – to prove that I *don't* have epilepsy.' This could be done. The so- called patient could prevail; in fact, if he was right, he would be sure to prevail. But how does a person accused of schizophrenia prove that he doesn't have schizophrenia? So, we are back to square one, to the myth of mental illness.

Obviously, insofar as we are dealing with demonstrable bodily conditions that may affect other people – for example, epilepsy or infectious pulmonary tuberculosis – medicine has a very important social- protective function to play. But let's be clear what that function is and is not. That function is a public health function: protecting society from the patient, from the patient's illness. That's a valid and important function. But it is different from a therapeutic function, from helping the sick patient. There may even be a conflict between these two functions. Let me emphasise once more that I am wholly in favour of the public health functions of medicine. Physicians and biological scientists have a moral duty to provide their services for the protection of society – from infectious diseases, industrial pollution, radiation hazards, and so forth. In that case, the physician assumes the role of a protector of society – like the policeman or the soldier. I don't see any problems with that. That is not what I have been objecting to in legal psychiatry.

Let's go back to mental illness and let's take an actual example, or else this is going to be too vague. You remember what happened to Ezra Pound? He was charged with a crime but was not allowed to stand trial. There have been many such cases. Now it's happening in Russia. I'll summarise the scenario. A Russian writer, a so-called dissident, is arrested and is charged with some crime. The prosecutor or the judge says: 'We can't try him because he is crazy, he has schizophrenia.' The defendant says: 'Please let me stand trial because (a) I haven't got schizophrenia, and (b) I am innocent.' Now, that is the sort of situation that exposes the real problems, the characteristic problems, of psychiatry. That is the sort of situation I would prefer to talk about.

MILLER   You seem to hinge much of your argument on the existence of some objectively identifiable lesion. In someone who has jaundice and nausea and pale stools and so forth we expect to find corresponding disorders in the liver. But let's go back to the days *before* the findings at autopsy in the liver had been shown to have an association with the cluster of symptoms which patients presented in hospital. Now you wouldn't want to say that before the liver had been identified as the source of the illness, patients with jaundice, nausea, and so forth, were *not* in fact sick?

SZASZ   Of course not.

MILLER   Well, in exactly the same way, might it not be the case that certain consistencies of aberrant conduct and thought should be regarded as illnesses even though it is impossible at this particular point in time to find a lesion at autopsy?

SZASZ   Well, let's pursue this for a minute. Let's assume that that is the case – that certain identifiable patterns of behaviour, which psychiatrists now call schizophrenia, are indeed the symptoms of a very subtle disease of the nervous system. Precisely speaking, we should call this a putative disease, a suspected disease. It's not a proven disease. Okay. Let's assume that schizophrenia is such a putative disease. The question remains: What would happen if this were so? What would be the consequences? After all, there is no point in arguing about words; but there is a point in arguing about deeds. So what would be the consequences of treating schizophrenia as a real disease, as a brain disease? They would be of two kinds: one would concern the so-called patient, what he would do about it; the other would concern society, what other people would do about it.

So, let's try to spell out those consequences, otherwise it won't be clear what the fuss is all about. Because if a psychiatrist on Harley Street or at the Maudsley or wherever wants to believe that schizophrenia is a disease, why should I care. That's his business. He may also believe that Jesus is the Son of God, which I also don't happen to believe. So, what's next?

MILLER   All right. What is next then?

SZASZ   Well, we are back to the question of what does the patient want to *do*? If schizophrenia is an illness, if we are going to use the medical model – we are talking about patients in England or America, not Russia – then, it follows, doesn't it, that the patient is a free agent. Just as if he had, say, pneumonia. So you tell the patient: 'Mr Jones, you have got pneumonia, you should take some penicillin for it.' And the patient says: 'Thank you, Dr Miller, but I don't like penicillin. I'll go home and take aspirin.' Now, psychiatrists tell schizophrenics to take thorazine. And the patients often say, 'no I won't take thorazine.' Okay? Next chapter.

Now, let's assume that this gentleman with schizophrenia kills his wife or kills someone else. Why should he be able to plead schizophrenia as an excuse for such a crime, but not be able to plead diabetes or Parkinsonism, for that matter? Why should mental illness be an excuse for crime, but not bodily illness? You see, although I don't think schizophrenia is a disease, I don't have any objection to treating it, in some ways, *as if* it were a disease. But if schizophrenia were a disease, 'like any other', then it would not be an excusing condition for crime, as it now is.

So, if we want to treat schizophrenia as a disease, we must ask ourselves: what are the consequences of that idea? Of that linguistic practice? Let me dramatise this. A person can have all sorts of diseases today, even infectious diseases that are curable – certainly, this will be true for the United States – for example, a person can have active, infectious syphilis – and yet he cannot be treated for it against his will. Such a person could walk around in New York City and no doctor could forcibly inject him with an antibiotic. Why? Syphilis is not a putative disease; it's a proven disease. You can make sure whether someone has got it or hasn't got it. And it is safely curable. So why can't it be treated involuntarily? Partly, because everyone – for practical purposes everyone – who has syphilis is quite happy to have it treated. But that's not the only reason. It is also because faced with a conflict between individual liberty and medical therapy, our whole moral and political tradition, our customs and laws rank liberty higher than therapy.

So, syphilis you can identify objectively and scientifically, whereas schizophrenia you cannot – but schizophrenia you can treat involuntarily. Isn't that interesting? Well, to finish my comment on this subject, let me just add that as soon as psychiatrists would eschew – or, better, would refuse – hospitalising and treating people involuntarily, I would have much less objection to whether or not they call something a disease.

MILLER   If we can leave the juridical questions on one side for the moment . . .

SZASZ   We can't do that because psychiatry *is* juridical, through and through. We can only pretend to leave out the juridical.

MILLER   No, but if we can leave the more confined aspects of the juridical, in the sense of the . . .

SZASZ   The juridical hangs over psychiatry. Like a pall. When a social worker tells poor Mrs Jones to come to the hospital, she goes along, meekly. Mrs Jones knows very well that she can't successfully resist such an invitation, that the social worker can get the machinery rolling to get her certified.

So long as there are laws for involuntary mental hospitalisation, there can be no truly voluntary mental hospital patients. Strictly speaking, there are no voluntary mental hospital patients in Great Britain – even though most of them are officially, ostensibly voluntary. Just as there are no voluntary taxpayers. Of course, we all pay our taxes – in order not to go to jail. I don't call that a voluntary act.

MILLER   You mean that because there is the threat of *involuntary* commitment . . .

SZASZ   Indeed. Because of the threat of compulsory hospitalisation; because of the long history of it; because of the harsh reality of it, it's not an empty threat.

MILLER   No, but if I can shift the ground slightly and say there is nevertheless the problem of helping the apparently helpless, the agonised, the distressed, and those who are not merely agonised and distressed themselves, but those who agonise and distress their relatives, who for reasons of their madness – whether you call it illness or not – are not in a position to offer themselves as plaintiffs in the way that a patient suffering from physical disease is able to do. What do you do on the basis of philanthropy, on the basis of helping, in terms of kindness, about such people?

I agree with you, that there is always the threat of the tyranny of the involuntary commitment – of simply taking away someone's liberty merely because you have identified them one way rather than the other. But what do you do about those people who, for reasons which we needn't discuss – either because of brain disorder or something else, some existential disorder – have become mad, and mad in a way which renders them incapable of asking for the help which the medical profession might be able to give.

SZASZ   Your question is, again, very well taken. I would like to say all sorts of things about this, and I will. But let me first say that this is precisely why psychiatry is such an important social institution and why psychiatrists are so powerful. Because they *are* useful. I like to paraphrase Voltaire, in this connection. Voltaire, you remember, said that if there were no God, it would be necessary to invent him. Well, if there were no psychiatry, no mental illness, it would be necessary to invent it. Because, today, it is psychiatry, not religion, that comes to the rescue in many existentially difficult, tragic situations. Whether the way psychiatry resolves certain tough, vexing situations is the best way to resolve them; whether we could do better differently, without psychiatry – well, that is certainly debatable. Honest people can have honest differences about that. Many thoughtful people believe that, in certain situations, psychiatry now offers the best solution, the most humane or most practical answer. Before we can go any further with this, we must again break down the conglomeration of phenomena we are talking about and take each one separately.

You emphasised the patient's – the so-called patient's – helplessness, his inability to act as his own agent, to seek help. Now, that's certainly a part of the problem. It's a tusk or a leg, but it is surely not the whole elephant. Actually, insofar as people behave the way you described – insofar as they are so helpless that they cannot seek help – there is no great problem. In this respect, there is no difference between my views and the views of other psychiatrists. I believe that such a person should be treated pretty much the same way that a person knocked unconscious by a taxi is treated. The ordinary channels of medicine, law, compassion, and decency should be opened. The resources available in society should be mobilised on his behalf. He should be treated and cared for in whatever way makes sense in and to that society – humanely, caringly, therapeutically. There is no great problem here.

MILLER No, I see that.

SZASZ But you know, this sort of problem makes up only a very small part of psychiatric practice. It is a tiny part of the psychiatric elephant, so to speak; it is not a tusk or a leg, it's more like a toe-nail – if the elephant has a toe-nail. Why do I say that? Because although it is true that involuntarily hospitalised mental patients are often helpless, don't take good care of themselves, and don't seek help – ironically, there is one thing they are often very sure and decisive about. And that is, that they don't want to be in a mental hospital, that they don't want anything to do with psychiatrists.

But we still haven't touched on the sorts of human situations – on the conflicts that tear apart families, on the dilemmas that persons must face – in which psychiatrists typically intervene, in which they are typically expected to intervene. We need some examples again. I like to use literary examples. That way everyone knows what one is talking about. Now, who is a good example of a person, who would now be called a mental patient, presenting a distressing problem all around? Lady Macbeth. What's wrong with her? Well, I won't rehash the story. The point is that here is Macbeth who has finally made it, all the way to the top. Now he can't enjoy his success because of his wife. She is upset. She can't sleep. She sees blood where there is no blood. Psychiatrists would now say she suffers from an agitated depression. But why is she depressed? Is she sick? That's what her husband would like to believe. He calls the doctor. But the doctor – that was 400 years ago – knows why Lady Macbeth is depressed. Because she is guilty. So the doctor tells Macbeth that this is not a medical problem and beats a hasty retreat. Now, precisely that which the doctor in *Macbeth* says *is not* a medical problem, doctors now insist *is* a medical problem. This is as good an example of the medicalisation of morals as I can think of.

Of course, if you want to make the sort of problem that the Macbeths are having a medical problem, that can be done. Many people – many of the ostensible or designated patients and their families – actually invite such a medical definition of their life problems. It is also possible to do things to women like Lady Macbeth as a result of which their husbands are likely to feel better. For example, it is possible to give her drugs so she won't remember and won't remind her husband of all the things they ought to feel guilty about. It is possible to give electric shocks to her brain – and that will work even better in wiping out her painful memories. I don't think these are good things to do to people. But many people think otherwise. These are judgements about which honest people can disagree. For example, some of my psychiatric colleagues say: 'After Lady Macbeth gets electrotherapy – that's what they call it now – she'll feel better, she'll feel grateful for the treatment she got.' Perhaps. But what does that prove? To me, it certainly doesn't prove that she was ill or what was done to her was a treatment. There is a reason, after all, why Shakespeare didn't make Lady Macbeth come down with the plague, or make her run off with one of her husband's lieutenants. Those things would have spoiled Macbeth's success also. But they would not have made the point that Shakespeare wanted to make, that the play makes. The medicalisation of morality is the point. That's what we are talking about.

MILLER   So what do you feel *ought* to be on offer to those people who are exhibiting either very florid and peculiar and distressing mental symptoms, or florid disorders of behaviour, or thought, which are distressing either to them or to their relatives?

SZASZ   To begin with, I would want to separate those two categories. We are dealing with two quite different populations here. Let me first say something about people who upset other people.

Some so-called mental patients – people who are now called schizophrenic, depressed, Lady Macbeth, for example – may themselves suffer. Or they may not suffer – for example, people with so-called grandiose delusions. The point is that we are dealing here with a group of people whose pattern of behaviour upsets those with whom they live. Psychiatrists call such people disturbed, but it would be more accurate to call them disturbing. Now, for the sake of simplicity, let us assume that the so-called patient does not seek any help – at least, not via medical or psychiatric channels. In that case, I believe it is up to the disturbed relatives, friends, employers, and so forth to decide what they want to do, how they want to conduct themselves towards the disturbing, upsetting person. The upsetting person may, of course, be counselled or cajoled to change his behaviour, to pursue one or another course; but, in my opinion, nothing should be done to him by force, against his will – as long as he does not break the law. *Primum non nocere* – first of all, do no harm – that is the classic Latin precept for the doctor in quandary. It's a good precept. I think it could and should be applied to the way we treat so-called psychotic persons. Of course, if the person consents . . . well, then, there is no problem.

MILLER   No, but I'm trying to indicate a type of patient who is not simply obstreperous, he's not causing distress to his relatives because he makes their life distressing . . .

SZASZ   Give me an example.

MILLER   Well, I'm talking about the personality changes which lead the relatives, the parents, the siblings to say *not*: 'Please cure my brother, sister or father, because they are making our life appalling,' but: 'Please restore to us the person whom we love.' Not: 'Please make them less obstreperous – less insulting, less disgusting,' but: 'We would like back the lovable person with whom we've been associated all our lives.'

SZASZ   Ah! Hard as I may try – and without wanting to appear difficult about this – I can't deal with that. I can't deal with it, in that form, because a relative who would speak like that would already be denying the reality, the truth of what is happening in his life and in the life of his so-called loved one. Just as Macbeth was denying, or was trying to deny, how he got to the top – his bloody deeds.

       You still haven't given me a concrete example. It's all too abstract. We have got to have a concrete example. May I suggest one? Here is a fine young woman. She had been a good, healthy, lovable child. She was fine when she was ten, eleven, twelve years old. Then, when she gets to be thirteen, fourteen, fifteen, she begins to starve herself. She hardly eats. When she eats, she throws up. Pretty soon she looks like a skeleton. The psychiatrists say: 'Ah, she has got anorexia nervosa.' The parents say: 'Give us back our wonderful daughter, just the way she was before she became ill; she was a healthy little girl, she ate normally, everything was fine.'

MILLER   Yes, but isn't that a perfectly legitimate and reasonable request?

SZASZ   It looks like a legitimate request, but it's not because it denies all the reasons why this young woman doesn't eat – which, from her point of view, are just as legitimate as why a hunger striker in Northern Ireland doesn't eat.

MILLER   But surely there is a fundamental distinction. Admittedly the reasons why the patient suffering from anorexia nervosa is deliberately abstaining from food may be metaphorically similar to the way in which the prisoner in the H-block is abstaining from his. She may be trying to get some sort of deal. But in the case of the H-block prisoner, the concessions which would call off the strike are clearly known. They're on the table. But in the case of the *anorexic* patient it's almost impossible for anyone other than an expert, and perhaps a medical expert, to find out what concessions would get them to call off the strike.

SZASZ   That's not so. Excuse me for being so direct. I think this may be a very instructive parallel, between anorexia nervosa and anorexia politica, as it were. The point you make is partly – and that part is correct – that nothing in the motivation or goal-structure of the Irish hunger striker is mysterious or repressed. We know why he doesn't eat. People can now accept and tolerate all the ideas involved in such a drama – who the hunger striker is, what he wants, what his adversaries want. That's where the difference lies between the self-starvation of a political prisoner and of a young woman in contemporary society. I'll have to over-simplify here a bit, but what I will say is, I dare say, correct. Whereas people now accept the motivation of an Irish hunger striker, they do not accept – they reject, repress, deny, call it what you will – that there are many young people today who, during adolescence, have one overriding goal – and that is not to grow up! Now, that is a pretty unpleasant fact, all right. And people can't tolerate it. So we call it schizophrenia, we call it anorexia nervosa, we call it all sorts of things, depending on how the young person displays his or her refusal to grow up.

So, the point is that most people can't tolerate that there are some young girls who don't want to become adult women, with everything that role implies for them; they don't want to become second-class citizens. Can you blame them – when that's how they have been treated for so long? They don't want to be sexually attractive, perhaps because that leads to having babies, which they may not want and so forth. You are right, of course, that what these women want is not a relatively straightforward political deal, like a prisoner might want. It is a more subtle existential deal; the protest is symbolic, is more disguised. People are not prepared to hear such demands, much less to meet them; it may be impossible to meet them.

MILLER But nevertheless, as regards the family, what you have is a painful situation and apparently one which will eventually lead to a fatal outcome.

SZASZ But it's not a fatal outcome.

MILLER Well it *may* be a fatal outcome.

SZASZ No, no. Please. You are in the word business, you deal with language. When you speak about a fatal outcome, you make it sound as if we were dealing with something like cancer or end-stage renal disease. But what we are talking about is a person, a young woman, who may prefer death to growing up as a woman. In 1400, she might have been called a saint. You know. 'Give me liberty or give me death.' There have been lots of people throughout history who have preferred one or another goal, even if it meant death, to a life on terms they deemed unacceptable, which raises the whole question of suicide – and that is a question which our society is especially loath to look at. We deny the legitimacy or rationality of suicide. It's a mental illness. I am not particularly advocating suicide . . .

MILLER No, but without denying the legitimacy of it one can understand relatives who would prefer it not to take place and say: 'Please do something to persuade our daughter *not* to kill herself.'

SZASZ Now we are off to the races. The parents of a young woman or man may prefer all sorts of things; they may prefer that their son, if he is a nice Jewish boy, should not marry a Gentile girl; or that their daughter, if they like their son-in-law, should not get a divorce. Now we have shifted to talking about how some family members would like some other family members to behave; especially how older family members would like younger family members to behave. That's got nothing to do with disease; that's got to do with power. Suppose that the father is an orthodox rabbi and the son comes home and all he wants for lunch is a ham sandwich; so, where is the disease? But anorexia nervosa is? Why is that a disease?

MILLER Well, to whom do they go in order to talk about it?

SZASZ That's their problem, their decision to make. I am just trying to bring order to psychiatric chaos. I don't have an answer to every one of life's problems. I only know a stupid answer when I see one.

MILLER I recognise *that*. But in that case let us put ourselves in the position of the unfortunate complainer, whether it is a relative or the patient himself or herself. To whom do they turn? *You* say it's not your problem – whose problem is it?

SZASZ Well, let me try to answer that in greater depth. You see, before we can deal with that question, we must distinguish between problems and problems. There are lots of problems in life. Let us distinguish between two quite different types. Let's call the first kind of problem scientific or technical, and the second kind moral or personal.

Suppose a person has pneumococcal pneumonia and he wants help with that problem. Then he should turn to someone who is an expert on treating pneumococcal pneumonia – and who has the appropriate chemicals, to which pneumonia responds.

But suppose someone has a family problem – about having children, divorce, religious differences. To whom should such a person turn for help? If the person who has got this problem is going to do this right – right, as I see it, of course – then the decision about whom he turns to for help must grow out of who he is. In other words, this is not a decision that can be made by determining who is technically most competent to help in such a situation; instead, it must grow – I am tempted to say, organically – out of who the person seeking help is. Let's assume that the troubled person is devoutly religious, that his whole family is devoutly religious – then, I think, it would be best for them if he sought help, if all of them sought help, from a priest or a rabbi. On the other hand, if our hypothetical clients are not religious but are psychologically inclined – then it may make sense for them to seek help from a psychotherapist or a psychoanalyst.

You see my point? . . . I could go on. If the person with the problem is in love with medicine, with drugs – then he could go to doctors, take thorazine, have a transsexual operation – people seek all kinds of solutions for their problems, for the way they interpret their problems.

Transsexual operations are a good case in point. I don't like them. But some people do. Officially, they are treatments. The American government, the American taxpayer now pays doctors to operate on perfectly healthy men in order to make them into fake women, and *vice versa*. So, that gives you some idea of the range of choices people have when they try to solve their life problems.

MILLER   So you're saying that whoever finds themselves distressed should seek relief from some ethical source, rather than from some medical one.

SZASZ   Yes, that's right. It's a mistake for people to seek relief for existential or spiritual difficulties through technological means. But it isn't just the medical methods that are faulty, that lead to a dead end. All the technicalised, pseudo-scientific methods – for example, psychoanalysis and the other so-called modern psychotherapies – are fundamentally flawed.

You see, I look upon all of psychiatry as a religion, with various branches and types. Biological psychiatry, Freudian, Jungian, Reichian, this kind of 'analysis' and that kind of 'analysis' – direct, rational, transactional, you–name–it – just so many creeds and cults. To all this, I try to bring the point of view of a psychiatric atheist: of someone who observes, studies, comments on all these creeds, but who refuses to accept any of the cult-founders, of the gurus, as scientists; who insists on calling their rituals rituals rather than therapies. This is why I said, a long time ago, that the trouble with evaluating psychiatric treatments is that in psychiatry everything works and nothing works. In short, all of the psychiatric 'treatments' are fine, for those who believe in them. If the psychiatrist wants to believe in a certain method – fine; if the patient wants to believe in it – fine. If they both believe in the same thing, let them get together – that's fine, too. All psychiatries, like religions, are okay, so long as they are practised voluntarily, without coercion, without state intervention. All are objectionable if the state promotes them and pays for them. And all of them become evil if the state imposes them on persons by force. That is my moral and political position on religions, psychiatry included. That position does not mean that I don't also have an intellectual opinion about them. I do, as I indicated already. I hold all contemporary psychiatric approaches – all 'mental-health' methods – as basically flawed because they all search for solutions along medical-technical lines. But solutions for what? For life! But life is not a problem to be solved. Life is something to be lived, as intelligently, as competently, as well as we can, day in and day out. Life is something we must endure. There is no solution for it.

Suggestions for further reading

1. GEORGE MILLER

G.A. MILLER and R. BUCKHOUT. *Psychology: The Science of Mental Life*, 2d ed. New York: Harper & Row, 1973; London: Penguin, 1966.
  A general introduction to psychology, with a historical perspective.

R. LACHMAN and J. LACHMAN. *Cognitive Psychology and Information Processing: An Introduction*. Hillsdale, NJ: Erlbaum, 1979.
  A survey of the changes that have occurred in experimental psychology since World War II.

2. JEROME BRUNER

J.S. BRUNER. *A Study of Thinking*. New York: John Wiley & Sons, 1956. (Out of Print.)
  One of the earliest examples of the application of the new 'informational' approach to human higher mental processes.

J.S. BRUNER, R.R. Olver, P.M. Greenfield (and others). *Studies in Cognitive Growth*. New York: John Wiley & Sons, 1966. (Out of Print.)
  These are studies of the development of children's cognitions by members of the Center for Cognitive Studies.

J.S. BRUNER. *Processes of Cognitive Growth: Infancy*. Worcester, MA: Clark University Press, 1968.

J. PIAGET. *Language and Thought of the Child*, 3d ed. Atlantic Highlands, NJ: Humanities Press, 1962; London: Kegan Paul and Co., 1926.
  This is the classic work that turned the field of child development towards concern with the systematic nature of intellectual development.

J.S. BRUNER. *Beyond the Information Given: Studies in the Psychology of Knowing*, ed. J.M. Anglin. New York: W.W. Norton, 1973.
  This is a collection of typical research studies on various aspects of cognitive development.

J.S. Bruner. *How Children Come to Talk*. New York: W.W. Norton, in preparation.

This is based on Professor Bruner's work at Oxford University on the social aspects of language acquisition.

3. RICHARD LANGTON GREGORY

R.L. Gregory and J.G. Wallace. *Recovery from Early Blindness: A Case Study*. Reprinted in *Concepts and Mechanisms of Perception*. London: Duckworth, 1974.

An exciting case history of a man born blind who recovered his sight in middle age.

R.L. Gregory. *Eye and Brain*, 3d ed. London: Weidenfeld and Nicolson, 1977.

A popular introduction to visual perception, available in ten languages as well as in Braille and "Talking Books."

R.L. Gregory. *The Intelligent Eye*. New York: McGraw-Hill pbk., 1970; London: Weidenfeld and Nicolson, 1970.

This concentrates on the way we make sense of the world from sensory signals.

R.L. Gregory and Sir Ernst Gombrich, eds. *Illusion in Nature and Art*. London: Duckworth, 1973.

A collection of chapters by various contributors, showing the power of illusion in perception.

R.L. Gregory. *Concepts and Mechanisms of Perception*. London: Duckworth, 1974.

A collection of research papers by Professor Gregory and various colleagues, concerning perception principles.

R.L. Gregory. *Mind in Science: A History of Explanations in Psychology and Physics*. New York: Cambridge University Press, 1981; London: Weidenfeld and Nicolson, 1981, and Penguin pbk., 1983. In Great Britain, a Macmillan Scientific Book Club choice, 1982.

This traces ideas and concepts in the physical world and compares them with how the observer perceives the visual world.

4. DANIEL C. DENNETT

F. Dretske. *Knowledge and the Flow of Information.* Cambridge, MA: Bradford Books/MIT Press, 1981.

A fascinating and ingenious attempt by a philosopher to build a theory of cognitive, or semantic, information on the foundation of the Shannon-Weaver information theory.

D.R. Hofstadter and D.C. Dennett, eds. *The Mind's I: Fantasies and Reflections on Self and Soul.* New York: Basic Books, 1981; London: Harvester, 1981.

An anthology of thought experiments and commentary designed to lead the reader to an appreciation and understanding of the new theories of the mind growing out of artificial intelligence and philosophy.

A. Woodfield, ed. *Thought and Object: Essays on Intentionality.* New York: Oxford University Press, 1982.

An anthology of philosophical essays, all quite technical, on the problems of attributing content to mental states and processes.

J. Haugeland, ed. *Mind Design: Philosophy, Psychology, and Artificial Intelligence.* Cambridge, MA: Bradford Books/MIT Press, 1981.

An introductory collection of classic papers on the conceptual foundations of artificial intelligence.

5. JEROME FODOR

N.J. Block, ed. *Imagery.* Cambridge, MA: Bradford Books/MIT Press, 1981.

An anthology of recent philosophical and psychological papers on mental images; the experimental findings and their philosophical implications are both extensively discussed.

N. Chomsky. *Language and Mind* (enlarged edition). New York: Harcourt Brace Jovanovich, 1972.

A brief introduction to contemporary syntactic theory, with a provocative discussion of implications for philosophical and psychological pictures of the mind.

J.A. Fodor. *The Language of Thought.* Cambridge, MA: Harvard University Press, 1979; London: Harvester, 1976.

A general philosophical discussion of the concept of mental representation and of associated issues about the structure and ontogeny of concepts, with special attention given to questions about innateness.

M. Piatelli-Palmarini. *Language and Learning: The Debate Between Jean Piaget and Noam Chomsky.* Cambridge, MA: Harvard University Press, 1980. (Out of Print.)

Proceedings of a conference that centered on issues concerning the innateness and modularity of linguistic capacities.

6. STUART HAMPSHIRE

S. Freud. *The Interpretation of Dreams.* New York: Avon, 1967; London: George Allen and Co., 1913.

This shows Freud's methods at work.

S. Freud. *Introductory Lectures on Psychoanalysis.* New York: Liveright/W.W. Norton, 1974; London: George Allen and Unwin, 1922, and Penguin, 1974.

The most authoritative general summary of Freudian psychoanalysis.

S. Freud. *An Autobiographical Study.* New York: W.W. Norton, 1963; London: Hogarth, 1935.

This is informative and reveals Freud's temperament.

R. Wollheim. *Sigmund Freud.* New York: Cambridge University Press, 1981.

The complete exposition of Freudian theory.

E. Jones. *The Life and Work of Sigmund Freud,* 3 vols. New York: Basic Books, 1957.

The authorised story of the psychoanalytic movement.

7. NORMAN GESCHWIND

N. Geschwind. *Selected Papers on Language and the Brain*, vol. 16 in the series Boston Studies in the Philosophy of Science. Hingham, MA: Reidel/Kluwer Boston, 1974.

This volume contains 26 papers published in 1973 or earlier dealing with a wide variety of topics relating to brain-behaviour relationships.

N. Geschwind. "Language and the Brain," *Scientific American* (April 1972), pp. 76–83.

A discussion of the anatomy and connections of the language systems and the clinical disturbances resulting from damage.

N. Geschwind. "Specialisations of the Human Brain," *Scientific American* (September 1979), pp. 180–99.

This article, appearing in an entire issue devoted to the brain, deals with the specialisations of the brain for emotion, face recognition, spatial abilities, and other functions.

N. Geschwind. "The Apraxias: Neural Mechanisms of Disorders of Learned Movement," *American Scientist* 63 (1975), pp. 188–95.

This article describes the organisation of the motor systems and the many different ways by which motor activity can be produced.

8. GEORGE MANDLER

G. Mandler. *Mind and Emotion*. Melbourne, FL: Kreiger, 1982.

Available only in a reprint of the 1975 edition, but a new book, *Mind, Consciousness and the Emotions*, which incorporates most of *Mind and Emotion*, will be published in late 1983.

R. Plutchik and H. Kellerman, eds. *Theories of Emotion*, vol. 1 of *Emotion: Theory, Research, and Experience*. New York: Academic Press, 1980.

A smorgasbord of the range of current speculations about emotion, with individual chapters by the respective theorists.

M.S. CLARK and S.T. FISKE, eds. *Affect and Cognition: The Seventeenth Annual Carnegie Symposium on Cognition.* Hillsdale, NJ: Erlbaum, 1982.

A collection of original essays on current research and theory.

9. ROM HARRE

P. Collett, ed. *Social Rules and Social Behaviour.* Totowa, NJ: Rowman, 1977; London: Blackwell, 1977.

A fairly detailed study of the way rules are used in the management of everyday life.

E. GOFFMAN. *Relations in Public.* New York: Torch Books/Harper and Row, 1972; London: Penguin Books, 1972.

The classic study of how people manage to achieve an orderly way of living when they are strangers to each other.

R. HARRÉ. *Social Being: A Theory of Social Psychology.* Totowa, NJ: Rowman/pbk. Littlefield, 1980; London: Blackwell, 1979.

The distinction between the expressive and the practical aspects of human action is used to analyse many different kinds of social episodes and to suggest ways of understanding social change.

P. MARSH, E. ROSSER, and R. HARRÉ. *The Rules of Disorder,* from The Social World of Childhood Series. Boston and London: Routledge and Kegan Paul, 1978/pbk. 1980.

Popular myth sees football violence as meaningless, but it is possible to discover the rules behind the riots.

V. REYNOLDS. *The Biology of Human Action,* 2d ed. San Francisco: W.H. Freeman, 1980.

Recently, animal studies have suggested new ways of looking at human behaviour. This book explores the uses and limitations of that idea.

10. ROBERT A. HINDE

R.A. HINDE. *Animal Behaviour: A Synthesis of Ethology and Comparative Psychology.* New York: McGraw-Hill, 1970. (Out of Print.)

Professor Hinde describes this as a textbook for students but considers that it is perhaps getting a little out of date.

R.A. HINDE. *Towards Understanding Relationships.* New York: Academic Press, 1980.

An attempt to lay a basis of description for a science of interpersonal relationships.

R.A. HINDE. *Ethology: Its Nature and Relation with Other Sciences.* New York: Oxford University Press, 1982.

A book for the intelligent layman surveying the nature of ethology and its relations to other sciences.

R.A. HINDE. *Biological Basis of Human Social Behaviour.* New York: McGraw-Hill, 1974.

This is a survey of the literature on non-human primates insofar as it is relevant to man.

11. CLIFFORD GEERTZ

E.E. EVANS-PRITCHARD. *Witchcraft, Oracles, and Magic Among the Azande.* New York: Oxford University Press, 1937/ pbk abr. ed., 1976; London: Clarendon, 1939.

A classic study of the modes of reasoning of a tribal African people in connection with a particular issue: the explanation of events that, in a Western society, would be attributed to 'chance' but here are causally ascribed to 'witchcraft'.

B. MALINOWSKI. *Magic, Science, and Religion,* from *Science, Religion, and Reality,* ed. J. Needham. Port Washington, NY: Kennikat, 1970.

A reprint of the 1925 Sheldon edition, this is a study of Trobriand Islanders' ways of coming to terms with uncertain events, and the role of formula, empirical knowledge, and ceremony in regulating social life.

S. LANGER. *Philosophy in a New Key: A Study in the Symbolism of Reason, Rite, and Art,* 3d ed. Cambridge, MA: Harvard University Press, 1957.

An interpretation of tribal myth and rite as symbolic modes of rendering experience intelligible.

C. Lévi-Strauss. *The Savage Mind*, from The Nature of Human Society Series. Chicago: University of Chicago Press, 1966/pbk., 1968; London: Weidenfeld and Nicolson, 1966.

An interpretation of tribal thought as 'concrete science', that is, the formulation of abstract ideas in terms of sensuous representations.

12. ERNST H. GOMBRICH

E.H. Gombrich. *Art and Illusion: A Study in the Psychology of Pictorial Presentation*, 2d ed. Princeton, NJ: Princeton University Press, 1961.

A comprehensive study of the development of representation in the history of art from ancient to modern times.

E.H. Gombrich. *The Image and the Eye.* London: publ. n.a., 1982. In the U.S., *A Sense of Order: A Study in the Psychology of Decorative Art.* Ithaca, NY: Cornell University Press, 1979.

Most of the topics touched upon in Sir Ernst Gombrich's discussion with Jonathan Miller are here discussed at greater length.

R.L. Gregory and E.H. Gombrich. *Illusion in Nature and Art.* New York: Scribner pbk., 1974; London: publ. n.a., 1973.

13. BRIAN A. FARRELL

S. Freud. *Introductory Lectures in Psychoanalysis.* New York: Liveright/W.W. Norton, 1974; London: George Allen and Unwin, 1922, and Penguin, 1974.

Freud is the best popular exponent of his own work, and these lectures present his position in his middle period.

E. Nagel, 'Methodological Issues in Psychoanalytic Theory', in *Psychoanalysis, Scientific Method and Philosophy*, ed. S. Hook. New York: New York University Press, 1959. (Out of Print.)

This essay is the *locus classicus* of the criticism that psychoanalysis and Freud's work are not scientifically respectable.

D.H. Malan. *Individual Psychotherapy and the Science of Psychodynamics.* Woburn, MA, and London: Butterworth, 1979.

A book that presents a stimulating and valuable insight into the ways in which a contemporary analyst uses and applies the concepts and generalisations of psychoanalysis and psychodynamics.

J. SANDLER. *The Patient and the Analyst: The Basis of the Psychoanalytic Process.* New York: International Universities Press, 1973; London: Allen and Unwin, 1973.
A lucid attempt to clarify the basic clinical concepts used by analysts to describe and explain what happens in psychoanalytic treatment, in the course of which the authors reveal how they view their own practical work.

B.A. FARRELL. *The Standing of Psychoanalysis.* New York: Oxford University Press, 1982.
This is an introductory study, which examines the epistemological status of psychoanalysis and psychodynamics in general by concentrating on the person who started all the trouble—Freud.

14. HANNA SEGAL

H. SEGAL. *Introduction to the Work of Melanie Klein*, 2d ed. New York: Basic Books, 1980; London: Hogarth, 1973.
An account of Kleinian theories illustrated by Dr. Segal's own work and based on a series of lectures given to students at the Psychoanalytic Society.

H. SEGAL. *Melanie Klein*, from the Modern Masters Series. New York: Viking, 1980/Penguin pbk., 1981; London: Penguin, 1979.
A biography, including an account of the development of her work.

H. SEGAL. *The Work of Hanna Segal: A Kleinian Approach to Clinical Practice.* New York: Aronson, 1981.
A collection of selected papers on psychoanalysis, both clinical and applied.

15. THOMAS S. SZASZ

G. RYLE. *The Concept of Mind.* New York: Harper and Row, date n.a.; London: Hutchinson's University Library, 1949.

302 · STATES OF MIND

The classic account of the 'category error' and its implications for explanations of human behaviour.

T.S. Szasz. *The Myth of Mental Illness: Foundations of a Theory of Personal Conduct,* rev. ed. New York: Harper and Row, 1974; London: Secker and Warburg and Paladin, 1972.

His most systematic effort to show that mental illnesses, as literal diseases similar to bodily illnesses, do not and cannot exist, and a discussion of the implications of this idea on the profession and 'science' of psychiatry.

T.S. Szasz. *Law, Liberty, and Psychiatry.* New York: Macmillan, 1963/pbk., 1968.

An account of the numerous interpenetrations of law with psychiatry, demonstrating how and why psychiatric ideas and interventions are fundamentally inimical to the concepts of individual freedom and responsibility and the political institutions based on them.

T.S. Szasz. *The Myth of Psychotherapy.* Garden City, NY: Anchor Books/Doubleday, 1979.

An account of what psychiatrists do when they are said to be 'treating' mental illnesses or mental patients, showing that so-called psychiatric therapies are not methods of treating disease, but religious, rhetorical, and repressive acts couched in pseudo-medical terminology, socially accredited as medical treatments.

R.M. Weaver. *The Ethics of Rhetoric.* Chicago: Regnery-Gateway, 1953.

A seminal book on the strategic use of language and its relations to politics, morals, and the social sciences.

The contributors

Professor Jerome BRUNER was born in New York in 1915. He was educated at Duke University and Harvard University. After the war, during which he worked on political intelligence and psychological warfare, he was appointed Professor of Psychology at Harvard University. From 1972 to 1979 he was Watts Professor of Psychology and Fellow of Wolfson College, Oxford University, and from 1979 to 1981 he was a Sloan Foundation Fellow at Harvard University. In 1981 he became George Herbert Mead University Professor at the New School for Social Research.

His publications include *Mandate from the People*, *A Study of Thinking*, *The Process of Education*, *On Knowing: Essays for the Left Hand*, *Toward a Theory of Instruction*, *Processes of Cognitive Growth in Infancy*, *The Relevance of Education*, *Under Five in Britain*. His forthcoming books are *Learning to Use Language* and *Quest for Mind: Autobiographical Essays*.

Professor Daniel DENNETT was born in Boston in 1942, and was educated at Harvard and at Oxford, where he worked with Gilbert Ryle, and received his Ph. D. in philosophy in 1965. He is currently Professor of Philosophy at Tufts University, in Medford, Massachusetts, and has taught at the University of California at Irvine, Harvard University, and the University of Pittsburgh. He is the author of *Content and Consciousness*, and *Brainstorms: Philosophical Essays on Mind and Psychology*, and the co-editor with Douglas R. Hofstadter of *The Mind's I: Fantasies and Reflections on Self and Soul*. He has also published numerous journal articles in philosophy and psychology.

In 1978 he was a Fulbright Research Professor at the University of Bristol, and in 1979 he was a Visiting Fellow at All Souls College, Oxford, and a Fellow at the Center for Advanced Study in the Behavioral Sciences in Palo Alto. In 1983 he will give the John Locke Lectures at Oxford.

Mr B. A. FARRELL was born near Cape Town in 1912. He was elected Rhodes Scholar from the University of Cape Town. After a period in England he became Lecturer in Philosophy at the University of the Witwatersrand, Johannesburg, until 1947. He left South Africa, and after spending a year in Cambridge, England, he was elected Reader in Mental Philosophy at the University of Oxford. He was elected Fellow of Corpus Christi College in 1965 and retired from the readership in 1979.

His publications include *Experimental Psychology*, the Introduction to Freud's essay 'Leonardo da Vinci' in *Leonardo* ed. with B. Babington Smith, *Training in Small Groups* and *The Standing of Psychoanalysis*.

Professor Jerome FODOR was born and raised in New York City and educated at Columbia College. His Ph.D. is in philosophy from Princeton University. With the exception of occasional visiting appointments, he has spent his entire academic career at the Massachusetts Institute of

Technology, where he holds a joint appointment in Philosophy and Psychology. About fifteen years ago, he unexpectedly got involved in laboratory psychology. Since then, most of his research has concerned one or another aspect of the theory of cognitive processes, which he has approached sometimes from a philosophical and sometimes from an experimental point of view.

His major publications include the books *Psychological Explanation*, *The Language of Thought*, *The Psychology of Language* (with Professors M. Garrett and T. Bever), *Representations*, and a forthcoming monograph called *The Modularity of Mind*.

Professor Clifford GEERTZ was born in San Francisco in 1926 and after serving in the US Navy during World War II was educated at Antioch College and Harvard University. He has done extensive anthropological field research in Indonesia and Morocco, and has taught anthropology at Harvard University, the University of California, Berkeley, the University of Chicago, and, as Eastman Professor, Oxford University. He is at present Harold F. Linder Professor of Social Science at the Institute for Advanced Study, Princeton, New Jersey, and is the author of *The Religion of Java*, *Agricultural Involution*, *Peddlers and Princes*, *The Social History of an Indonesian Town*, *Islam Observed*, *The Interpretation of Cultures*, *Kinship in Bali* (with H. Geertz), *Meaning and Order in Moroccan Society* (with H. Geertz and L. Rosen) and *Negara: The Theatre State in Nineteenth Century Bali*, as well as numerous articles. Another collection of his essays, *Local Knowledge*, will appear next year.

Professor Norman GESCHWIND was born in New York City. He attended Boys High School in Brooklyn, Harvard College in Cambridge, and the Harvard Medical School in Boston. He had postgraduate training in Boston, at the National Hospital, Queen Square, London, and at the Massachusetts Institute of Technology. He was formerly in the Department of Neurology at the Boston University School of Medicine where he eventually held the post of Professor of Neurology and Chairman of the Department. Since 1969 he has been James Jackson Putnam Professor of Neurology at the Harvard Medical School and is also Neurologist-in-Chief of the Beth Israel Hospital. He is also Professor of Psychology at the Massachusetts Institute of Technology. He has published over 100 papers. His major interest has been the understanding of behaviour on the basis of the organisation of the brain. He has worked on language disorders, anatomical asymmetries of the brain, the corpus callosum and split-brain syndromes, immune disorders and migraine in left-handers, behavioural changes in epilepsy, the evolution of language, the history of studies of brain–behaviour relationships, and epilepsy in Dostoievsky's life and writings.

Sir Ernst GOMBRICH, CBE, was born in Vienna in 1909 and educated at Vienna University. In 1936 he came to England to work at the Warburg Institute (which had emigrated from Hamburg to London) with which he has been associated ever since. During the war years he was with the BBC Monitoring Service. After the war he returned to research and teaching. He has been Slade Professor of Fine Art at the Universities of Oxford and Cambridge and held guest professorships in America and elsewhere. He is a Fellow of many learned Societies and the recipient of no less than twelve honorary degrees.

His many publications include *The Story of Art*, *Art and Illusion*, *Meditations on a Hobby Horse*, *Aby Warburg, an intellectual biography*, *The Sense of Order*, *Ideals and Idols*, and *The Image and the Eye*.

Professor Richard Langton GREGORY was born in 1923 and educated at King Alfred School, Hampstead. He served in the 1939–45 war in the RAF, passing through No. 1 Signals School, Cranwell, in Signals and Radar. From 1947 to 1950 he attended Downing College, Cambridge, where he read Moral Sciences. From 1950 to 1953 he was Research Worker in the Medical Research Council Applied Psychology Laboratory, Cambridge. He was seconded for one year to the Royal Naval Physiological Laboratory, Whale Island, Portsmouth, to run an experiment on escaping from submarines, following the 'Affray' disaster.

From 1953 to 1958 he was University Demonstrator at the Department of Psychology, Cambridge, and from 1958 to 1967 he was University Lecturer at the Department of Psychology, Cambridge. From 1962 to 1967 he was Fellow at Corpus Christi College, Cambridge, and from 1967 to 1970 Professor of Bionics, Department of Machine Intelligence and Perception, University of Edinburgh. He started the Department with Professor Donald Michie and Professor Christopher Longuet-Higgins.

In 1970 he was elected Professor of Neuropsychology, and Head of Brain and Perception Laboratory, Department of Anatomy, University of Bristol, a post which he currently holds.

His publications include: *Eyes and Brain*, and *The Intelligent Eye*.

Sir Stuart HAMPSHIRE was born in 1914 in Lincolnshire. He was educated at Repton and Balliol College, Oxford. He was a Fellow of All Souls College, and Lecturer in Philosophy, Oxford, from 1936 to 1940. After the war he was elected Lecturer in Philosophy at University College, London, a post which he held from 1947 to 1950. From 1963 to 1970 he was Professor of Philosophy at Princeton University. In 1970 he became Warden of Wadham College, Oxford.

His publications include *Spinoza*, *Thought and Action*, *Freedom of the Individual*, *Modern Writers and other essays*, *Freedom of Mind and other essays*, (ed jtly) *The Socialist Idea*, *Two Theories of Morality*, (ed) *Public and Private Morality*.

Mr Rom HARRÉ was born in New Zealand in 1927 and educated at Kings College, Auckland, and Auckland University where he read engineering and mathematics. He taught mathematics for some years including a year at the University of Punjab, Lahore. He read philosophy at Oxford and subsequently had posts at the University of Birmingham and Leicester, returning to Oxford in 1960 as University Lecturer in the Philosophy of Science. His current post is Fellow of Linacre College, a position which he has held since 1963. Since 1974 he has been Adjunct Professor of the History and Philosophy of the Social and Behavioural Sciences at the State University of New York at Binghamton. He was co-founder of the *Journal for the Theory of Social Behaviour* and was author of the Introduction to the *Logic of the Sciences*, *The Philosophies of Science*, *The Principles of Scientific Thinking*, *Social Being*, and co-author of *Causal Powers* (with E. H. Madden), *The Explanation of Social Behaviour* (with P. F. Secord), *The Rules of Disorder* (with P. Marsh and E. Rossern) and *Nicknames* (with J. Morgan and C. O'Neil).

He is currently working on the theory of personal psychology and co-editing the *Blackwell Encyclopedic Dictionary of Psychology*.

Professor Robert A. HINDE was educated at Oundle School, St John's College, Cambridge, and the Edward Grey Institute of Field Ornithology, Oxford. He served as a pilot in RAF Coastal Command during the Second World War. He has been a member of the Cambridge University Department of Zoology since 1950, first as Curator of the Madingley Ornithological Field Station (subsequently the Sub-Department of Animal Behaviour) and more recently as Honorary Director of the Medical Research Council Unit on the Development and Integration of Behaviour. He is a Fellow of St John's College, Cambridge. His research has been concerned with various aspects of behaviour and endocrinology of birds, with the social development of monkeys, and with social behaviour and interpersonal relationships in man. He was appointed a Royal Society Research Professor in 1963. He is a Fellow of the Royal Society, a Foreign Honorary Member of the American Academy of Arts and Sciences, an Honorary Foreign Associate of the National Academy of Sciences, and an Honorary Fellow of the American Ornithologists' Union and of the British Psychological Society. He holds honorary doctorates at the Université Libre (Brussels) and Nanterre (Paris).

He is the author of *Animal Behaviour*, *Biological Bases of Human Social Behaviour*, *Towards Understanding Relationships*, and *Ethology*, as well as of numerous scientific papers.

Professor George MANDLER was born in Vienna in 1924, emigrated to England in 1938 and thence to the United States. He received his doctoral degree from Yale University and subsequently taught at Harvard University, University of Toronto and the University of California at San

Diego, where he is currently Professor of Psychology and director of the Center for Human Information Processing.

His publications include *The Language of Psychology* (with W. Kessen), *Thinking: from Association to Gestalt* (with Jean Mandler), and *Mind and Emotion*. He is currently at work on another book on mind, consciousness, and the emotions, which is planned for publication in 1983.

Professor George MILLER was born in Charleston, W.Va., on 3 February 1920, and educated in the public schools of Charleston. He graduated with a BA degree from the University of Alabama in 1940 and went to Harvard for graduate study in psychology. After spending World War II doing research on voice communication systems for the military, he received his Ph.D. degree from Harvard in 1946. Professor Miller taught at Harvard until 1951, when he moved to MIT. In 1955 he returned from Massachusetts Institute of Technology to Harvard. In 1960 J. S. Bruner and Professor Miller founded the Harvard Center for Cognitive Studies and continued as co-directors until George Miller left Harvard in 1968 to go to the Rockefeller University in New York. Then in 1979 he moved again, this time to Princeton, where he is now the James S. McDonnell Distinguished University Professor of Psychology.

In addition to some 200 articles, Professor Miller has written a few books and edited several more. The first was *Language and Communication* and the most recent is *Language and Speech*.

Dr Thomas SZASZ was born in Budapest, Hungary, in 1920 and emigrated to the United States in 1938. After receiving an MD degree from the University of Cincinnati in 1944, he specialised in psychiatry and psychoanalysis. In 1956, following a period of teaching and private practice in Chicago, and service in the United States Navy in Bethesda (Maryland), Dr Szasz accepted a professorship in the Department of Psychiatry at the State University of New York Upstate Medical Center in Syracuse, a position he still holds. He is a Life Fellow of the American Psychiatric Association and a Life Member of the American Psycho-analytic Association. In addition to his university post, Dr Szasz maintains a part-time private practice of counselling and lectures widely.

He is the author of *The Myth of Mental Illness* and sixteen other books and of hundreds of articles and book reviews in professional journals, popular magazines and newspapers. He is the recipient of numerous awards, among them two honorary doctorates and the American Huma-nist Association's 'Humanist of the Year Award'.

Dr Hanna SEGAL was born in Poland in 1918. She qualified as a doctor in the Polish Medical School in Edinburgh during the war, and in 1947 qualified as a psychoanalyst at the British Psychoanalytic Society. She was analysed by Melanie Klein and later qualified as a child analyst and

became a training analyst. She was president of the British Psycho-
analytical Society and Vice President of the International Psychoanalytic
Association. She was Visiting Professor Freud Memorial Chair at
University College, London, from 1977 to 1978. She is a Fellow of the
Royal College of Psychiatry.

She has written extensively on Melanie Klein.

Acknowledgments

Page 7 Photo Clive Barda
  13 Photo Michael Athay
  43 Photo Laurie Sparham/Network
46–59 Line drawings Tony Spaul
 101 Photo Laurie Sparham/Network
 120 Illustration Alan Burton
 128 British Museum (after Reinach, *Répertoire de Reliefs*)
 137 Photo Laurie Sparham/Network
 155 Photo Oxford *Mail* & *Times*
 175 Photo Laurie Sparham/Network
185–187 Diagrams Tony Spaul
 213 Photo Laurie Sparham/Network
 216 Diagrams Tony Spaul
 220 Mansell Collection
 228 Mansell Collection
 233 Photo Laurie Sparham/Network
 243 Mary Evans/Freud copyright/W E Freud
 251 Photo Laurie Sparham
 261 Institute of Psychoanalysis

The publishers wish to acknowledge that the footnotes on pages 16, 21, 37, 60, 97, 102, 196, 203 (top) and 205 are from *Chamber's Biographical Dictionary*; on page 203 (bottom) from *Makers of Modern Culture* ed. J. Wintle, Routledge and Kegan Paul; on page 91 from *The Fontana Dictionary of Modern Thought*; on pages 18, 198, from *Encyclopedia Britannica*; on page 143 from *A Dictionary of Psychology*, Penguin.

Index

psychotic illness 272
punishment 279
purpose 24, 26, 32

radar 24–5
rain dancing 203–4, 207
rationality 206, 208–9
reality sense 268–9
Reflections on Art (Langer) 203n
reflexes 9, 19–23
Riegl, Alois 215
Reinach, Salomon 229
relationships 183–6
religion 197, 201, 275, 279, 290
Rembrandt 227
replicability 181–2
representation, mental 14, 91, 103
repression
  function of 104, 107, 236, 265–6
  and neurosis 110–11
  of sexual impulse 241–2, 246
  and unconscious mind 103–4,
    114, 171, 252
retina 49–50
Reynolds, Sir Joshua 227
ritual 194, 202–9, 290
romanticism 9–10, 102
Rosicrucians 10
Roth, Sir Martin 238–9
Rubin Vase 50
Russell, Bertrand 35
Ryle, Gilbert 60–1, 77, 90, 272–3,
  301

schizophrenia 281–3, 288
Schoenberg, Arnold 143
sciences 17, 37, 208, 224
*Scientific Credibility of Freud's
  Theories and Therapy* (Fisher,
  Greenberg) 242n
scientific observation 157
'Scientific Project' of
  Freud 114–15
Second World War 14, 23, 103,
  152
Segal, Hanna 306
  dialogue with 250–69
selective advantage 195
sense organs 9
*Senses Considered as Perceptual
  Systems* (Gibson) 224n
sensory discrimination 9
sentences 91–3, 108, 160
separation experience 178, 181
separation of child from
  mother 178

servo-mechanism 23–4, 26, 103
servo-system 24
sexual activity 237
sexual interest 236
sexuality 111, 162
  female 242, 254
  infantile 10, 106, 236–47
shame 156
Shannon, Claude 72
Shannon-Weaver theory of
  information 72, 74
Sherrington, Sir Charles 19–21
signal detection 24–5
signal-to-noise ratio 25–6
Simon, Herb 35
  Size Constancy Scaling 47–8
Skinner, B. F. 77
socialisation 124
social norms 186
social representations 166, 171
sociopaths 151
somatic nervous system 139, 141
soul 196
speech perception 95
spinal cord 131
spinal injuries 146–7
Spinoza, Benedict 111
'splitting' 255, 259, 265–6
stimulus and response 14, 19–22,
  32–3
Story of Art, The (Gombrich) 229
stroke 126–7
structuralism 73
'Structure and Origin of the Anal
  Character' (Beloff) 240n
Study of Instinct (Tinbergen) 176
Study of Thinking, A (Bruner) 35
subjectivity 33
sucking 40, 237, 262
suicide 288
superego 235–6, 238, 253, 259–60
superstitions 205
*Symbol Formation and Its
  Importance for the Development of
  the Ego* (Klein) 267
*Symbol Formation and Its
  Relationship to the Growth of the
  Ego, The* (Klein) 266
symbolisation 28, 265, 267
symbolism 252
sympathetic nervous system 140,
  147
Syntactic Structures
  (Chomsky) 91n
syphilis 283
Szasz, Thomas 305

dialogue with 270–90

tabula rosa 260, 262
talk 160
technology 34
Thatcher, Margaret 239
Theory of the Earth (Hutton) 8
Thorpe, W. H. 176
thought 94
Thought and Action
  (Hampshire) 103
three-dimensional images 219, 221
*Three Essays on the Theory of
  Sexuality* (Freud) 237
Tinbergen, Niko 176
'top-down' strategy 69–73, 75–6,
  80
Totemism (Frazer) 196
Totemism and Exogamy
  (Frazer) 196
Treatise on Painting (Leonardo da
  Vinci) 224
tribal mind 194
Turner, Victor 202
two-dimensional image 219, 221
*Two Principles of Mental
  Functioning* (Freud) 264
Tylor, E. B. 196, 199, 204

unconscious mind 102–11
unconscious thought 107
unemployment 275
universal language 109–10

values 142
Virchow, Rudolph 273
vision 45, 214
visual perception 37–8
voice recognition 95
Voltaire 284
Vygotsky, Lev S. 41, 169

Wallenberg, Raoul 277
Watson, John B. 21
Weaver, Warren 72
Whitehead, A. N. 35
Wilkins, John 109
will, human 18, 60
Winnicott, D. W. 260
*Witchcraft, Oracles and Magic
  among the Azande* (Langer) 203
writing 201–2
Wundt, Wilhelm 16

Yorkshire Ripper 278–9